PENGUIN BOOKS

MALE HOMOSEXUALS

Martin S. Weinberg is Senior Research Sociologist at the Institute for Sex Research and Professor of Sociology at Indiana University. He has coauthored a number of books, including *The Study of Social Problems: Five Perspectives; The Solution of Social Problems: Five Perspectives; Deviance: The Interactionist Perspective;* and *Homosexuality: An Annotated Bibliography.*

Colin J. Williams is Research Sociologist at the Institute for Sex Research and Associate Professor of Sociology at Indiana University–Purdue University at Indianapolis. He is coauthor, with Martin S. Weinberg, of *Homosexuals and the Military: A Study of Less Than Honorable Discharge.*

MALE HOMOSEXUALS

THEIR PROBLEMS AND ADAPTATIONS

Martin S. Weinberg and Colin J. Williams

PENGUIN BOOKS INC New York • Baltimore

Penguin Books Inc
72 Fifth Avenue
New York, New York 10011

Penguin Books Inc
7110 Ambassador Road
Baltimore, Maryland 21207

Penguin Books Canada Limited
41 Steelcase Road West
Markham, Ontario, Canada L3R 1B4

First published by Oxford University Press, Inc., New York, 1974
Published by Penguin Books Inc, 1975

Printed in the United States of America

Map design by David Lindroth

CONTENTS

FOREWORD

In Europe and the United States there has been an increasing public concern with homosexuality, a concern which was first openly visible in scandals such as the Wilde case. Subsequently, homosexuality became more widely tolerated as a subject for discussion, providing it was in a medical or psychoanalytic context and thereby relegated to the area of social problems comfortably removed from the mainstream of life occupied by ourselves, friends, and neighbors. This defensive insulation from homosexuality was shattered by Dr. Alfred Kinsey, who in a flood of publicity, forced upon our society the realization that homosexuality was far more prevalent than thought, and that our families, friends, and associates were not exempt. His studies accelerated the growing concern, and soon prestigious groups such as the American Law Institute, the Group for the Advancement of Psychiatry, and the Wolfenden Committee were openly dealing with the social and legal implications of homosexuality. At the same time homophile organizations were founded, and certain clergymen began re-examining the moral and theological aspects.

A major landmark in this growing wave of public attention to homosexuality was the appointment of the National Institute of Mental Health Task Force on Homosexuality. This represented a courageous act by Dr. Stanley Yolles, the Director of N.I.M.H., who felt that this federal agency must forthrightly deal with a phenomenon that affected the mental health of millions. This stamp of federal validation and supporting grant monies led to an increase in scientific studies of homosexuality, and the already massive body of literature was further augmented.

Unfortunately, most of the growth has been in volume rather than quality, and there has been a preoccupation with etiology and therapy, while adaptations within a homosexual life style have been largely ignored. Consequently, this book, which deals primarily with the study of homosexual adaptations, is all the more welcome. The authors had made previous studies of "deviance" of a nonsexual nature and hence came to this study with a broad perspective. Unlike many authors, they are not fascinated by the seeming exoticism of the subject but treat homosexuality in a matter-of-fact but sympathetic way.

A foreword is no place to preview the substantial and often unique contributions presented in this volume, but it is a place for broad evaluation. First, Weinberg and Williams are good ethnographers. Rather than simply sending questionnaires out into an unknown world, transmuting the returned data into cards and tapes, and then proceeding with analyses as though reality existed solely in computer print-out, these investigators also studied the milieu occupied by their respondents. Recognizing that the present is built upon the past, they also investigated the recent social history of homosexuality, and in doing so, have given an excellent and concise description of homophile organizations and movements.

The study is characterized by thoroughness and fairness. The authors present various possibilities and alternatives rather than pursuing some favorite explanatory theory or inference. The data analysis is responsibly done, and the volume is replete with careful qualifying statements. The authors develop sophisticated and complex ideas regarding the relationship of the homosexual to both the homosexual and heterosexual worlds, and the effect of this on his psychological adjustment. And in their research, they call into question many examples of stereotypic thought.

The book is also important in two other respects. First, it is a cross-cultural study and, to strengthen their methodology, one which compares three, rather than the usual two, cultures. Moreover, the study was done using the same instrument in all three cultures and at the same period in time, so the reader does not have to wonder whether variation is attributable to instrumental differences or temporal change. Second, the authors courageously end their book with useful practical conclusions.

In summary, this is the sort of study and publication which the Institute for Sex Research has held as its ideal: quantified data intelligently, but not ostentatiously, analyzed, combined with humanistic ethnographic observations. It is only with such a combination that social scientists can approximate reality, that elusive but ultimate subject of all our studies.

PAUL GEBHARD

Director
Institute for Sex Research
Indiana University
Bloomington, Indiana

PREFACE

In the spring of 1966, a male homosexual spoke to a Social Problems class that we were teaching. He was quite ordinary in appearance and behavior, and his very ordinariness reduced the aura of mystery surrounding the exotic label "homosexual." He seemed quite happy and not particularly bothered about being homosexual in a society we knew to be very antihomosexual. His air of well-being led us to re-evaluate our own thinking.

Our speaker invited us to visit the New York Mattachine Society, a homophile organization, where we met other homosexuals. We also had the opportunity to accompany him to homosexual bars and clubs. It became readily apparent to us that the term "homosexual" covers a tremendous heterogeneity of persons, persons who live their lives in a variety of ways and with varying degrees of success.

These experiences sowed the seeds of the present study. Given that there are many styles of "being homosexual," do some homosexuals adapt more easily than others to their homosexuality? If so, what are the social conditions for these more successful adaptations? These are the primary questions we sought to answer in this study.

We first looked for answers to these questions in the United States. After doing this, we decided to extend our study to the Netherlands and Denmark, countries reported to be less intolerant of homosexuals. By comparing subjects in the three countries, we could see whether the well-being and way of life of homosexuals reflect differences in societal tolerance. In addition, we could see whether conclusions based on the United States data also hold in other countries.

Many people and organizations contributed to this study through their support, encouragement, and advice. We would like to thank our homosexual speaker for sparking some of the ideas with which we began; the National Institute of Mental Health (MH 13556), the West European Studies Program of Indiana University, the Hugh M. Hefner Foundation, and an anonymous source in Los Angeles for financial support; the Mattachine Societies of New York and San Francisco, the Society for Individual Rights of San Francisco, C.O.C. of the Netherlands, and Forbundet of Denmark for their help and cooperation; Melvin Kohn for data used in Chapter 11 and Albert D. Klassen and Eugene Levitt for data used in Chapter 7; Torrington Watkins, Carolyn DeMeyer, and Harry Silverman for their research assistance; Lois Downey for her computer assistance; Alan P. Bell, Paul Gebhard, and Harriet Serenkin for their editorial suggestions; Ronald Gold, Larry Littlejohn, James L. Kepner, Jr., and Neal Preller for their recommendations regarding the paperback edition; and Elizabeth Ketchen, Marianne Siegmund, and Karen Ruse Strueh for their secretarial and proofreading assistance. We would like to express special thanks to Sue Kiefer Hammersmith for her careful review of the manuscript and invaluable help in reworking it. Many other people, too numerous to mention, also were helpful to us. We would like to single out the following for their comments on early drafts: Harold Christensen, Barry Dank, Richard Green, Martin Hoffman, Evelyn Hooker, Laud Humphreys, Judd Marmor, William Simon, and Robert Stoller.

The paperback edition of *Male Homosexuals* is slightly revised from the Oxford University Press hard-cover edition.

MARTIN S. WEINBERG
COLIN J. WILLIAMS

Bloomington, Indiana

PART I

INTRODUCTION

CHAPTER 1

THE STUDY OF HOMOSEXUALITY

Homosexuality has been studied primarily by psychiatrists and psychologists. Most see homosexuality as a psychopathological condition.[1] For example, major proponents of this view state:

> We consider homosexuality to be a pathologic, bio-social, psychosexual adaptation consequent to pervasive fears surrounding the expression of heterosexual impulses.[2]

> All psychoanalytic theories assume that adult homosexuality is psychopathologic.[3]

Underlying this conception is the notion that heterosexuality is the normal, natural outcome of sexual development against which other forms of sexual expression are to be compared.[4] Furthermore, the idea of a "cure" is implied when homosexuality is viewed as pathological.[5] Of course, not all psychiatrists and psychologists subscribe to this perspective, but a sufficient number do to have greatly affected the way many persons conceive of homosexuality as well as the direction research has taken in this area.

Since homosexuality is defined as pathological, discovering the cause of it becomes a major concern. The Institute for Sex Research bibliography on homosexuality shows that a great deal of attention has been paid to the question of etiology.[6] Moreover, as the theoretical approach to homosexuality has been primarily Freudian, child-parent experiences have been concentrated on as the major etiological factors.

By defining heterosexuality as the norm, there also has been the tendency to view persons as *either* heterosexual or homosexual. This not only poses the danger of ignoring the great range and heterogeneity of homosexuals (and heterosexuals, for that matter), but in turn creates an erroneous stereotype of "the homosexual." Certainly it highlights the persistent problem of the definition of homosexuals and homosexuality that has confused much research.[7] Finally, the emphasis on cure has often inhibited theoretical progress and a better understanding of homosexuality and the homosexual.

Psychiatry and psychology also have been remiss in their methodology. The Institute for Sex Research bibliography is replete with examples of work which do not measure up to minimal canons of scientific research.

First, the samples used have been extremely small. This in itself need not always be a serious defect, even if it does limit more complex analyses of the data. A much more important problem is that such samples are usually made up of persons who are patients of the clinicians doing the research and cannot provide much knowledge about homosexuals in toto. While a representative sample of homosexuals may be impossible to achieve, certainly less biased groups can be obtained.

Another major defect of such studies has been that control groups are rarely used. Comparison groups are crucial if, for example, one is concerned with determining the degree to which homosexuals are maladjusted (instead of claiming it by fiat). A heterosexual control group is essential to answer this question as well as etiological questions. Finally, most studies of homosexuality have been culture-bound. Few attempts have been made to study homosexuals outside of the United States.[8]

In comparison with the fields of psychiatry and psychology, there has been little sociological research on homosexuality. The initial breakthroughs in sex research in the United States were made by more established disciplines such as medicine, biology, and zoology.[9] The first behavioral science to concern itself seriously with sex was psychiatry, which, given Freud's pioneering work and the link between medicine and psychiatry in the United States, promoted the "medical model" of homosexuality. Homosexuality was viewed as an arrest of sexual development, and many of the studies conducted were based on this assumption.

In addition, as psychiatry grew as a "helping" profession, it began to take over the treatment of "sexual deviance," which previously had been handled punitively. Thus, many types of sexual behaviors came to be considered psychiatric problems, partially by default (in that punishment was ineffective) and partially through the professional interests of psychiatrists.

The first sociological approach to the study of sex came from social anthropology. Because anthropologists dealt with cultures outside of the United States and, furthermore, cultures that were seen by many people as "uncivilized," they tended to receive less censure for their studies. At the same time, the intensive study of sex was most easily "legitimized" in the field of psychiatry. As for sociology, sex was generally considered to be outside its province; it had no mandate to counsel or cure and no theoretical framework that at the time was conducive to such study.

The first large-scale study of sex and homosexuality was a sociological one, however, even though it was done by a zoologist, Alfred C. Kinsey. (Although Kinsey's studies were not directed primarily at homosexuality, they alone provided data on the extent of homosexuality in the United States, its diverse forms, and its distribution among various social strata.) [10] Only recently have sociologists begun to turn their attention toward the study of sex and homosexuality, in part because of an increased acceptance of such research. Also, recent sociological conceptualizations provide a theoretical framework for doing research in this area. These formulations contain assumptions which, with respect to homosexuality as well as other phenomena, conflict with the views traditionally held by most psychiatrists and psychologists. (It should be noted, also, that some psychiatrists and psychologists are moving away from the traditional model.[11])

First, homosexuality is not seen as ipso facto pathological but rather as a variant of sexual expression. It is assumed that there are many types of homosexuals, some with fewer psychological problems than others; and on the part of those with more problems, homosexuality is not necessarily a symptom or cause. Generally, we find agreement with Hooker's conclusion: "Homosexuality may be a deviation in sexual pattern which is within the normal range, psychologically."[12] Understandably, there is also a greater appreciation of the role played by a variety of social factors in individual adjustment:

> We are now beginning to realize that social forces have an influence on all kinds of phenomena which we have hitherto analyzed in individual terms. We are beginning to understand, for example, that even physical illnesses such as heart disease and cancer may be influenced by sociological factors. . . . If this be the case, as is plainly indicated by recent studies, then it ought to be clear that the relationship of the homosexual to a larger hostile society must have profound effects on his life.[13]

Second, if homosexuality is to be considered as a variant of sexual expression rather than a sickness, then there is no mandate to search for cures. And finally, there is no need to posit heterosexuality as a norm other than in a statistical sense.

This perspective affects etiological conceptions. Persons are viewed as being born with an undifferentiated sexual potential that becomes attached to certain objects and situations through a complex learning process. Thus, becoming homosexual has similarities to becoming heterosexual. It does not necessarily involve pathological predisposing conditions—for example, a pathological family situation.

Perhaps the major emphasis of the sociological perspective is that later events are as important in understanding the homosexual as are initial or original causes and "the patterns of adult homosexuality are consequent upon the social structures and values that surround the homosexual after he becomes or conceives of himself as homosexual. . . ." [14]

This focus points to the social context within which the homosexual's adaptations take place. It also demystifies the homosexual by underlining his commonality with all persons. Simon and Gagnon state: "It is necessary to move away from an obsessive concern with the sexuality of the individual, and attempt to see the homosexual in terms of the broader attachments that he must make to live in the world around him." [15]

Taking into account the social context in which the homosexual lives leads to a fundamental change in the conception of research. Instead of talking about homosexuality as a condition (which a person has to a greater or lesser degree) and seeking the causes of the condition, primary attention is directed to the ways in which the homosexual is affected by his social situation, for example, how the connotations and expectations surrounding homosexuality affect the homosexual's behavior and self-concept.[16]

Since in this society the status given the homosexual is a deviant one, such research can draw on the sociology of deviance, especially societal reaction theory.[17] Reaction theory does not view "deviance" as inhering in particular types of behaviors. Rather it sees "deviance" as a sociological phenomenon, being defined by the evaluations and responses of people to various behaviors. For example, what makes homosexuality "deviant," according to reaction theory, is not anything about the behavior per se but rather the fact that people differentiate, stigmatize, and penalize alleged homosexuals.

Other people's reactions can involve assigning someone a deviant status which often overrides his other statuses. This can influence him to identify and associate with other "deviants" and affect the view he has of himself and the world.

This framework can be used to study homosexuals. Although earlier research could be reconceptualized within this framework, as yet there are few studies of homosexuality that explicitly employ it.[18]

The Present Study

This study is guided by societal reaction theory. In the context of this perspective, we conceptualize the homosexual's situation according to three parameters: relating to the heterosexual world, relating to the homosexual world, and psychological problems.

Relating to the Heterosexual World

The paramount problems faced by homosexuals are a function of the social and cultural contexts within which they pursue their sexual expression. In Western societies, characterized by the Judeo-Christian tradition, homosexuality is publicly disapproved of and often officially condemned. Such negative reactions, however, vary in their intensity among societies. At one extreme is the United States, where homosexuality is not only publicly disapproved of but officially penalized in that such behavior in most states is a criminal offense. A less extreme situation exists in the Netherlands and Denmark, where homosexuality between consenting adults is not against the law, where authorities are aware of the homosexual's problems, and where public opinion is more tolerant. Relating to the heterosexual world would therefore appear to be different in the United States than in these European countries. One might expect different consequences for the homosexual's well-being in societies that vary in their reaction. Since this is a major implication of the societal reaction perspective, we examine it in studying these three societies.[19]

Within any society, we assume that the following considerations are of importance in affecting the homosexual's life. Being known about is an essential factor in the homosexual's public identity. It can propel a person whose homosexuality is of little salience for him into a homosexual role. Being publicly identified as homosexual means that others may relate to him in terms of this status rather than his other statuses and attributes. If homosexuality is devalued within the society, new forms of interaction with heterosexuals may ensue; moreover, a change in "reputation" may close off a variety of conventional avenues.[20] Even the homosexual who accepts the personal identity of homosexual may do all that he can to avoid a public homosexual identity. Thus, fear of exposure and concern with secrecy may determine in important ways the manner in which the person's homosexuality is managed and may affect his psychological well-being.[21]

Homosexuals are not encompassed by a homosexual subculture; even those most involved with the subculture cannot completely avoid associating with heterosexuals. Homosexuals thus face a "predicament of encirclement" by the conventional world.[22] Nonetheless, associations with heterosexuals can be manipulated within certain limits and within certain contexts by the homosexual, and the ability and opportunity to do this provide for different ways of relating to the heterosexual world.[23] At the same time, homosexuals are socialized or exposed to traditional values and moralities, and these life perspectives produce a conflict between conventionality and homosexuality.

Social characteristics and background also have effects. For example, regardless of sexual orientation, a person's age, race, and religious background affect his behaviors, interpretations, and life style in certain ways. It is to be expected that adaptations to homosexuality will be similarly affected.

Relating to the Homosexual World

The manner in which a homosexual relates to the homosexual world is usually more a function of his own choice than is the case of his involvement in the heterosexual world. The limiting conditions, of course, are whether such a community exists within the reach of the homosexual and how developed it is. The homosexual world in its publicly accessible aspects has been described minimally as follows: "The world of 'being gay' becomes reduced to their meeting places—the gay bar, the cruising street, the gay party. . . . It is a world highly eroticized because its . . . purpose is to find a sexual partner as desirable as possible." [24]

With its more complete development, the homosexual world also contains a significant social dimension—a milieu that includes homosexual clubs, coffee houses, homophile organizations, newspapers, and so forth. We must also include here the less publicly accessible homosexual cliques and friendship groups. The homosexual, therefore, can structure his relationships to the homosexual world in a variety of ways. These can range from rapid, impersonal sex in public restrooms to political activism on behalf of the homophile movement. Other combinations of sexual and social desires can produce "one-night stands," affairs, nonsexual friendships, and homosexual "marriages." [25]

Various factors determine the extent and kind of association a homosexual has with other homosexuals, the most important perhaps being his concern with secrecy. The most covert may primarily confine his homosexual contacts to sex and make use of public restrooms and steam baths, relatively anonymous settings in the homosexual world.[26] For those who accept the private identity of homosexual while avoiding the public identity, association with other homosexuals and membership in a homosexual clique is another mode of relating to the homosexual world.[27]

The homosexual world, then, allows for a range of ways of being homosexual. This is especially the case in larger cities where specialized coteries of persons within the homosexual population exist; where, in effect, a large variety of tastes are catered to. Outside of large cities this is not as much the case. The homosexual world of smaller towns and cities may include at the most the rest room at the bus station, the corner of a public park, a small group of acquaintances.

Any analysis of the way homosexuals relate to the homosexual world cannot be self-contained. The homosexual world is shaped very strongly by the heterosexual world, and most homosexuals travel between both spheres by necessity and by choice. Thus, modes of adaptation and their success involve the particular forms of interaction and transaction the homosexual employs in bridging these worlds.

Psychological Problems

Social ideologies and responses determine the way an individual conceives of himself. The homosexual, therefore, surrounded by notions of reprobation, is thought to be particularly prey to a demeaning picture of himself. As one homosexual writes: "A person cannot live in an atmosphere of universal rejection, of widespread pretense, of a society that outlaws and banishes his activities and desires, of a social world that jokes and sneers at every turn, without a fundamental influence on his personality." [28]

Such is the power of heterosexual society that the homosexual may take over the beliefs that it propounds, creating problems of self-acceptance for himself. He may feel forced to hide his sexual orientation, often beset with fears and anxieties about its exposure. A variety of psychological problems may result.

If psychological problems result from the reactions of the heterosexual world, such difficulties may be only partially allayed by support from other homosexuals, even though, as Simon and Gagnon state: "Minimally, the [homosexual] community provides a source of social support, for it is one of the few places where the homosexual may get positive validation of his own self-image." [29]

It is also true, however, that this community itself is affected by the condemnation of the heterosexual world. Fear of exposure may contribute to anonymity in sexual contacts and difficulties in establishing intimate, lasting relationships. This latter problem, too, is partially the result of the assimilation of heterosexual views, causing the homosexual to devalue other homosexuals who might provide positive support.[30]

Finally, it has been noted that homosexuals can take over the characteristic psychological problems of other minorities.[31] This means that involvement with other homosexuals may alleviate some problems while producing or sustaining others.

Plan of the Book

We are interested in studying the social correlates of the adaptations the homosexual makes to the heterosexual world, to the homosexual world, and to potential psychological problems. We conceptualize such relationships through the utilization of the societal reaction perspective as formulated in contemporary sociology.

Three societies—the United States, the Netherlands, and Denmark—were chosen so as to provide variation in societal reaction. The United States, in terms of its laws and public opinions, is one of the most antihomosexual of modern Western societies. The Netherlands and Denmark, on the other hand, are relatively liberal in this regard.

We provide ethnographies of the homosexual's situation in these societies and, more specifically, his situation in New York, San Francisco, Amsterdam, and Copenhagen. For each locale we describe the social institutions which surround the homosexual. Following these descriptions, we present an account of the method and the manner in which respondents were obtained for a questionnaire study. Data on the characteristics of the samples are given as well as an analysis of the types of homosexual obtained from each of our sample sources—homophile mail organizations, homosexual bars, and homosexual clubs.

We then discuss the results of our questionnaire study, looking first at the differences found between homosexuals from the American and the European locales. After examining the locale differences, the book examines similarities. Here our cross-cultural data provide replications for the United States findings. First, we compare our homosexual samples with general population samples from the same locales. Next, we examine the correlates of self-other processes and of passing and being known about. We then examine the relationship between the respondents' adaptations and their degree of social involvement with other homosexuals, exclusiveness of homosexual orientation, age, occupation, living arrangements, religious background, religiosity, and race. In these comparisons the data are organized in the tripartite manner outlined previously: patterns of relating to the heterosexual world, the homosexual world, and psychological problems. In the concluding chapters we discuss the implications of our research for societal reaction theory and for possible social action.

PART II

THE HOMOSEXUAL'S SITUATION IN THREE SOCIETIES

CHAPTER 2

THE UNITED STATES

It has often been pointed out by foreign observers of American society that our sexual morality is significantly different from that found in any European country. While the American society has its historical roots in Europe it has, over time, developed many moral patterns peculiar to itself.[1]

American attitudes toward sex in general have been termed "erotophobic"—that is, involving exaggerated anxieties and fears of sexual behavior of all types with inordinate attempts to place such activities under societal regulation.[2] Paramount among such concerns has been male homosexual behavior. According to Kinsey:

In our American culture there are no types of sexual activity which are as frequently condemned because they depart from the mores and the publicly pretended custom as homosexual activities. There are practically no European groups, unless it be England, and few if any cultures elsewhere in the world which have become as disturbed over male homosexuality as we have here in the United States.[3]

Such attitudes are agreed by most commentators to be influenced by the Judeo-Christian tradition.[4] Originally an accepted part of ancient Jewish life, homosexual practices were condemned as a form of idolatry in the seventh century B.C. as part of an attempt by the early Jews to disidentify with their neighbors. Hebraic attitudes toward such behavior found their way into early Christian codes and were elaborated upon by St. Paul. Still associated with paganism, homosexual acts were defined as foreign, unfamiliar, and eventually, unnatural. With the spread of Christianity, homosexual behavior was condemned by ecclesiastical law, which later became the basis of English common law and American state law.

The United States and Europe both have the Judeo-Christian attitude against sex in general and homosexuality in particular. In addition, however, these were perpetuated and strengthened in the United States by American Puritanism.[5] The Puritans viewed sex as evil and dangerous and as strongly as possible encouraged its repression. Sexual acts should not be a source of pleasure, they believed, and should occur only within marriage for procreation. Thus, homosexual behavior was regarded as a classic sin.[6] Held by one of the earliest and one of the most powerful groups in the country, Puritan beliefs influenced the culture of the United States profoundly:

More than any other power, the United States was founded on traditions of Puritanism. The concept of sex as a necessary evil, an ugly pursuit, enjoyed by man because of the devil incarnate in the flesh, was taught by the early cultural leaders of this country. The varying and diverse elements that made up the American melting pot vied with one another to appear before the masses as pure and good, one group not to be outdone by another in the antisexual repudiation of physical desire. Thus the struggle of the Protestant Puritans to maintain a rigid and self-avowedly virtuous ban on all things sexual was strengthened by the several minorities that found conformance the road to acceptance and possibly integration into American life.[7]

Consequently, throughout most of its history as a nation, the United States has maintained an official antisexual morality. Not surprisingly, in such a climate minority forms of sexual expression are penalized. In the great majority of states, homosexual acts between males are felonies, with maximum penalties in some cases of life imprisonment. In some jurisdictions, discovery of such an act is enough to require a person to register as a "sex offender"; in others, the risk exists of being defined as a "sexual psychopath," which involves involuntary hospitalization until "cured." Whoever commits a homosexual act (or in some instances just exhibits homosexual "tendencies") fares no better with the federal government. Such behavior can lead to dismissal of any federal employee, rejection at draft induction, separation from the military with a less than honorable discharge,[8] and, among immigrants, deportation.[9]

Public opinion is consistent with official morality. The few studies which attempt to discover the attitude of the general public toward homosexuality show great consistency in delineating the negative reaction of most persons toward this type of behavior. Simmons published a study in 1965, for example, in which a quota sample of 180 persons were asked to list the things or persons they regarded as deviant. Even though there were over 200 such acts and persons considered deviant, the most frequent response (49%) was "homosexuals." [10] In connection with a television program on homosexuality, CBS commissioned the Opinion Research Center to study public attitudes toward homosexuality. From a nationwide probability sample of 946 persons 18 or older conducted in 1966, homosexuality was chosen by a third of the public as detrimental to society and also placed third among a list of nine sex-related items considered as social threats.[11] In a Harris poll published in 1965 which asked persons what they considered most harmful to the nation, homosexuals were placed third (behind communists and atheists) by 82 per cent of the males and 58 per cent of the females.[12] In a Harris poll conducted in 1969, 63 per cent of Americans considered homosexuals harmful to American life.[13]

Research has also depicted the views of homosexuality which underlie these negative attitudes. In the CBS poll, 71 per cent saw homosexuality as an illness, 10 per cent as a crime, 9 per cent as a sin, and only 8 per cent as a preference. Simmons asked a sample of 134 respondents to select from a list of traits those which best characterized homosexuals. A great deal of consensus was found, with 72 per cent seeing homosexuals as sexually abnormal, 52 per cent seeing them as perverted, and 40 per cent seeing them as mentally ill.[14] In 1966, Rooney and Gibbons published a study in which 87 per cent of their sample of 353 residents in the San Francisco area agreed that homosexuals are psychologically disturbed and should seek psychiatric help in order to become adjusted to a normal sex life.[15] They concluded: "The stereotyped view of the 'sick' homosexual whose sexual activities reflect personality pathology was held by nearly all of the subjects." [16]

Such negative perceptions of homosexuality also affect the public's attitudes toward its legalization. For example, the CBS poll showed that nationally there is little support for removing legal barriers surrounding homosexuality; less than one in five were in favor of legalizing private homosexual behavior among adults.[17] The report concludes that homosexuality is a phenomenon that upsets large numbers of the American public who react to it in stereotyped ways and who demand its punitive suppression: "The findings show that homosexuality is seen as an unquestionably negative phenomenon of our society, strongly rejected as a concept and as a practice, and is to be dealt with punitively when it is discovered." [18]

Finally, the latest study done in 1970 at the Institute for

Sex Research by Albert D. Klassen and Eugene Levitt with a nationwide random sample of 3,018 adults, aged 21 and over, shows:

> Two-thirds of our respondents regard homosexuality as "very much obscene and vulgar," and less than 8% endorse the view that it is not at all obscene and vulgar. As corollaries, about two-thirds of the respondents state that they have never liked homosexuals, over 80% express a reluctance to associate with them, and more than half do not believe that they "should be regarded as any other group."
>
> [Also] substantial majorities of the respondents agree that homosexual men should be allowed to work as artists, beauticians, florists, and musicians, but almost equally substantial majorities do not believe they should be permitted to engage in occupations of influence and authority. Three-quarters would deny to a homosexual the right to be a minister, a school teacher, or a judge, and two-thirds would bar the homosexual from medical practice and government service.
>
> Nor are our respondents willing even to support the legal right of consenting, adult homosexuals to engage in sex acts in privacy. Nearly 60% disapproved of the permissive statutes that currently prevail in Illinois and Connecticut. . . .
>
> [Also] a majority view homosexuals as tending to "corrupt their fellow workers sexually," and nearly half are willing to adopt to some extent as strong a statement as "homosexuality is a social corruption which can cause the downfall of a civilization." Finally, a majority of our respondents believe that at least some homosexuals "are born that way," but that a majority of them have "a curable illness." [19]

Whereas these findings represent the feelings of most Americans, the increasing "live and let live" attitude on the part of some younger Americans may, in the future, decrease the preponderance of the above negative attitudes.

Homosexuality and the Law in the United States

One of the most important differences between the United States and the Netherlands and Denmark concerning the homosexual's social situation is that in the United States his sexual behavior is a crime in most states, whereas in the latter countries it is not. It has been hypothesized that this difference is correlated with many differences in the social psychological well-being of homosexuals in the different societies.

The legal prohibitions against homosexual acts in the United States, usually found under the sodomy statutes, can be summarized as follows:

> Almost all homosexual acts—except in . . . [a few states]—are felonies, though in law . . . [a few states] offer a misdemeanor option; and in practice, all states permit adult consensual sodomy to be prosecuted as a misdemeanor through the use of alternative sections of the penal code.[20]

Illinois in 1962 was the first state to legalize consensual homosexuality between adults in private. Similar legal changes have been made in seven other states as of 1974. There is thus a climate of legal change beginning in the United States. Most of the laws prohibiting homosexuality are, however, very unclear as to the actual behavior they seek to enjoin; for example, in some states the term "crime against nature" is all that exists without any behavioral referent whatsoever.[21] The situation has been summarized thus:

> Sodomy historically and medically refers to anal intercourse, or buggery, but [now] the statutes on sodomy include all manner of sexual activity conceived by someone, somewhere, at one time or another, to be "unnatural"; and this means, of course, in this sexually repressed society, almost every variety of sexual activity other than "natural coitus." [22]

The legal penalties in some states can be harsh. The maximum penalty is life imprisonment in five states, 20 years in 13 states, and between 10 and 15 years in another 20 states.[23]

Despite the frightening import of these felony statutes, it should be noted, however, that the enforcement of sodomy laws is sporadic and rare, and the greatest involvement of homosexuals with the criminal law occurs under misdemeanor statutes. These statutes proscribe solicitation, disorderly conduct, lewd and lascivious behavior, and vagrancy, all of which are used ostensibly to control the homosexual's sexual behavior and the public pursuit of sexual partners. Often the "disorderly conduct" laws are used to arrest persons for acts for which no other punishment is provided in the code. "Lewd and lascivious behavior" provisions are used to punish acts which range from dancing and hand holding to more explicit sexual behavior. "Vagrancy" laws are a convenient catchall used in a variety of instances to harass homosexuals. It should be noted that most homosexuals are charged on misdemeanors rather than felony offenses not only because these laws are easier to apply but also because it is easier to get a conviction on a misdemeanor charge with its lesser penalties.

In addition to these criminal statutes, there are "sexual psychopath" laws which provide for an indefinite term of "treatment" (which may range from one day to life) for those defined as "sexual psychopaths." [24] It has been noted that the homosexual can bear the brunt of such laws even when engaging in acts with other consenting adults. In some states, those who are merely accused or suspected of homosexual behavior may be legally proceeded against as sexual psychopaths, that is, they may be incarcerated because of their "condition," *not* for any criminal acts. Courts sanction this procedure on the grounds that commitment as a sexual psychopath is usually a civil rather than criminal procedure:

> On the basis of suspicion alone, without any proof or direct evidence that an offense has actually taken place, a person may be taken into custody, denied his freedom indefinitely, and put through a rigorous psychiatric investigation. If he is adjudged a

"sexual psychopath," he need not be released until several psychiatric authorities are able and willing to attest that he has been "cured." [25]

Such provisions still exist even though the sexual psychopath laws have received a good deal of criticism because of their vagueness of definition, violation of civil rights, and the ineffectiveness or inapplicability of "treatment."

Enforcement of the Law

It is crucial to appreciate the role of law enforcement in evaluating the social situation of the homosexual in the United States. It is here—in the practical moralities of law enforcement agents—that he confronts the formal manifestation of public sentiment toward homosexuality.

In this regard, however, one must realize that it is impossible to effectively enforce antihomosexual legislation despite the variety of provisions in the statutes. First, there are literally millions of homosexual acts performed but only a limited number of police. Second, the majority of these acts are performed in private and between consenting adults and hence lack a complainant. Of necessity, therefore, the police are reduced to selectively enforcing the laws against homosexuality in ways that are often surreptitious and degrading.

The major means of enforcement include the following: [26]

(1) *Police decoys*/These are police officers who intentionally lend themselves to receiving homosexual solicitation by walking, talking, and dressing as they think homosexuals do. The decoy will loiter in a public rest room, park, or street where homosexuals are known to congregate. Then, gestures, conversations, and so on by the apparent homosexual can be taken as evidence of solicitation and

grounds for arrest. The U.C.L.A. study showed that in Los Angeles, 51 per cent of the homosexual misdemeanor arrests (243 out of 475) were made by police decoys.[27] Evidence centers around the officers' testimony that solicitation occurred, and corroboration is seldom asked for by the court. Behind this technique lies, of course, the issue of entrapment—was the enticement to commit the crime perpetrated by the officer or the defendant? Homosexual defendants frequently claim entrapment to be the case while the police just as frequently deny it; not surprisingly, the officer's story is believed in most cases.[28] This technique is highly questionable in that the nature of the charge is extremely tenuous, the evidence is often suspect, and the whole procedure is open to abuse by the police.[29]

(2) *Police observation*/Though the majority of homosexual arrests are made for misdemeanor violations, mainly through police decoys, most *felony* arrests result from direct observation by the police of homosexual activities, usually in public rest rooms.[30] Clandestine observations can take many forms, the most popular being peepholes, one-way mirrors, television cameras, and photographs. These techniques usually involve the police waiting many hours in the hope of catching someone engaged in a homosexual act. Because these procedures have raised questions of unreasonable search and invasion of privacy, courts have restricted their practice to some degree but not enough to eliminate it as a common method.

(3) *Other practices*/These include routine patrol of places where homosexuals are known to congregate, and harassment, for example, arresting patrons of homosexual bars on any legitimate grounds.[31] Harassment of homosexual bars, baths, private clubs, and so on is a quite common practice used in "controlling" homosexuals.

Antihomosexual actions as described above can come

about as the result of pressures from the District Attorney's office, complaints of businessmen, politicians, or "concerned citizens." Then again, the election of a new mayor or the appointment of a new police chief or even precinct captain can alter the homosexual's situation overnight. This list of contingencies can be extended further, with changes in enforcement resulting, on the one extreme, from the election of a new national administration or, on the other, from the individual policeman deciding to "get tough." Furthermore, changes in expressions of official morality can also be accompanied by changes in a variety of private sanctions (blackmail, extortion, "queer baiting") on the part of other citizens toward the homosexual. The complexity of official reaction, therefore, accounts for a built-in uncertainty in the social situation of the American homosexual which Dutch and Danish homosexuals do not face. It is for this reason, too, that attempts to talk about an "improving" or "deteriorating" situation for the homosexual run into trouble. A period of tolerance can virtually disappear overnight and vice versa, although it seems that each local and national cycle of improvement and deterioration has in the long run resulted in a net gain for the homosexual.

Homophile Organizations

The homophile movement in the United States began on the West Coast after the Second World War. The reasons it emerged then include (a) the re-evaluation of sexual mores following the upheaval of the war, (b) the Kinsey report on the male published in 1948 which showed homosexuality to be a not uncommon phenomenon, and (c) the homosexual-hunting activities associated with the McCarthy era of the early 50's.[32]

The first major United States homophile organization was the Mattachine Foundation, established in 1950 in Los Angeles as a secret society to promote discussion groups and educational efforts regarding homosexuality. Eventually the secrecy was dropped, and the organization became chartered as a corporation in 1954 in California with the title of Mattachine Society, Inc. The headquarters were soon moved to San Francisco.[33] (In 1955, the Daughters of Bilitis—D.O.B.—was established in San Francisco, independent of Mattachine, as the first all-female homophile organization.) The Mattachine Society also established a number of chapters in cities around the country, but internal schisms within the movement led to their being dropped. Some of these continued as autonomous organizations in the early 1960's, the two main ones being Mattachine of New York (M.S.N.Y.) and Mattachine of Washington. Consequently, Mattachine of San Francisco, though a parent body, no longer controls its offshoots.

Activities of homophile organizations in the 1950's were generally introspective, concerned with the "why" of homosexuality and the counseling of members in trouble. In the 1960's the movement really began to be a "movement"; the number of homophile organizations was over 40 by the end of 1968 and growing all the time. Impetus for reform came with the publication of the Model Penal Code draft by the American Law Institute in 1955 and the Wolfenden Committee's recommendations in England in 1957. This and the general atmosphere of protest in the 60's led to the demand that the homosexual's legal and social position be improved. Mattachine Society of Washington, for example, took on the Civil Service Commission and the Department of Defense for their exclusionary policies; the White House, the State Department, and Independence Hall were picketed by homosexuals. The Mattachine Society of New York staged a successful "sip-in" in 1966 to challenge regulations affecting homosexuals' right to drink in public establishments and to influence the city administration's policy toward homosexuals. (As well as these political activities, homophile organizations were also increasing counseling and recreational services to their members—see the next two chapters.)

The scope of the movement also expanded. In 1963 a regional association was formed, East Coast Homophile Organizations (E.C.H.O.), which, though short-lived, did give impetus to a movement for national meetings of homophile organizations. This was realized in 1966 with the establishment of the North American Conference of Homophile Organizations (N.A.C.H.O.), which organized annual national meetings where position statements were adopted, administrative committees established, and press conferences and television and radio interviews held. N.A.C.H.O., however, fell prey to the schism in the homosexual movement between liberal and radical homosexuals and is now defunct.

A new wave of homophile groups composed of younger, more militant homosexuals, had exploded upon the national scene by the early 1970's. Many traced their origin to the violent Stonewall riots that occurred in New York in June 1969 (see next chapter). These groups consciously sought to distinguish themselves tactically and ideologically from previous homosexual organizations. The very word "homophile" was widely supplanted by the more provocative "gay liberationist." It is difficult to generalize about the groups involved because they comprised so many different aims and organized themselves in so many different ways. One thing, however, that these groups had in common was the willingness of their membership to identify themselves as homosexual and to seek, sometimes in militant ways, an end to the social discrimination against the homosexual. These ideals are reflected in slogans still popular today—"Gay is good" and "Out of the closets and into the streets." [34]

This new militancy in the homosexual movement was itself part and parcel of the widespread gradual radicalization of many people, especially the young, around that period. Radicalized by political events of the sixties and especially influenced by the model of black militancy, a more varied and numerous breed of homosexual activist made an appearance, imbued with a different sense of tactics than homosexuals of the past. For example, the New York Gay Liberation Front (G.L.F.), a short-lived but highly influential organization, declared:

GLF differs from other Gay groups in our realization that homosexual oppression is a part of all oppression. We are denied our basic humanity by the same system that oppresses blacks, women, and other minorities. We believe that our liberation is tied to the liberation of all peoples and that we must, therefore, seize the time and demand our rights now! [35]

Similarly, the constitution of the Gay Activists Alliance, also a New York organization, begins with the words:

We as liberated homosexual activists demand the freedom for expression of our dignity and value as human beings through confrontation with and disarmament of all mechanisms which unjustly inhibit us: economic, social, and political. Before the public conscience, we demand an immediate end to all oppression of homosexuals.

The essential word in the G.A.A. statement is "confrontation." Once fully out of the closet, the inevitable tactic of the fledgling gay liberation movement involved highly dramatic and often highly successful confrontations with discriminatory institutions.

During the period of initial antagonism and disruption, the relationship between the new gay liberation groups and older, more conservative groups like Mattachine was something like that existing between black militants and white liberals, each vacillating between alliance for specific goals and outright rejection as part of their general ideology.[36] This is not difficult to understand when the different membership compositions are considered. Mattachine was then predominantly composed of older, mainly middle-class covert homosexuals, and the Gay Liberation Front of young, déclassé, militantly overt homosexuals.[37] After working long and hard for acceptance by the heterosexual world, the old-style activists felt that the young militants were "rocking the boat" and making life more difficult for homosexuals; they resented the attempt to set homosexuals apart as a separate group. Quite simply, they saw hard-won rights being jeopardized.[38] The radicals, on the other hand, felt the early groups were too apologetic and too involved in the antisexual attitudes they should have been attacking.

Since the time of this study, however, in many ways the distinction between the "radical" and the "establishment" homophile groups has become far less sharp, and consequently less applicable. As of 1974, there are probably more than one thousand grass-roots gay liberation groups in the United States, and very few of them resemble the Mattachine or the G.L.F. of the Stonewall days. For example, the Los Angeles Gay Liberation Front, patterned after the militant New York group, gradually shifted its concern away from confrontation tactics and reorganized itself as the Gay Community Services Center, which provides counseling and diverse social services to needful people within the gay community. Similarly, the Gay Activists Alliance in New York, which perfected the technique of "zapping" political figures with demonstrations when they least expected it, now employs lobbyists to keep state and local politicians informed about the different bills G.A.A. supports. Surprisingly, nearly half of the most recent homosexual groups are located on college and university campuses and function as recognized parts of student activities programs. In the major cities, nearly every sort of specialization has been taken up: These range from gay religious groups to gay therapy and counseling organizations, from gay political clubs to groups for gay blacks and

Hispanics, from gay newspaper collectives to city- and statewide gay coalition groups. The emergence of gay professional groups is also part of the current trend. At present, there are active gay task forces within the teaching, library, media, legal, nursing, and medical professions.

Homosexual Bars

In all major cities in the United States the gay bar is the cornerstone of the gay community.[39] Because there are few public locations where homosexuals are able to present their sexual orientations and preferences, the bar emerges as probably the single place that provides the terms and conditions necessary and sufficient for large numbers of homosexuals to congregate in public, engage in leisure-time socializing, and pursue sexual relationships.

Thus, homosexual males frequent gay bars for the consumption of alcohol, for meeting new friends and old, for entertaining and being entertained, for sitting, dancing, and getting drunk, for something to do, and, especially, for meeting sexual partners. The bars provide a variety of entertainment, decor, types of clientele, and prices for a variety of interests and idiosyncrasies. The homosexual patron may remain anonymous and be generally or particularly accepted for his sexual orientation and preferences. Travelers from other areas, urban and rural (and even transnational), find readily available sources of social and sexual interactions. Some gay bars cater solely to males. Others, termed "mixed" bars, cater to heterosexuals as well. Some cater to certain types of homosexuals. For example, "leather" bars cater to those homosexuals interested in a hypermasculine atmosphere, "nellie" bars for an effeminate atmosphere. Some bars center around the provision of specific services, for example, "hustler" bars. Ecological factors such as neighborhood type and distance from the city center can also affect the characteristics of bars and the nature of their clientele. Thus, the gay bar can provide many of the essential components necessary for the homosexual's social and sexual satisfaction.

Second to the bar (although only as places for meeting and/or consummating a sexual contract) are those places where "cruising" takes place. Cruising refers to the pursuit and solicitation of sexual partners in public places, usually being a patterned activity in that particular places are known to homosexuals as likely areas to meet other homosexuals. These would include various streets, neighborhoods, parks, public toilets, steam baths, and transportation centers. In addition to these cruising areas, there are other locales that serve as gathering places for homosexuals—for example, certain restaurants, cafés, and hotels—but none are as important as the bar.

CHAPTER 3

NEW YORK CITY

New York is considered to be one of the best cities in the United States for homosexuals. As a cosmopolitan commercial, cultural, and entertainment center, it has a lot to offer anyone. In addition, the homosexual finds a larger number of fellow homosexuals as well as a variety of homosexual bars, clubs, baths, and other meeting places.

Our description of New York is based on field work conducted between 1966 and 1968 when we began the project and were residing in that area and two weeks of more intensive field work in 1970. In addition, we provide documentary evidence from homophile magazines, newspapers, and the professional literature wherever possible and appropriate.

The Legal Situation

A commission was established by the state of New York in 1961 to revise the criminal law, statutes, and procedures. Its report in 1965 led to the Revised Penal Law of 1965, which took effect on September 1, 1967.[1] Under the new code, the term "crimes against nature" is dropped from the law, and sodomy is defined as "deviate sexual intercourse," meaning "sexual conduct between persons not married to each other consisting of contact between the penis and the anus, the mouth and penis, or the mouth and the vulva [Section 130.00]." [2]

A further provision concerns adult consensual sodomy. Originally the commission reported to the legislature that the criminal prosecution of consenting adult homosexuals served no purpose and that New York should follow the Model Penal Code and the Illinois Criminal Code Revision of 1962, which eliminated such provisions. In May of 1965 the legislature attempted to remove consensual sodomy from the list of criminal offenses, but opposition, especially from the Catholic Church, prevented its passage at the eventual vote. At this writing, therefore, adult consensual sodomy is still a crime in New York (Section 130.38); however, the penalty is less severe (up to three months imprisonment) than in other states which still criminalize adult consensual sodomy.

As elsewhere, however, most prosecutions for homosexual behavior in New York come under the disorderly conduct statutes. The new penal code created the crime of loitering, which deals with those who linger in public places for the purpose of engaging in or soliciting another person to engage in deviate sexual intercourse, punishable by a maximum of fifteen days imprisonment (Section 240.35). It is this provision that is usually invoked against those homosexuals who pursue partners in public places, especially public rest rooms and parks.

For the New York homosexual, therefore, despite a diminution in penalties for certain offenses he might be likely to commit, the effect of these legal changes was not significant. As we have suggested, it is how such laws are enforced (in jurisdictions which criminalize homosexual behavior) and how law enforcers use auxiliary laws to arrest homosexuals that provide the homosexual with a major source of problems.

Enforcement of the Law in New York City

It is not the laws themselves that tell us much about the homosexual's situation but rather the nature of their enforcement. This is most clearly seen with the election of John Lindsay as mayor in 1965. Lindsay completely changed the existing policy toward homosexuals, which had relied heavily upon entrapment and harassment. Since April 1966, through orders of the police commissioner, any arrest for homosexual solicitation (under Section 240.35[3]) must be accompanied by a complaint signed by a private citizen. Otherwise, entrapment is now permitted as a defense in court. Other actions by the administration also signaled a more permissive policy toward the homosexual. However, the complexity of official reaction in a large city with a chain of command and overlapping (sometimes autonomous and competing) authorities cannot be fully understood solely by looking at a mayoral decision. Even with the best intentions of higher authorities, the homosexual is often subject to repressive action on the part of those who actually enforce the law.

For example, in an effort to break the monopolization of gay bar ownership by organized crime, a New York homophile society, the West Side Discussion Group, formed what was known as the Corduroy Club. Admission was restricted to members and guests, and since no liquor was sold on the premises, no liquor license was required. Instead, members brought their own liquor which was kept at the bar. It was a private social club chartered as such by the state. Nevertheless, on October 4, 1969, the Corduroy Club was raided on the basis of some unpublicized legislation, Section 646 of the Alcoholic Beverage Commission (A.B.C.) Code, which made it illegal to *store* liquor on a premise without a license. Since no other club, to our knowledge, has been treated in this way, it appears the Corduroy Club was selected out for special attention by the State Liquor Authority (S.L.A.). Thus, despite a liberal city administration, an autonomous state agency can take a different tack. Such a policy of harassment by S.L.A. officials had been in effect for some time.

Another example was the police raid on the Continental Baths, a very popular homosexual steam bath, on February 20, 1969, in what appeared to be a case of entrapment. An "innocent person" (police officer) had gone into the baths, was "shocked" by what he saw, and complained to the police. The ensuing raid, which led to twenty-two arrests, was the first major entrapment since mid-1966 (when Lindsay changed police policy) and thus provided the first test of the antientrapment law. The police denied entrapment, centering their argument on the Continental's advertisements in the *Village Voice*. Nonetheless, the majority of arrests were dismissed through lack of evidence, which must have upset the police in that locale, as there followed a campaign of harassment involving many arrests for "solicitation." This was contrary to the police commissioner's orders, and the district attorney refused to prosecute. Eventually, pressure from higher authority did cause harassment to cease (especially when those arrested began to file suits against the city for false arrests).

One's understanding of the conflict between homosexuals and law enforcement agencies in New York would not be complete without our mentioning the Transit Police. This police force (about 3,500 strong at the time of writing) was organized after the building of the I.N.D. subway, when the subway was seen to attract various "undesirables." The subways, especially the rest rooms, have long been a popular place for many homosexuals, and the Transit Police have had the job of controlling homosexuals by arrest and other measures. The Transit Police face the same difficulties as the city police in finding evidence of an illegal act involving homosexuals, and they have employed similar techniques of observation and entrapment. They are not bound, however, by the ruling that restricts city police that arrests for solicitation be accompanied by a complaint signed by a private citizen.

Homophile Organizations

At the time of our study, the Mattachine Society of New York (M.S.N.Y.) was one of the largest and most influential of American homophile organizations. The M.S.N.Y began in 1955 as a branch of the Mattachine Society of San Francisco but later became independent. Its main aim is to fight laws that make homosexual acts criminal and generally to oppose intolerance, discrimination, and misinformation with regard to homosexuality. Modeling itself as a civil rights group, M.S.N.Y. keeps its social functions to a minimum and organizes its relationships to its members primarily by mail. Excluding females, in 1967, at the beginning of this research, the organization had over 2,700 persons on its mailing list, approximately 950 of whom lived in New York City and 350 in New York State, Connecticut, and New Jersey. The remainder came from nearly all the states in the union.[3]

It is in its civil rights activities that M.S.N.Y. is best known. Perhaps the most important civil rights work is carried out by the Mattachine Legal Committee, which, for example, has sponsored a case which challenged the constitutionality of New York's antidrag law (making it illegal for a male to dress as a woman), and has acted as amicus curiae in an appeal to the New Jersey State Supreme Court when gay bars were being raided for permitting homosexuals to congregate on their premises. Citing the First and Fourteenth Amendments concerning the rights to free speech and peaceful assembly, they argued that the state was infringing upon those rights. The court agreed.

Cases concerning employment of homosexuals have been a main target for Mattachine. In 1969, for example, they participated in a fight with the city Civil Service Commission to change hiring practices to allow homosexuals employment in jobs under its jurisdiction.[4] M.S.N.Y. attorneys also filed suit against the Selective Service Commission and CBS over possible discrimination against homosexuals.

In addition to these direct efforts, M.S.N.Y. also functions as a pressure group in indirect ways. Its complaints and representations to the mayor and police commissioner and joint activities with the New York Civil Liberties Union and the Episcopal Diocese of New York helped end police entrapment by decoys in 1966. A "sip-in" by organization members assisted in making the S.L.A. recognize the legality of gay bars. Organization members also participated in demonstrations for homosexuals' rights at Independence Hall and the White House.

Although primarily a civil rights organization, Mattachine also provides some social and recreational opportunities for its members, such as costume balls at Halloween, beach parties, and a travel service.

The M.S.N.Y. also has a Social Service Division which helps homosexuals with their problems. It receives referrals from professionals, such as physicians and psychiatrists, who have homosexual patients whom they feel they cannot help. The M.S.N.Y. then directs the person to someone who can counsel his particular problem—sometimes a professional, sometimes a nonprofessional fellow homosexual. It also supplies speakers to various community organizations, church groups, schools, and the media.

The M.S.N.Y. is not the only homophile organization in New York City. One organization that is purely social and which does not involve itself with counseling or political activism is the West Side Discussion Group, established in 1956. It originated in an attempt by M.S.N.Y. to establish a number of informal neighborhood discussion groups in private houses. West Side was very successful and eventually decided to separate from M.S.N.Y., officially establishing itself in 1956. A different topic is discussed each week, and after the discussion there are refreshments and dancing. Often a representative from the city Department of Health is available to arrange for blood tests for V.D. About 100 persons were in attendance at the meeting we observed, and we were told that this is about the average attendance at the weekly meetings throughout the year.

As previously described, the West Side Discussion Group formed a new social club, the Corduroy Club. The club offered to members and their guests room for dancing, drinking, and socializing in an atmosphere different from most bars where homosexuals gather.

Also in New York City, the Gay Liberation Front came into existence with an incident on June 28, 1969. The city police made an early morning raid on the Stonewall, a homosexual bar on Christopher Street, a popular cruising area in Greenwich Village. The manager and employees were arrested on the grounds of selling liquor illegally, and the patrons were ordered to leave, which they did. They gathered outside, however, where they were joined by a variety of others who shared their consternation at the raid. On emerging from the Stonewall, the police were pelted with pennies, cans, rocks, and other objects and were driven back into the Stonewall, which was locked from the outside and set afire. The Tactical Police Force (riot police) was summoned, and several hours of street fighting ensued, resulting in many arrests and beatings.

The following night, the more militant homosexuals (under the slogan of "Gay Power") decided to "liberate" Christopher Street. Their activities swelled the crowds again, this time including Black Panthers, "yippies," and "crazies." A riot situation developed, and again the Tactical Police Force was called to clear the streets.

June 28, 1969, and the Stonewall incident became one of the major symbols of the gay liberation movement. On its anniversary one year later, Gay Liberation Day was proclaimed with a march that has been repeated every June to the present; the number of participants has ranged from about five thousand to fifteen thousand. Whatever the merits of the Stonewall event, it was a turning point that brought many disaffected young homosexuals into the mainstream of the homophile movement.[5]

The Gay Liberation Front, the first large group to spring from the radical agitation following the Stonewall riots, never developed an organizational structure that could assure its stability. Despite its catchall emphasis on the common struggle of all oppressed peoples for human rights, G.L.F. usually functioned as a number of independent cells, working in relative ignorance of each other and often ideologically opposed to each other. During its short existence, the Gay Liberation Front established rudimentary contacts with the radical black and women's liberation movements, it staged a number of successful demonstrations, and, perhaps most important, it publicized the drama of homosexual oppression and liberation in a way that has seldom been equaled.

Because of its internal conflicts, however, G.L.F. dropped out of sight shortly after an alternative organization, the Gay Activists Alliance, was formed. G.A.A. was conceived as a tightly structured, nonideological, and nonviolent group, with the objective of promoting solely the civil rights and welfare of homosexuals. G.A.A. operates out of its unofficial gay community center, a refurbished firehouse, which provides space for its many committee and general meetings and also for the Saturday night dances that provide most of G.A.A.'s regular income.

Although G.A.A.'s activities over the years have been extremely diverse, its forte has always been practical politics. Numerous small "zaps" and full-scale demonstrations were planned and carried out, all based on the premise that if antihomosexual politicians and institutions could only be forced onto the defense, their lack of any valid logical or ethical basis for their actions would be exposed, to others if not to themselves. Parallel with this strategy has been the belief that the mass of closeted and oppressed homosexuals can be reached only through the established radio, television, and printed media. G.A.A.'s News and Media Relations Committee has kept up a constant stream of gay-related news bulletins and press conferences. Because of the concentration of the national news media in New York City, these efforts have a potentially important effect on the rest of the country.

Lastly, the Gay Activists Alliance has served the New York movement as a training ground for gay liberationists, and it has spawned a number of different homosexual groups. One such group, which developed after the time period of this study, deserves mention. The National Gay Task Force was established in 1973 out of the Gay Activists Alliance for much the same reasons G.A.A. developed out of G.L.F. in 1969—frustration over internal conflicts and organizational inefficiency, compounded with a strong sense that changing times require changing tactics. Structurally, the Task Force is modeled after the American Civil Liberties Union, with which it has a close working relationship. After one year of existence, the Task Force had some two thousand dues-paying members, including many highly prominent homosexual and heterosexual men and women. Because of expertise, contacts in the media and in political circles, and organizational mobility, the Task Force seems optimally situated to act as a catalyst on the national level. Already, it has had some important successes. It has been instrumental in the decision of the American Psychiatric

Association to remove homosexuality from its handbook of mental disorders, extracted promises from the major television and motion-picture producers to adhere to certain guidelines in their depiction of homosexual men and women, and negotiated favorable editorials in *The New York Times* and the *Post,* later purchasing an unprecedented full-page ad in the *Times* to publicize the need for an antihomosexual-discrimination bill in New York and elsewhere. Among the Task Force's on-going projects are court suits to overturn state sodomy laws throughout the nation, the formation of gay caucuses within major professional organizations, the preparation of test cases to alleviate the plight of homosexuals caught in child custody suits, the introduction of Congressional job protection legislation, and the initiation of legal arguments to change the present discriminatory practices of the federal Civil Service, the immigration authority, and the armed forces.

Needless to say, New York City has also developed a wide variety of small, specialized homosexual groups. Aside from college and high-school groups and many purely social groups, New York has four gay religiously oriented groups, five gay counseling groups, four switchboard and referral services, two gay liberation bookstores, and numerous other special-interest groups.

Homosexual Bars

To provide a specific picture of the gay bar scene in New York that would hold over a period of time is problematic because of its transient nature. We rely mainly on our informal observations gathered over the years 1966 to 1970. (Additional information was obtained from homosexual publications and interviews with homosexual subjects active in the gay life of New York.) During this period the number of gay bars operative in Manhattan remained relatively constant. However, this number was made up of different bars at different times:

Bars that change clientele/Establishments that previously did not attract a homosexual clientele begin to do so. This occurs for a variety of reasons. For example, the bar changes ownership and the new owner is homosexual or sympathetic to homosexuals; a gay bartender gets a job at a bar and brings with him some of his old clientele; a gay "crowd" decides to start using a particular bar and the word spreads.

Gay bars that cease to be/Mortality rates among gay bars are frequently high. Until recently the activities of the State Liquor Authority (S.L.A.) and the police department meant that the continued existence of a gay bar was precarious in New York City. Even now, as the Stonewall case shows, gay bars still may be subject to official harassment. Today, the demise of a gay bar is more likely to be due to its lack of popularity or to financial crises of one kind or another. The fact that many gay bars in New York are owned by organized crime, which is more interested in profit than in providing services to its clientele, probably contributes to the instability of the gay bar situation.

One factor that distinguishes gay bars in New York is the number of bars in which organized crime is involved. Gay bars in New York City have been a lucrative investment for syndicate funds. More respectable businessmen, disinclined to deal with homosexual clients, leave a vacuum which is quickly filled by organized crime. The growing tolerance toward gay bars, however, has changed the extent to which this kind of development occurs.

S.L.A. rulings now make the serving of known homosexuals no longer a violation; nor can authorities suspend or revoke the license of a bar on the basis of an alleged solicitation by a homosexual. At present, the S.L.A. brings disciplinary proceedings only on evidence that the licensee permitted lewd or obscene behavior. Court decisions have exempted same-sex dancing,[6] kissing, and physical contact such as embracing or holding hands from the definition of lewd behavior (touching genitals or engaging in overt sex acts are still crimes). The result is that the bar scene is more "open" in New York City than it used to be. Running a gay bar has become less risky, and legitimate businessmen have begun to move into this area, breaking the monopoly that organized crime has enjoyed for many years.

At present, underworld money is being reinvested in private clubs, many designed to retain their homosexual clientele. Since these clubs are private, they are immune from routine police and S.L.A. inspection. Most do not operate with a liquor license and many have "orgy rooms," darkened recesses where sexual behavior takes place. The police find it difficult to move against unlicensed liquor sales and homosexual behavior since courts will not issue warrants without specific complaints, and, naturally, these are difficult to obtain. Even those that have been raided take advantage of the delays in court appearance and the relatively minor penalties by remaining open for business, or by reopening again in a short time. Some of these places also, of course, "buy immunity" in the form of payoffs to the local police. This would appear to have been the situation on the night of July 17, 1971, when federal agents raided nine after-hours gay bars. It was reported that the patrons were not arrested or harassed since the targets were the alleged Mafia-linked managements. It was further stated that such intervention came as a complete surprise to the local police who, it was believed, were involved in extensive payoffs.[7]

One past president of M.S.N.Y. has claimed that about a third of homosexual bars, restaurants, and clubs are operated by underworld figures. Most of these establishments are found in Manhattan. A common strategy is to buy a straight bar in financial difficulties, redecorate it, and bring in a few "tame" homosexuals, thus establishing a gay bar. As soon as it starts making money, they sell it to a legitimate businessman at a large profit.[8]

We estimated that at least seventy gay bars were in operation in Manhattan over the period 1966–70.[9] To describe their distribution we divided New York into the following areas (see map):

Area 1—The Upper West Side/This area contains twelve bars on the list, two of which are in Harlem and the others of which seem to be concentrated between West 62nd and West 68th Streets. Many gay persons live in this area, parts of which, though once fashionable, have greatly declined of late and are experiencing an influx of poor Puerto Rican immigrants. Another change is the influx of young heterosexual singles in the recent past.

One private club, three steam baths, and a number of coffee houses and gay hotels are situated in this area. The eastern boundary, between 70th and 80th Streets, is Central Park West, which has been called "the longest cruising area in the world." On the west side of the park are also two areas that are popular for cruising and having sex. Another popular cruising location is Riverside Drive between 79th and 96th Streets along the eastern boundary of Riverside Park.

Area 2—The Upper East Side/This area contains fifteen bars on the list. This section, from the East 60's to the East 80's, is one of New York's most fashionable, with its "sophisticated" life style, its emphasis on the contemporary "chic," and the latest in the arts. The bars are elegant in their decor and usually require a coat and tie of their clientele. Also, these bars, because of their reputations and longevity, attract many out-of-towners. For the younger

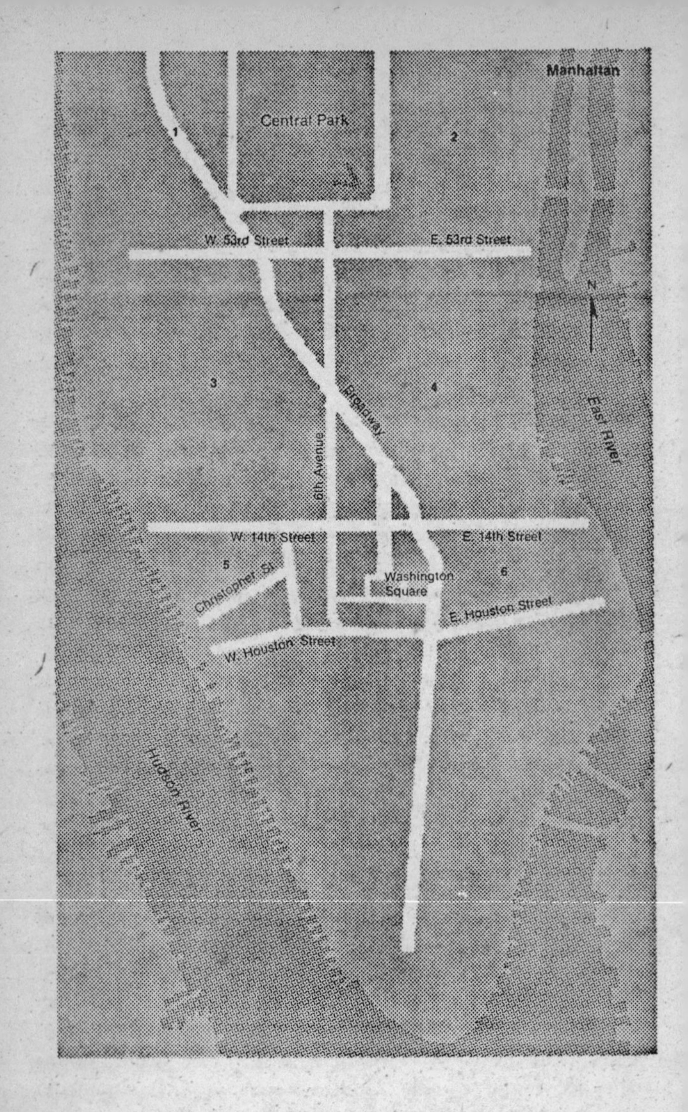
Manhattan
Central Park
1
2
W. 53rd Street
E. 53rd Street
N
3
4
Broadway
6th Avenue
East River
W. 14th Street
E. 14th Street
5
6
Christopher St.
Washington
Square
E. Houston Street
W. Houston Street
Hudson River

crowd, the area also includes a number of dance bars, possible since the easing of restrictions.

The Upper East Side contains expensive restaurants, antique shops, and various specialty shops, especially clothing, many of which are run by homosexuals or which attract a predominantly homosexual clientele. Especially important are homosexual restaurants and coffee houses. Here the area of most concentrated cruising is 3rd Avenue between 50th and 72nd Streets.

Area 3—Midtown West/Only five bars on our list are located in this area, which, unlike the previous two, contains no large concentration of homosexuals and their institutions, that is, no "lavender ghettos." Most of these bars are "neighborhood" bars whose clientele is not exclusively homosexual; in appearance they seem little different from the run-of-the-mill New York bar. Two restaurants on the list are also found here, however, as well as two private clubs and two hotels.

Running east-west through the middle of this area is West 42nd Street and the Times Square area. This locale is famous as a hang-out for so-called lower-class deviant types. Many of the erotic literature stores on 42nd Street have sections set aside for homosexual publications and photographs. The homosexuals in the area are mainly the poor and footloose young. Black drag queens are a feature of the street scene as well as young hustlers who lean against the entrances to cheap restaurants, amusement arcades, and bookstores plying their particular business. Cruising goes on up and down the street and in movie houses, some of which often show homosexual movies. The Port Authority Bus Terminal on 41st Street is also a place for street cruising.

Area 4—Midtown East/This area is somewhat similar to the Upper East Side except that it is less affluent and less residential. It includes large office buildings like the Chrysler

Building, Empire State Building, and Rockefeller Center and large concentrations of shops and stores on 5th Avenue, Madison Avenue, and Lexington Avenue. There are many apartments here, of course, but rents in the main are lower than those on the Upper East Side.

Thirteen bars on our list and two restaurants are located in this area. The bars in this section are very pleasant and do much of their business in the daytime; thus, a bar might have a "mixed" clientele by day whereas at night it may be predominantly gay. Because of its central location there are different types of bars in this area, ranging from the most elegant to neighborhood bars and a dance bar that is active in the very early hours of the morning.

Other homosexual institutions in this area include two private clubs and a steam bath. Finally, cruising areas include Bryant Park on 42nd Street and various sections of the avenues.

Area 5—Southwest Manhattan (Greenwich Village)/The most concentrated area of homosexual institutions has been in the Greenwich Village area—an area renowned for unconventional life-styles. At one time labeled Bohemian, then beat, it now rejoices under the appellation of hip or hippie to describe its particular culture. Various "subterranean traditions" find their home, even their origins, in the Village—the radical political, romantic poetic, mystical religious, and so forth. It is not surprising that in such an atmosphere homosexual institutions should take root to such a degree. Twenty-six bars on our list are located in this area and twelve nightclub/restaurants. (The extent of concentration cannot be adequately shown by the *number* of bars but rather by the fact that in terms of area or city blocks, the Village area is one-half to one-third the size of the areas previously mentioned.)

The fulcrum of homosexual life in the Village is Christopher Street, running southwest of 6th Avenue. The majority of bars, restaurants, and clubs on our list are located within one or two blocks of here. Christopher Street itself is a popular cruising area. At the western end of the street are the "docks" or "trucks" at the waterfront. The trucks parked here are a locale for much homosexual activity. Left unattended at night, they are often used as convenient places in which to engage in sex. Sometimes they will be used by those who have been cruising on Christopher Street and have picked up a partner but have no place to go. On other occasions persons will wander about the parked trucks waiting for an invitation or will just jump into a truck when they hear sounds of activity and take "pot luck." Often particular trucks become the scene of orgies that continue for hours with a stream of new participants.

Bars at the western end of Christopher Street and northward along the waterfront have little in the way of decor, just a long bar with little furniture and sometimes a sawdust floor. Reflecting the "tough" tone of the area, this area has two leather bars on the waterfront which attract the hypermasculine type of homosexual. On the same street is a gay discotheque featuring go-go boys and a "back room" for impromptu orgies. This is a good example of the new after-hours places and was one of the bars raided by federal agents to which we referred earlier.

The Village contains all types of homosexual bars. In addition to the leather bars, the five lesbian bars on our list were all located in this area. Approaching Sheridan Square, the bars (and homosexual restaurants) improve in decor, and the clientele is older and sometimes more "mixed."

Other bars in this area include the Stonewall on Christopher Street (now closed), which was the center of the riots in 1969, and a long-established and very popular bar on West 10th Street.

Four hotels which cater to homosexuals can be found in the Village area; two private clubs but no baths are also situated here. Cruising areas abound: Washington Square

Park, West 8th Street between 5th and 6th Avenues, Greenwich Avenue from 6th to 7th Avenues, Bleecker Street between 7th and 8th Avenues, and, as previously mentioned, Christopher Street from Greenwich Avenue to the Hudson.

*Area 6—Southeast Manhattan (The East Village)/*East of Greenwich Village is the East Village, a deteriorating area of New York, undergoing a rapid change as older, Lower East Side ethnic immigrants move out and are replaced by Puerto Rican immigrants and young white "hippie" types. Only one gay bar is listed as being in this area, along with a popular bath. There is also a private club. Though not a particularly "gay area," it should perhaps be noted that the East Village is the home of what has been called the "new homosexual," a young person who is said to be bisexual because of the value he places on sexual expression of any kind.

*Area 7—Outside Manhattan/*In the boroughs outside of Manhattan there is no appreciable concentration of homosexuals and their institutions with the exception of the Heights in Brooklyn and Kew Gardens and Forest Hills in Queens.[10] Bars used by homosexuals are more often neighborhood bars with a "mixed" clientele. Outside of Manhattan there are recreation areas such as parks and beaches where, especially during the summer, a great deal of cruising is done and where "open air sex" is enjoyed. The boardwalk at Coney Island is a particularly popular cruising place as well as Riis Park Beach in the Rockaways.

CHAPTER 4

SAN FRANCISCO

San Francisco is generally considered the best city in the United States for homosexuals. Its tradition of tolerance toward nonconforming life styles is well known. In addition, San Francisco is smaller and less residentially dispersed than New York and thus is more conducive to a tightly knit homosexual community. Our description of San Francisco is based on our familiarity with the city in connection with this study during 1968–69 and on field work completed for another large survey study being carried out by the Institute for Sex Research.

The Legal Situation

Unlike New York City where homosexuality is regulated by city as well as state codes, the legal regulation of homosexuality in San Francisco comes under general state law. Legislation regarding criminal sexual behavior was preempted by the state in 1962 when the California Supreme Court ruled that the legislature intended a "general scheme for the regulation of this subject." Local regulations concerning illegal sexual activity are therefore void.[1]

The two felony statutes that are applied most often to homosexuals are Sections 286 and 288a of the California Penal Code.[2] Section 286, Sodomy, refers to the "infamous crime against nature" which court practice has come to interpret as anal intercourse involving men, women, or beasts. The penalty for such offenses is imprisonment for not less than one year, with a maximum potential sentence of life. Section 288a, Oral Copulation, is punished by imprisonment in the state prison for up to fifteen years or in the county jail for up to one year.

At the court's discretion, homosexual behavior may be treated either as a felony or a misdemeanor, which makes the penalty for such acts more liberal than those found in many other states. In fact, the most widely used provisions for punishing homosexuals is Section 647, Disorderly Conduct. The majority of arrests occur under 647a and 647d, which state:

> Every person who commits any of the following acts shall be guilty of disorderly conduct, a misdemeanor: (a) Who solicits anyone to engage in or who in any public place or in any place open to the public or exposed to public view engages in lewd or dissolute conduct. . . . (d) Who loiters in or about any toilet open to the public for the purpose of engaging in or soliciting any lewd or lascivious or any unlawful act.[3]

This statute is used rather than the felony provisions of 286 and 288a because the courts are unwilling to impose severe penalties for activities that are consensual.[4] Section 647a is the provision invoked most often, frequently in connection with arrests involving the soliciting of decoys by homosexuals.

A further hazard exists for the San Francisco homosexual: conviction under 286, 288a, 647a, or 647d means that within thirty days he must register with the chief of police or sheriff where he resides. Because of this provision, police often make arrests under a section that requires registration. The registration procedure involves fingerprinting, photographs, and notifications of any change of residence. While there may be some question about the extent to which this system deters homosexual activity, it clearly acts as a form of harassment for the homosexual, leaving him open to the possible misuse of these records through disclosures made to unauthorized persons.

Enforcement of the Law in San Francisco

Although subject to the same state laws, California cities differ from each other in the way that antihomosexual legislation is enforced. In San Francisco, an event occurred in 1965 that led to a less stringent police policy, and since then enforcement of laws against homosexuals appears not to have been very intense (although the situation does fluctuate).

A benefit ball was held on the eve of New Year's Day 1965 on behalf of a new homophile organization, the Council on Religion and the Homosexual (C.R.H.). This organization was established by clergymen who were concerned with the fact that the church's negative attitude toward homosexuality had alienated many homosexuals. Although a delegation of ministers and leaders of the homophile community had cleared their plans for the ball with the police department, the police turned up in force, took pictures of the participants, and demanded the right to enter the hall. This was denied them by three lawyers on the grounds that the affair was private and that no warrant had been issued. The lawyers were then arrested for interfering with the police, who entered the hall and, a while later, arrested two men for committing lewd acts.

A loud hue and cry followed. Six ministers publicly accused the police of harassing homosexuals, and the local newspapers reported the event in great detail, with the police generally appearing in a bad light. As a result, new officers were assigned to the Bureau of Inspectors ("Sex Detail"), which has the responsibility for enforcing anti-homosexual laws, and the patrolling of rest rooms as well as other forms of harassment decreased. In addition, later that year an organization was formed by concerned homophile members called "Citizens Alert," a twenty-four-hour answering service set up to report police misbehavior. In order to further improve police-homosexual relations, the Community Relations Division of the San Francisco Police Department has assigned one of its members to work full time with the gay community. In general, therefore, law enforcement problems faced by homosexuals in San Francisco seemed to have decreased over the last seven years or so.

Events in the summer of 1970, however, illustrate the fragility of the homosexual's situation vis-à-vis law enforcement practices. In June of that year, the number of arrests for homosexual conduct increased sharply. Reports of harassment at gay bars and baths were also received (for example, patrons of the baths received traffic tickets at 3:00 A.M.) as well as reports of enticement and entrapment.

What accounted for this increase in police activity against homosexuals? Two explanations were provided by *Vector*, the magazine of the Society for Individual Rights (S.I.R.), a San Francisco homophile organization.[5] On the one hand, it was noted that many of the arrests were made by a new police motorcycle unit, the Parks and Beach Detail, recently formed on a trial basis to discourage muggings and rapes in parkland areas. It was suggested that in order to justify their continued existence, officers on this detail maintained their arrest records by concentrating on homosexuals who used these parks as popular cruising areas.

A second explanation centered around the appointment of a new police chief who was eager to "do something" about the city's crime rate. It was suggested that to show his effectiveness, homosexuals were chosen as easy targets to increase the arrest and conviction rate. Furthermore, a referendum for more police funds had been defeated that June, and the suggestion was made that the crackdown could have been initiated to "prove" the need for more resources.

The upshot of this was that San Francisco homophile societies instigated a meeting with the police chief to discuss the issue. It has been reported that since this meeting reports of harassment by police in these areas have diminished.

Events in the summer of 1971 also help illustrate the boundaries of tolerance with regard to police–homosexual relations in San Francisco. The Castro Street area of the city has recently emerged as a new center of homosexual activity, especially for the more youthful "hippie" type of homosexual. The influx of new people into the area, and their public manifestations of homosexuality, apparently upset the residents of the area (both homosexual and heterosexual). Complaints from merchants, parents, and other residents led to increased police activity in the area (police undercover agents in bars, prowl cars in the streets, harassment of homosexuals by the police, and entrapment methods in a nearby park were reported).

Though not all the facts are at our disposal, it would seem that police reaction was caused by complaints received from "respectable" residents of the area with a channel to City Hall and the fact that San Francisco's usual "containment" policy, where homosexuals are left relatively undisturbed in their "own areas" by the police, was breached by the new homosexual influx. Thus, again we see that "tolerance" is always tentative. A reversal can come about as the result of changing administrations and also as a result of the public's notions of how and where minorities should conduct their lives.

Another source of problems for homosexuals in San Francisco has been the Alcoholic Beverage Control Agency

(A.B.C.), which is responsible for licensing establishments that sell alcoholic beverages and seeing to it that their practices conform to state laws. To enforce such laws, the A.B.C. has a corps of inspectors. For some time, apparently, A.B.C. inspectors paid particular attention to bars patronized by homosexuals. Some of their activities, resembling the police practices of enticement and entrapment, resulted in arrests and often the revocation of the bar's license. Other practices included repeated and extended surveillance and raids resulting in mass arrests (the charge often being "frequenting a disorderly house").[6]

Such inequitable methods of law enforcement have, however, according to most observers, declined in recent years. Nowadays, entrapment and enticement are seldom practiced, and A.B.C. inspectors generally no longer seem to be a source of trouble to owners of gay bars. This change in policy seems to be associated with the general adverse publicity over law enforcement against homosexuals that began in the sixties. In addition, owners of gay bars organized the "Tavern Guild" in 1961, which attempted to change A.B.C. practices. Eventually a cooperative partnership was established between the A.B.C. and the guild, which resulted in the establishment of a code of conduct for its membership and new efforts by the owners themselves to control "criminal" behavior in their bars.

Homophile Organizations

The Mattachine Society of San Francisco, which has already been described, is now, in the words of the president, a "public service agency" with no membership participation. The organization is supported financially by dues from its membership, unsolicited donations, and a legacy set up in trust. It does not actively recruit members and is quite small as an organization (approximately 200 "supporting members"). Its most important function is as a counseling and referral service. It offers lay counseling, draft counseling, and makes referrals to attorneys, bail bondsmen, and psychiatrists. A lot is done on an individual basis by members of the Mattachine Board who develop and maintain contacts with influential people in the community. The Society also provides speakers to such groups as the Lions and Kiwanis.

The largest homophile society in San Francisco, and one that also claims to be the largest in the country, is the Society for Individual Rights (S.I.R.). Founded in 1964, it is concerned with protecting homosexuals' civil rights and providing a social life for homosexuals other than that provided by gay bars. With an active leadership, a large membership was quickly obtained and a variegated social organization established. Most important, the organization was able to rent a large hall in the heart of downtown San Francisco, which was made into a community center for homosexuals including offices, a dance floor, stage, some conference rooms, and food facilities.

As of 1969, there were 782 dues-paying members in the San Francisco area and many more who held subscriptions to *Vector* (the organization's monthly publication) or who lived outside of San Francisco.[7] The results of a reader survey in the June 1969 *Vector* showed that the membership was predominantly white and middle class. Few distinctions are made between members and nonmembers in terms of the services S.I.R. provides except that members are given preference for admittance to dances.

S.I.R.'s activities are social and political. Its social activities include concert series, weekly dances, flea markets, skating parties, bowling, theater parties, dinners, discussion groups of all kinds, speakers (the August 1970 edition of *Vector* notes that Troy Perry, the well-known gay minister, and Laud Humphreys, the author of *Tearoom Trade*, were to be speakers), weekly tours of the San Francisco homosexual scene (the "Gay Time Tour," from "lavender to leather"), and rehearsals for their annual song and dance revue ("Sirlebrity Capades"). The organization is able to provide a full program of recreational and cultural events scheduled for every day of the week.

S.I.R. also provides the homosexual community with a variety of services, mainly of a referral type—to attorneys, psychiatrists, suicide prevention agencies, counselors of all types, and so forth. They also keep close contact with the relevant community agencies such as the Center for Special Problems in San Francisco.

Politically, the organization has been active in a number of ways. For example, it joined other homophile organizations in the area to picket San Francisco's Federal Building (over the exclusion of homosexuals from federal employment) and Macy's department store in downtown San Francisco. The rest room at the store had been a popular place for homosexual activities, and Macy's began a crackdown by having their guards arrest anyone involved in such behavior. More than forty persons were arrested, most of them on felony charges. Annoyed by the clumsy handling of the situation (S.I.R. claims an easier solution would have been to post warnings and to have a uniformed guard patrol the premises) and the possible fate of those arrested, the homophile organizations in the area responded by urging homosexuals to send back their credit cards, boycott the store, and picket outside. This latter tactic, although performed mainly by younger militant homosexuals, went on for weeks, with the aim of forcing the store to reduce the legal charges against those homosexuals it had had arrested.

More conventional political activities are in line with S.I.R.'s style, however. These include, for example, efforts to alleviate the homosexual's legal situation by challenging the constitutionality of some of the antihomosexual laws.

S.I.R.'s Legal Committee filed a suit in the United States Federal Court for the Northern District of California to decide the constitutionality of Sections 286 and 288a of the California Penal Code. These, it will be remembered, are the felony statutes which prohibit anal and oral copulation (S.I.R. was joined as plaintiff in the case by the Sexual Freedom League, the Modern Sex Institute, and various individuals).[8]

One important political event is "Candidates Night," held before local elections when all candidates are invited to appear at the community center to express their views on issues relevant to the homosexual community (these are then published in *Vector*). This is held in conjunction with a voter registration drive. Given the large number of homosexuals in San Francisco, the organization has potential for exerting considerable political power and already claims to have had some success in influencing the outcome at the polls, although this is difficult to demonstrate.

Another homophile organization is the Council on Religion and the Homosexual (C.R.H.), founded in 1964. In an attempt to create a bridge between homosexuals and the church, under the auspices of Glide Methodist Church, a week-long retreat was set up for ministers and representatives of various homophile organizations (S.I.R., D.O.B., Mattachine). The outcome of these meetings was C.R.H. The aim of the organization is to promote a "continuing dialogue between the church and the homosexual." There are about 100 to 150 members and 700 on the mailing list for C.R.H. publications. The organization's services are primarily for the community at large—providing speakers for interested groups, holding symposia, and publishing informational pamphlets. It has also published, as a result of the police raid on its ball, "A Brief of Injustices," which outlines the problems of unequal law enforcement faced by homosexuals. It also established "Citizens Alert."

Citizens Alert was formed in August 1965 through the efforts of S.I.R. and C.R.H. as the culmination of specific experiences of police violence and unequal law enforcement practices which had begun at the C.R.H. Ball early in the year. The original aim of this organization was to report on police misbehavior. Its modus operandi was a twenty-four-hour answering service manned by volunteers. Complaints were channeled through attorneys, physicians, and ministers and filed with the police department. Not only homosexuals but also any concerned citizen was welcome to use the service. In fact, the volunteers who answered the phone were mainly nonhomosexual college students. Later blacks and hippies rather than homosexuals were the most frequent users of the system, and most dues-paying members were not homosexual. (Within a short time after the period of our study, however, Citizens Alert was no longer in existence.)

Another important homophile organization is the Tavern Guild. Founded in 1961 as a social organization for owners and employees of gay bars, the Tavern Guild has become a trade organization for those involved in the running of gay bars. Important to its strength as an organization was the effect it had on policies of harassment which gay bars were subject to both by the police and A.B.C. officials. Concerted action by members of the Tavern Guild was influential in eliminating these practices, which made the organization attractive to other owners of gay bars not originally involved. It cooperates with the A.B.C. in controlling criminal behavior on the premises of its members and has established regulations for them to follow. Though it has little in the way of sanctions to control its members, it has been observed that one bar expelled from the organization did suffer a loss in clientele. The Tavern Guild has about 60 member bars and 150 to 200 individual members. Services for members include a group insurance plan for health and life insurance (most gay bars are nonunion, and many bar owners pay fees for their employees) and an unemployment fund.[9]

In summary, it can be said that the San Francisco homosexual is well represented by a variety of organizations that attempt to make life easier for him. Many of these organizations are vigorously and efficiently run and are known and respected by the majority of San Francisco homosexuals, as well as by many heterosexuals. S.I.R. appears to be particularly effective. It has made great strides in providing social facilities for the gay community and, working in concert with other organizations as a pressure group with local authorities, it has, to some extent, made the city a better place for the homosexual to live.

Not only is the San Francisco homosexual served by a number of self-help organizations, but he can also utilize many professional services that cater specifically to his needs. As there are sound working relationships, especially concerning referrals, between homophile organizations and these services, we would say that San Francisco meets the needs of its homosexual citizens better than any other place in this country.

Medical services/A prominent medical problem among homosexuals is V.D. The San Francisco Health Department provides professional and clinical services for V.D. which are quick, thorough, and sympathetic. There is no need for an appointment, and a person can be quickly diagnosed and treated. Social workers provide referral services for other problems, and a close working relationship is maintained between the clinic and other services meeting the needs of the homosexual community.

Also, certain urogenital and anorectal problems such as infections, fissures, and ruptures are sometimes associated with homosexual activities. Some physicians in San Francisco are known by the gay community to be sympathetic and responsible people to consult with regard to these problems. The homophile organizations keep a list of such physicians and refer people to them.

Suicide Prevention, Inc./This is a twenty-four-hour telephone service for potential suicide victims. In an attempt to prevent suicides, the service provides an understanding listener who consoles, advises, and refers the potential victim. San Francisco has a very high suicide rate, and it has been observed that many of the victims are homosexual.

San Francisco Police Department/The San Francisco Police Department has assigned a member of its Community Relations Division to deal with the special problems of the homosexual. Working in the downtown area with its large transient population of youthful homosexuals, he often refers those with problems to the relevant social agencies and also acts as an intermediary between the police and the homosexual community.

Glide Foundation/The most active private organization is the Glide Foundation and its affiliated organizations, especially Glide Methodist Church and the Council on Religion and the Homosexual. Glide has been a leader and promoter of special services to the homosexual community and is often sought out for professional consultation and referral.

San Francisco City and County Department of Public Health/The Community Mental Health Division of the city's health department provides professional services which are especially directed toward the homosexual and his problems. The vanguard of these community mental health services is the city's Center for Special Problems, established in 1965 as a clinic for the specialized treatment of drug problems, "sexual deviance," and in general, the types of problems suffered by those persons usually disqualified for psychiatric services in most public and private clinics. Its policy of not seeing homosexuality as evidence of an emotional problem per se has made it attractive to many homosexuals. As the word spread, more homosexuals came, and the center recruited staff who were familiar with various aspects of homosexuality. The center now offers a variety of services to homosexuals: individual and group psychotherapy, vocational and educational counseling, daily contact and volunteer groups, in-community mental health services, street workers, and organizational liaison. Also included is conjoint therapy for homosexual couples. Referral to the center is also often a condition of probation and parole.

Homosexual Bars

There are many risks involved in instituting and managing a gay bar. Licensing of various kinds, meeting municipal code requirements, and following the formal and normative regulations of operating public accommodations are all more difficult for the homosexual bar than for other bars—public agencies are disinclined to directly facilitate procedures for the opening and operation of a gay bar. In the operation of the bar, the management must be constantly concerned about the enforcement of rules, ordinances, and laws and usually must be more stringent and strict. For example, most gay bars will close their doors before the California 2:00 A.M. closing time, because Alcoholic Beverage Control and local police enforcement agents will use an infringement of this state law as grounds for revoking the license. Under similar circumstances, other bars might be overlooked or at most reprimanded. Such difficulties have led to the organization of many of San Francisco's gay bar managements, especially in the Tavern Guild, and these organizations have been an important part of the general organization of the homosexual community in San Francisco.[10] It appears that all homosexual bars are owned and operated by local ownerships and partnerships; at the time of writing, there are no absentee owners to our knowledge.[11]

The relationships between the heterosexual and homosexual communities (and the lawfully constituted agents of the former), between the gay bar and the changing interests of homosexual urbanites, and between factors associated with the larger economic scene can produce a precarious situation for the owner of a homosexual bar. The market changes, as do public enforcement policies, as well as more elusive conditions like possible "payoffs," the in-fighting among owners and competitors, and the whims of clients. As an example of fluctuating conditions, the rapid-transit excavation in the downtown area of San Francisco left two homosexual bars with few clients.

It might seem that homosexual bars in San Francisco could not remain open without payoffs to public officials who could bring legal sanctions against them. Verification of this was, however, very difficult to obtain, and it seems that, unlike New York, San Francisco bars are not involved with organized crime and that such things as payoffs to the police have been generally rare in recent years.[12]

At the time of our study, the longevity of the San Francisco homosexual bars ranged from six months to ten years. Owners and managers of gay bars stated that the probability of surviving in this business is a function of several factors, the most important of which are their ability to attract youthful homosexuals, space for cruising, and a rapprochement with the official local "establishment." During the last few years the dance and "hip" bar has opened or reopened most frequently. These bars have grown immensely throughout the city and at this time appear to have a monopoly of the young market. The drinking establishments which have been most successful over time have been the bar-restaurant combinations (one of these establishments has been in business for twenty years). The large number of such establishments is a feature of the San Francisco bar scene that distinguishes it from New York.

We estimated that between fifty and seventy-five gay bars were in operation in San Francisco during the years 1966–70.[13] They cluster in the following areas. (See map.)

Area 1: Downtown San Francisco/This area includes that part of San Francisco referred to as the Tenderloin.[14] Inside that area are located eleven of the bars on our list. Included among them are both long-established bars and relatively recent arrivals. The bars in this area range from places where good food is served to dancing bars and plain cruising bars. Since this area is a major cruising area, the traffic between bars is quite heavy. Also of note are the many hustlers who wait outside these bars, especially around closing time. One or two blocks to the west of this area there are five more bars. A similar distance northward are two other bars; two steam baths are also located in the Tenderloin area.

Area 2: Polk Street/Whereas the Tenderloin area has aspects of Skid Row, including a high crime rate, Polk Street appears to be a locale that appeals to the older and more affluent homosexual. This is reflected in the type of bars found here. They are more comfortable and sociable, reflecting the presence of a more residentially stable homosexual population. Eleven bars on our list were located on Polk Street or within one or two blocks of it. One bath was located near this area.

Area 3: Cole Street–Haight Street/This changing area, once the center of the hippie cult, contained four of the bars on our list.

Area 4: South of Market Street–Folsom Street/Four bars are located south of Market Street (the main downtown street) in close proximity to Mission Street, and seven bars

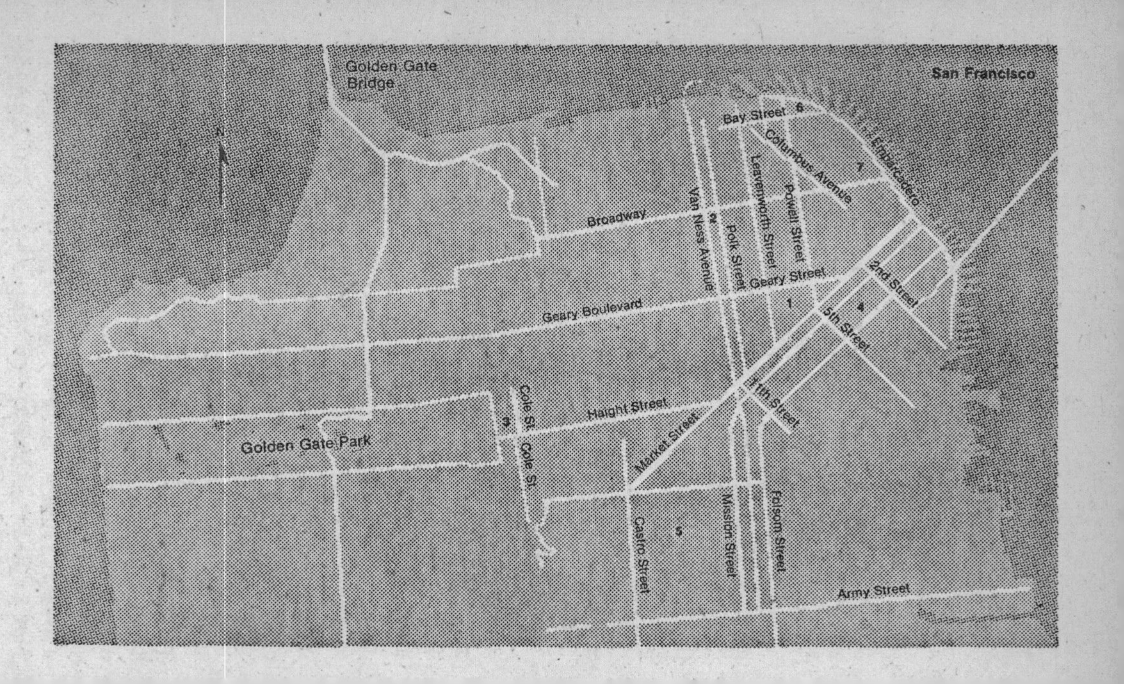
San Francisco
Golden Gate Bridge
Bay Street
Columbus Avenue
Embarcadero
Leavenworth Street
Powell Street
Broadway
Van Ness Avenue
Polk Street
Geary Street
2nd Street
5th Street
Geary Boulevard
11th Street
Haight Street
Cole St
Cole St
Golden Gate Park
Market Street
Castro Street
Mission Street
Folsom Street
Army Street
N

are located on Folsom Street on what homosexuals call the Miracle Mile. The Folsom Street bars cater to the "hyper-masculine" homosexual. The bars exhibit a motorcycle or Western theme which is reflected in their names. Two bars are located southeast of Folsom on Bryant Street. Nearby, too, is a popular bath. At the extreme northeast of this area is a Y.M.C.A., a popular cruising place for homosexuals.

Area 5: Mission–Upper Market Street–Castro Street/Five bars on our list are located in the Upper Market Street area, and six are in the Mission district. A homosexual bath is also located at 21st Street and Mission. Five bars and one bath on our list are found on Castro Street. The Castro Street area, as we earlier described, has only recently emerged as a center of homosexual activity. As noted, the area has experienced an influx of younger homosexuals who are open about their homosexuality (as well as an influx of "hippie" types), and these changes have resulted in strong negative reactions from some of the established residents of the area and in increased activity against homosexuals on the part of law enforcement agencies. It has been reported that undercover agents scrutinize the bars in the area very carefully (for example, citing owners for allowing dancing on the premises), and fire inspectors are constantly "dis-covering" violations. At the time of writing this area is undergoing considerable flux.

Areas 6 and 7: Elsewhere in San Francisco/No other appreciable concentration of bars seems to exist in San Francisco. Four bars, however, were found near the waterfront (Area 6). Four bars, one private club, and a popular bath are located northeast of Columbus Avenue in North Beach (Area 7). This area is the center of tourist night life in San Francisco, featuring "topless-bottomless" bars, night clubs, and so forth.

We now turn to the social world of the homosexual in the

Netherlands and Denmark, two societies in which the homosexual confronts a different situation from the United States. Again, we shall be concerned with the helps and hurdles that surround his attempt to reach a manageable and satisfactory life-style.

CHAPTER 5

THE NETHERLANDS

This description of the Netherlands is based on four weeks of intensive field work during the summer of 1969. It depicts the public's attitudes toward homosexuals and describes other facets of the homosexual's social situation.

With regard to attitudes of the Dutch toward homosexuality, we were fortunate to have the results of a recently completed study sponsored by the Dutch Department of Culture, Recreation and Social Work. This study collected data in 1966–67 on attitudes toward various minorities, including homosexuals, from a representative national sample involving some 1,671 respondents, men and women over twenty-one years of age.

Although we do not have the specific results, a summary of the findings of this study stated that, in comparison to other minority groups, homosexuals are viewed as being similar to "mentally disturbed persons, and to groups who readily yield to satisfying nonprimary needs. . . ." As to the question of their acceptance, there "emerged a picture of incomprehension and aversion . . . but also of sympathy as long as the homosexual remains in his own group." According to the director of the study, the Dutch attitude is,

"We should be tolerant toward abnormals." From these results and our own investigations, we would summarize the attitude of the Dutch toward homosexuality as one of tolerance but not acceptance.[1]

At the same time, Amsterdam is reputed to be one of the most liberal cities in Europe. It was one of the first cities where Jews could live according to their own religion and where other religious minorities could find a home (the Huguenots from France, Catholics and Puritans from England). Historically, it has been a refuge for philosophers and persecuted writers (Descartes, Spinoza), and it is one of the few places where censorship has been almost unknown (the works of Voltaire and de Sade were first printed here). Its general tradition of toleration in many different areas encompasses various aspects of sexual expression as well. Not only does Amsterdam have a large and legal "red light" district which caters to heterosexual prostitution, but it also has an extensive array of pornography shops. One must be careful, however, in generalizing from the city of Amsterdam to the rest of the Netherlands, even to other large cities in the country. The relationship between Amsterdam and the rest of the Netherlands was succinctly put to us by a lawyer who said, "The central government and the people feel that one Amsterdam is enough; 'people can get what they want in Amsterdam' is the feeling." The homosexual in Amsterdam benefits from this liberalism. Although most cities allow homosexual bars to operate, gay bars are less hidden in Amsterdam; cruising occurs in other cities, but it is interfered with less by the police in Amsterdam.

Some discrimination against homosexuals does exist in the Netherlands. For example, advertisements for heterosexual partners are allowed in newspapers, but similar ones for homosexuals are not. In fact, the large Dutch homophile society, Cultuur-en Ontspanningcentrum (C.O.C.), has run into problems with the government over a related issue.

C.O.C. has been trying to become a "legal personality," or chartered company. This requires the consent of the Queen through the government. Such permission was refused, however, on the grounds that some married members of C.O.C. had advertised for homosexual partners. We were told that one newspaper wrote a long article on this exchange between the government and C.O.C., suggesting that the Dutch people are not as liberal as they like to think. Also, as we shall discuss later, there has been a number of instances of legal discrimination between heterosexuals and homosexuals (for example, regarding the age of sexual consent).

One cannot depict the Dutch as being without prejudice against homosexuals. The populace, however, seems, in general, to be apathetic toward homosexuals and not intolerant; few wish to discriminate against them, and among the government and professional classes, a great deal is being done to help the homosexual with his problems. Of great importance, and different from the American situation, for example, is that organized religion in the Netherlands is *officially* on record as being concerned with helping homosexuals and in general does not display a moralizing stance toward them. Dutch churches are generally known for their liberalism regarding many things, not simply homosexuality. The birth control movement in the 1930's and its success inside and outside the church disjoined the relationship between sex and procreation and allowed both Catholic and Protestant churches to work for a more tolerant attitude toward various kinds of sex-related phenomena, including homosexuality.

In the late 1950's both Protestant and Catholic churches began "study groups" for members of their churches who were homosexual. A number of such groups have continued in various cities throughout the Netherlands for persons who are both religious and homosexual and who prefer to discuss their problems within these groups. In addition, a close relationship is kept by religious organizations with the Dialogue Foundation (part of C.O.C.), whose aim is to spread information about homosexuality by supplying speakers to groups and radio and television, and by providing other educational services.

Interestingly, the Catholic Church has been more forward than the Protestant churches in its dealings with homosexuals. This appears to be due to the fact that activities are carried out by the more liberal priests and bishops without reference to the wishes of local congregations or of the Pope. One priest we spoke to said he was asked by Rome to leave Amsterdam because of his work with homosexuals. His bishop supported him, however, and he has continued his work. Protestant ministers are more likely to encounter problems with, and are also less likely to receive support from, higher church authorities. There also appears to be more factionalism in the Protestant Church—the Reform Church (Calvinist) has recently had a conservative group dissociate and form their own church, the "Reformed Reformed Church," to protest liberal trends. One study group sent a letter to the synod of the Reformed Reformed Church to ask that they cooperate in working with homosexuals, but the Church refused to support any of their ministers in such work. These impressions were also supported by the survey study referred to on page 83. To quote, ". . . the most tolerant attitude [toward homosexuals] was ascribed to the Humanist [Ethical Cultural] Society and the Roman Catholic Church. The least tolerant attitude [was ascribed to] the Calvinist Church."

In the past few years, the position of the Dutch homosexual has been improved by efforts of ruling elites. How this will affect the attitudes of the ordinary citizen in the long run is difficult to say. But the Dutch homosexual, particularly if he lives in Amsterdam, has benefited by positive attitudes of political, legal, and ecclesiastical authorities, a situation that so far has failed to occur in America.

The Legal Situation

Homosexuality between consenting adults has not been a punishable offense in the Netherlands for over 160 years, since the imposition of the Napoleonic Code in 1809. Before 1911, an "adult" was any person sixteen years and older. In 1911 the law changed the age of consent for homosexuals to twenty-one. The particular administration which passed this law was very conservative, also passing severe laws against prostitution and establishing vice squads which became known as morality police. Since that time, however, no laws have been passed specifically against homosexuals.

Recently, however, serious discussions have taken place about revising the law to what it was before 1911. Such a bill was before Parliament at the time of this study. A major argument in favor of this legal change is that the age of consent for both homosexuals and heterosexuals should be the same—sixteen. We were told that the revision would easily pass.

The present government and most of the major political parties seem to be in favor of liberalization. The only opponents seem to be the Farmers' Party and some very orthodox Protestant and Catholic groups. For politicians, it seems, being antihomosexual would be to their disadvantage politically.

Despite the fact that homosexual acts with those under twenty-one are punishable, it appears that this is rarely enforced. Commenting on the legal situation in the Netherlands, the Wolfenden Report (1957) concludes that the effect of the law "is that homosexual acts that take place between mutually consenting partners both of whom are over 21, or both of whom are between 16 and 21, are not punishable unless public decency is affronted or there are certain other aggravating circumstances." [2]

Nor does being homosexual preclude one from Dutch government jobs. No one can be fired for being homosexual, and the threat of blackmail seems to be discounted. No one mentioned to us any problem homosexuals have in obtaining or remaining in government jobs. Until recently, however, discrimination existed with regard to the military. In the Medical Examination Regulations of the Armed Forces, homosexuality was regarded as an illness and known homosexuals were rejected.

Enforcement of the Law in Amsterdam

In Amsterdam, not only is homosexuality permitted between consenting adults, but the definition of adult seems to include those over sixteen, de facto if not de jure. Homosexuals usually come to the attention of the police in one of two ways: first, through some public nuisance offense such as having sex in a public place. Many public toilets in Amsterdam were closed recently because of their use by homosexuals as meeting places and for having sex. This is against the law, and the police used to keep the toilets under surveillance. According to a Dutch criminologist, entrapment is not practiced, however. Indeed, he commented that he had never heard of the police using such practices. Second, there are those cases where homosexuals are involved in other crimes, usually as victims. As in the United States, "rolling homosexuals" is sometimes resorted to by younger criminals and has recently become a problem in Amsterdam. Vondel Park, a large wooded park in the city, is a favorite "cruising area" for homosexuals and has recently been the scene of attacks upon homosexuals. The attackers are not always Dutch but often workers from southern Europe and North Africa who emigrated because of labor shortages. Many have entered the Netherlands illegally and cannot obtain jobs. One outcome has been to resort to crime, "rolling homosexuals" being one instance.

On more than one occasion, from police and homosexuals themselves, we have heard that problems caused by homosexuals in Amsterdam are not caused by those who live in Amsterdam. Not only does the city attract homosexuals from other parts of the Netherlands on the weekend (Amsterdam is not more than about two hours away from most parts of the Netherlands), but due to its tolerant reputation and many facilities, it also attracts homosexuals from all over Europe (especially West Germany, where consensual adult homosexuality was, until recently, punishable by the law). It is this influx of foreign homosexuals (especially in the summer) in an open, anonymous locale that is viewed as causing problems, particularly the flaunting of homosexuality in public.

Police sometimes "sweep" Vondel Park before holidays, but even if they catch couples in flagrante delicto they are more likely to tell them to stop than to arrest them. Foreigners who are caught are told to leave the country. The police are not known to blackmail or to discriminate against homosexuals in their law enforcement. And laws such as those against loitering and disturbing the peace are not (and never have been) used selectively to harass homosexuals.

The legal situation and law enforcement practices, therefore, appear more or less to reflect public feeling toward homosexuals. Because this form of sexual expression is not criminalized, little sustenance is given for the more flagrant discrimination and abuse toward homosexuals on the part of law enforcement officials and the general public which we find in the United States. If Dutch homosexuals, specifically those living in Amsterdam, have problems, it would be hard to find their genesis in the legal situation.

Homophile Organizations

Amsterdam is the home of one of the largest and most influential homophile organizations in Europe, Cultuur-en Ontspanningcentrum, or "Center for Culture and Recreation" (C.O.C.). Started in 1946, the club at the time of this research had approximately 4,000 members (men and women), with branches in most of the main cities of the Netherlands. As well as campaigning for legal and social changes which would improve the homosexual's situation, the club is a meeting place (formal and informal) for homosexuals and a recreation center with a bar and restaurant.

The C.O.C. is acknowledged as a private homosexual club by both the police and the public. The Amsterdam police have, in fact, helped the organization establish branches elsewhere:

> Such establishment was by no means easy; local police attitudes have not always been as permissive as those of Amsterdam . . . but as the result of a favorable report on the movement written by Amsterdam's Chief of Police and circulated throughout the country, official acceptance of the C.O.C. as a socially useful body . . . has slowly begun to permeate throughout the country.[3]

The C.O.C. in Amsterdam occupies an unpretentious building in the Korte Leidsedwarsstraat. The bar and restaurant are downstairs; business rooms and a television room, upstairs. The C.O.C. building has just a small brass plate outside announcing its presence. The bar and dance floor downstairs have no sign at all, and those who enter must either be members or obtain a "visiting" membership. Foreigners who show their passports as proof of being over twenty-one can have a temporary membership. Thus, the club is not something that a person can stumble into off the street. One has to know what it is and where it is and be prepared to take out membership.

The bar and dance floor are open on most nights until 1:00 A.M. The large horseshoe-shaped bar is raised above the dance floor. The atmosphere is dark, and loud music is continually being played for dancing. Men dance together as do women, and occasionally men and women dance together. There are tables around the dance floor for those who prefer not to dance but would rather sit and drink; they can also sit at the bar.

During our visits, some kissing, usually not of a passionate nature, could be observed on the dance floor. No kissing was seen off the dance floor. In fact, people were acting and behaving as they would at any club where there is drinking and dancing. The club starts to fill at about 10:30 to 11:00 P.M. and gradually reaches its maximum capacity for the night about midnight. The most popular nights are Friday and Saturday. Based on the questionnaires that were given out, between 11:00 and 11:30 P.M. on any day between Monday and Thursday there might be 70 to 100 people in the club at any one time. On a Friday or Saturday the figure would be between 150 and 200. This is at any *one time*—people are coming and going so it is difficult to estimate the total number of people who use the club in any one evening.

The hour before closing is most popular because that is when sexual contacts are most likely to be made. Many C.O.C. members do not like using other homosexual bars and depend upon C.O.C. for cruising. For others who wish to continue their evening's entertainment, many homosexual bars and De Odeon Kring (D.O.K.), a well-known Amsterdam homosexual club, are open until 3:00 A.M. or later on weekends.

As a place for entertainment and the meeting of homosexuals for social purposes, C.O.C. is well known. We met no homosexual who had not heard of the club. The national survey referred to earlier found that 46 per cent of the general population had heard of C.O.C. This would be due to the organization's promotional activities (for example, newspaper articles and appearances of its members on television). It seems a mark of its effectiveness that C.O.C. could make itself known to nearly half of the population.

In addition to providing a political platform and a place of entertainment for homosexuals, C.O.C. has many other functions. Perhaps its principal function is helping homosexuals with problems, either directly by engaging its own lawyers and psychiatrists or indirectly by working with various social welfare agencies in the city. For example, the Schorerstichting (or Schorer Foundation), which opened in November 1968, is a consultation bureau directed toward homosexuals and their problems. Begun on the initiative of C.O.C., it is supported financially by the Ministry of Social Work. The Schorer Foundation was established when so many people came to C.O.C. with problems that C.O.C. asked the National Council for Social Work to help them. Part of the reason for the large number of people turning to C.O.C. for help was that the homosexual did not turn to other, more conventional helping agencies either because they were ill equipped to help and advise him or because he did not trust them. The Schorer Foundation's association with C.O.C. solved the problem of trust (it includes homosexuals on its staff). It has also advised other welfare agencies of the way to deal with homosexuals and their problems.

The foundation occupies a small building on Wolvenstraat. Its staff is small: two full-time social workers, one part-time psychiatrist, one part-time social psychologist, and one part-time psychologist. The two social workers do most of the work and are advised by the other professionals. In February of 1969 the foundation ceased taking clients because of its heavy case load. We were told that they hoped to begin taking clients again shortly; meanwhile there are plans to expand facilities by employing more full-time staff and by opening other offices throughout the Netherlands. It is interesting to note that staffing difficulties were said to arise because professionals feel there is a stigma attached to working with homosexuals. At the most recent count (February 1969, when they stopped taking clients) the foundation had a case load of 185 homosexuals, about 20 per cent of whom were women.

Another important function of C.O.C. is disseminating accurate information about homosexuality. This is done by the Stichting Dialoog (Dialogue Foundation), set up by C.O.C. Its aim is to improve relationships with heterosexuals, to begin a "dialogue" with them; thus, there are both heterosexual and homosexual members of the foundation. It publishes a magazine called *Informatie Bulletin Dialoog,* which relates the current activities and successes of the homophile movement, summarizes the latest scientific studies of homosexuality, and provides such information as bibliographies of recent homophile works. It is a more "serious" document than the general C.O.C. publication, *Vriendschap.*

Dialoog is more specific in its aims than C.O.C. While C.O.C. tries to reach the average heterosexual, Dialoog attempts to influence people at the "top"—opinion makers and professionals. It has various "working groups." For example, a library group (working with the Dutch Institute for Sexual Reform at The Hague) is putting together a library and preparing bibliographies. Another group puts out the magazine bimonthly. One group provides help at C.O.C. every week; psychiatrists and social workers associated with Dialoog provide counseling at C.O.C. every Friday evening. Another group organizes study days for homosexuals and heterosexuals (usually professionals) centering around a certain theme, for example, the married homosexual. There is a group which advertises the work of the foundation and which supplies speakers to schools, churches, and so on. Finally, there is a group that provides speakers (both homosexual and heterosexual) who go out and speak on homosexuality.

In conclusion, it is our considered opinion that C.O.C. is a very effective organization. It gets things done, and it works through official agencies when it can. It is very well run and serves as a model for other homophile organizations which it sometimes advises. Consequently, for the Dutch homosexual, there is an effective, efficient organization that is working toward the solution of some of his major problems. No American homophile organization is as large or involved in as many activities as C.O.C., though S.I.R., which resembles it, comes closest. The greatest difference is that C.O.C. is integrated more with governmental agencies and other institutions in the heterosexual world in its attempts to improve the homosexual's condition. Thus, it enjoys a status among the general public that none of its counterparts in the United States has been able to achieve.

Homosexual Bars

Homosexual bars, as previously discussed, are transitory institutions. They open, close, and reopen according to the vagaries of the situation, such as the attitude of the police or licensing authorities (though these are not important factors in Amsterdam) or the popularity of the bar among homosexuals. It is, therefore, difficult to estimate the number of gay bars in a city the size of Amsterdam. We had at our disposal various bar lists prepared for American homosexuals touring Europe. These, along with information given to us by the Dutch homosexuals, provided an indication of the number of such bars in Amsterdam. Since questionnaires were to be given out in bars, it was necessary to check further on the accuracy of these lists so that

bar in Amsterdam, that is, catering to subgroups among the homosexual population ("queens," hustlers, and so forth). Nearby is one of the most popular gay hotels in Amsterdam.

Area 2: Rembrantsplein/The next area of concentration has as its fulcrum Rembrantsplein. This is another area where entertainments are concentrated, though by no means a "red light" district. Here can be found many restaurants, sidewalk cafés, and movie theaters, as well as larger clubs that put on shows, and dance halls catering mainly to young people. The homosexual bars are smaller and less crowded than in the other areas. Many of the bars did not seem to be heavily frequented, even on Friday and Saturday nights. This area did contain, however, one of the newest and then most popular gay bars in Amsterdam, which was very crowded after 10:00 P.M. most of the week. The fact that this bar is close to D.O.K. might explain its popularity.

Area 3: Leidseplein/The final area of concentration are the streets that run off and north of Leidseplein. This area, just north of Vondel Park and roughly south of the other two areas, contains many of the better hotels, the Dutch Students' Hostel, the National Theater, and the more expensive restaurants and clubs. It is also the locale for Madame Arthur's, a heterosexual club (although often "mixed") which is famous for its drag shows, much like Finnochio's in San Francisco. Also, C.O.C. is located in the center of this area (see map). It is here that the homosexual social life centering around bars flourishes most. Here the bars are less mixed than those located in the other two areas. They also range from large, crowded bars to smaller, more intimate bars.

Not all homosexual bars are in these three areas, though most of them are. Interesting exceptions are two bars that cater mainly to the homosexuals in their late teens.

Bars in Amsterdam, both homosexual and heterosexual, are very strictly regulated. A person wishing to open a bar must be without a criminal record (no offense in the last ten years) and must get the consent of the police and other authorities. Even after this permission is granted, it can be withdrawn at any time. To obtain the license, the bar must satisfy certain physical conditions (for example, air conditioning, certain lighting arrangements, thirty-five square meters of space), and the prospective owner must pass an examination which requires a year's study and tests his knowledge of wines and beers, bookkeeping, the law, and so on.

Permission to open a bar must be obtained from several sources. Clearances must be given from such departments as the police, fire, and taxation. These are all brought together before a license is issued. This procedure helps prevent corruption in opening a bar because, as one barman told us, "You just couldn't buy them all off."

Once opened, a bar continues to be regulated. The bar must keep its music down to a certain number of decibels, prohibit dancing, and maintain a certain level of illumination. It must maintain order among its clientele, prevent fights and sexual solicitation, and close at the appointed time. Failure to comply brings a warning. If two warnings are given within five years, the bar is closed. Again the chance of bribery is reduced, as the various legal agencies send their inspectors around incognito.

A bar where the clientele is 100 per cent homosexual will not be closed as long as "propriety" is maintained. Also, no harassment occurs from authorities on account of a predominantly homosexual clientele. A bar, however, cannot advertise as a homosexual bar.

The effect of these regulations is that gay bars in Amsterdam, unlike many gay bars in the United States, are pleasant places to visit. Many of them are mixed (used also by heterosexuals and heterosexual couples). The atmosphere of the unmixed ones is also different. Instead of being blatantly sized up as a sexual partner as one walks in, any new entrant seems to be little noticed. Perhaps this difference reflects the different functions that homosexual bars serve in the two countries. In the United States, bars serve primarily as cruising locales. While they also have this function in the Netherlands, they provide more social functions than do the bars in the United States.

In addition to having a somewhat different bar scene than American cities, two other homosexual institutions, homosexual restaurants and steam baths, seem relatively undeveloped in Amsterdam. Only two baths patronized by homosexuals were found in Amsterdam. Neither was as plush as the better American baths or as conducive to socializing. Another important difference was their lack of "private rooms." No restaurants used mainly by homosexuals were found. Perhaps because Amsterdam serves as something of a mecca for European homosexuals, it is quite well endowed with hotels that are patronized mainly by homosexuals.

CHAPTER 6

DENMARK

As in the Netherlands, our observations were carried out over a period of four weeks in the summer of 1969 and were confined to one city, Copenhagen; our conclusions do not necessarily apply to the rest of Denmark. In most cases, attitudes and behavior in large cosmopolitan urban centers are more liberal than elsewhere. It is suggested, however, that because of the greater ethnic and cultural homogeneity which exists in Denmark, there is probably a greater similarity between Copenhagen and the rest of Denmark than between Amsterdam and the rest of the Netherlands.

A lack of solid popular roots for the Christian faith would seem to be one of the major distinctions between Scandinavia and the rest of Europe. In Denmark, although the majority of the population is Lutheran, Christianity does not appear to have great influence. The Lutheran State Church was introduced by royal decree after the Reformation, and although the church baptizes, marries, and buries the majority of Danes, religious indifference is widespread.[1] Historically, the Scandinavian people never fully embraced Christianity, which was practiced mainly by the court and upper classes. Most maintained their pre-Christian traditions, using the church only for special occasions. Consequently, the church, despite its efforts, has never achieved an effective regulation of sexual behavior in Denmark. Also, "the traditional Christian view of the woman as the servant of man has not penetrated deeply into the Scandinavian populations." [2] The relative equality of women in Scandinavia in comparison to the rest of Europe can be thought of as having important effects upon conceptions of sexual morality in general.[3]

Whatever problems homosexuals have in Denmark are neither ameliorated nor caused by religion. Unlike the Netherlands, there seems to be no general movement on the part of organized religion to help the homosexual.

Insofar as *heterosexuality* is concerned, Denmark is more "permissive" sexually than most European nations.[4] In the foreign press, such "permissiveness" is given extensive coverage without, however, the realization that such things as high rates of premarital sex and pregnancies represent a continuity in the marital customs of the culture rather than an ethos of "anything goes." [5] Also, the legalization of pornography by the Danish parliament in the late sixties reflected not so much an approval of pornography per se as a feeling that its prohibition stimulated unhealthy interests in sex and, even more important, infringed upon the freedom of the individual. (These issues were given little coverage in the American press.)

As in the Netherlands, the relative tolerance shown the homosexual is a by-product of this emphasis on personal freedom rather than of any acceptance of the behavior. Also, as in the Netherlands, such ideological pressure comes from above, from politicians and professionals and the higher strata of society. The result, again as in the Netherlands, is one of tolerance of homosexuals, but with little genuine acceptance of them.

With regard to the whole question of tolerance toward sexual matters, however, it should be emphasized that

Denmark, like the Netherlands, is tolerant only relative to such erotophobic societies as the United States. That is, not everyone in the country is tolerant, and tolerance varies according to groups and areas. For example, at the time the Danish government was considering removing restrictions from written pornography, a Gallup Poll was taken of a representative sample of the Danish population over age fifteen. To the question, should written pornography be prohibited, 44 per cent said *yes*, it should. Dividing the sample into Copenhagen, towns, and rural areas, the largest proportion in favor of legalizing pornography lived in Copenhagen, followed by those living in towns, and then by those residing in rural areas. Liberal attitudes were also found to be more prevalent among males and the traditionally liberal segments of the population, namely, the young (fifteen to twenty-four), the more educated, and the more politically left. A similar poll concerning pictorial pornography showed the same results. For example, 36 per cent of the population would allow complete freedom for pictures and books: for Copenhagen, 49 per cent agreed with this, for towns, 36 per cent, and rural areas, 24 per cent.[6] Thus, even Copenhagen, with its image as a cosmopolitan, liberal city, had less than half of its population agreeing with the easing of such restrictions.

The Legal Situation

In Denmark, as in the Netherlands, private homosexual behavior between consenting adults is not punishable by law. The legal age of consent is eighteen, which is lower than in the Netherlands. In both countries the age of consent is lower (only fifteen in Denmark) for heterosexuals than for homosexuals. Like the Dutch, the Danes are very liberal in their actual enforcement of the law. Apart from some concern with young male prostitutes in the early

1960's, homosexuals and legal authorities generally have not come into conflict. Homosexuality today seems of little concern to politicians. As in the Netherlands, being homosexual does not preclude a person's obtaining a government job (except in the Danish foreign service) but does lead to rejection by the military.

Enforcement of the Law in Copenhagen

There is little contact between the police and the homosexual in Copenhagen. The most concentrated police activity within recent times has involved the young male prostitute. In 1955, in collaboration with the Child Welfare Board of Copenhagen and under the jurisdiction of the Ministry of Social Affairs, a special section of the "Morality Police" was assigned this problem. Legislation, however, recently has been passed which repealed prohibitions against male prostitution; thus, even this is no longer a police matter.[7]

An important by-product of this concern was that the issue of homosexuality was given a public airing through newspapers, talks to parents, and so forth. Most important, the distinction was consistently made between the paedophile (a person whose main erotic pleasure is from sex with children) and what was called the "normal" homosexual.

At the time of our study, the main problems the police face with homosexuals are sex in public and keeping order in some of the more unruly homosexual bars. Public toilets are policed, not to harass the homosexual, but to inhibit behavior offensive to many heterosexuals. Discovering homosexual conduct in such a locale is followed by an automatic fine. The parks, where a good deal of homosexual behavior occurs, are pretty much left alone by the police, especially late at night when a tacit recognition exists as to the reason why they are used. No examples of police harassment were observed by, or reported to, us. As in the Netherlands, the homosexual comes into contact with the police usually when he is the victim, rather than the perpetrator, of a crime.

Homophile Organizations

The major Danish homophile organization is Forbundet af 1948, with about 1,000 members of both sexes. At the time of this writing, it is primarily a mailing organization and publishes a newsletter/magazine called *Pan*. It has no "business" premises like C.O.C., M.S.N.Y., or S.I.R. Thus, a member who is in trouble or has problems cannot "go" to the organization for assistance. There is no full-time paid staff like C.O.C. nor are there branch offices outside of Copenhagen.

Forbundet does have premises for social activities, however. There is a restaurant known as Club 48 which is situated at some distance from the main center of Copenhagen. Here meals are available and dancing is allowed. The place is small and well lit and open most days of the week, Friday and Saturday until 3:00 A.M.

Forbundet also owns the Pink Club, which is situated to the northeast of the central district (see map). The Pink Club is similar to the downstairs section of C.O.C., although it is smaller. It is dimly lit, with two bars, and seats around the wall. To use either the Pink Club or Club 48, a person must be a member of Forbundet. A Dane who visits for the first time is not allowed in but is given a card to fill out and must wait twenty-four hours before returning (a police rule that applies to all clubs). On receipt of the form and for under $10.00 he is made a member of Forbundet for six months. Foreigners have to show their passports and for a smaller fee are made temporary members for four weeks. During the times that we were present at the club, we found it to be extremely crowded and noisy, with a packed dance floor. Based on the number of questionnaires given out, on an ordinary week night there would be 60 to 80 people in the club between 11:00 P.M. and 1:00 A.M., while during that time on a weekend the number would be 100 to 140. Women as well as men are present, and in addition to same-sex dancing, there is dancing between the sexes. Unlike C.O.C., at both Club 48 and the Pink Club, there is little evidence that these are run by an organization devoted to the betterment of the homosexual's legal and social position. Except for some literature placed on a table at the entrance, there are no attempts to get participation in any activities from the members. Also absent are smaller rooms such as a lounge, television room, and coffee room which are found at C.O.C.

Differences between Forbundet and C.O.C., other than size and the relative lack of physical organization, are influence and integration. Forbundet appears to have less influence not only in persuading law makers and authorities to assist in improving the situation of the homosexual, but also in working with them in such endeavors. There is no equivalent to the Schorer Foundation, for example, nor any official body, political or religious, with whom Forbundet routinely works. As for its effect on the general public, it would appear that Forbundet is again less successful than C.O.C. For example, it is not nearly as well known in Denmark as C.O.C. is in the Netherlands. This is partially due to the lack of specific promotional arms such as Dialoog of C.O.C., as well as its lack of integration with the helping professions and political authorities. C.O.C. is aggressive as a pressure group; Forbundet seems more occupied with organizing in a way that will insure its survival.

Of course, we are only speaking relatively. Forbundet does have a political program and is not without any influence. At the time of this writing, it is attempting to change the penal code provision that prescribes different ages of consent for heterosexuals and homosexuals. Arguments against such discrimination have received support from the mass media, and Forbundet has contacted the Minister of Justice. Further aims include gaining the same tax status for homosexual couples as exists for heterosexual couples. Forbundet wants the survivor of a homosexual partnership of five years or more to pay the same inheritance tax as the immediate family (5 per cent), not the nonrelative rate of 40 per cent. Also, Forbundet is working to get homosexual couples the same rights as heterosexual couples in renting municipal housing. Public housing makes up most of the new housing in Denmark, which has a housing shortage, especially in Copenhagen. Single people under thirty-five can only get a one-and-a-half-room flat, which poses difficulties for homosexuals who want to live together. The last two aims reflect Forbundet's long-range goal of legalizing marriage between persons of the same sex.

Homosexual Bars

In American homosexual folklore, Copenhagen is portrayed as one of *the* places to be. This, it seems, is based upon the reputation the city acquired in the 1950's, partially due to the publicity brought about by Christine Jorgensen, who obtained her sex change there. In addition, the publicity surrounding heterosexual "permissiveness" gives the impression of a wide-open city. As one American homosexual publication put it, "Copenhagen is a fairy tale." It is stories like this that lure many single American males—both homosexual and heterosexual—to the city.

There is, however, nothing sexually spectacular about the city. The pornography shops are all that publicly distinguish Copenhagen from other large cities in this way; less public are live sex shows (most are now closed down) in night clubs. Nor is there anything unusual about the homosexual scene. Most homosexual bars are in a drab area north of Raadhus Pladsen (see map, area 1). Within this locale were approximately ten bars that catered to homo-

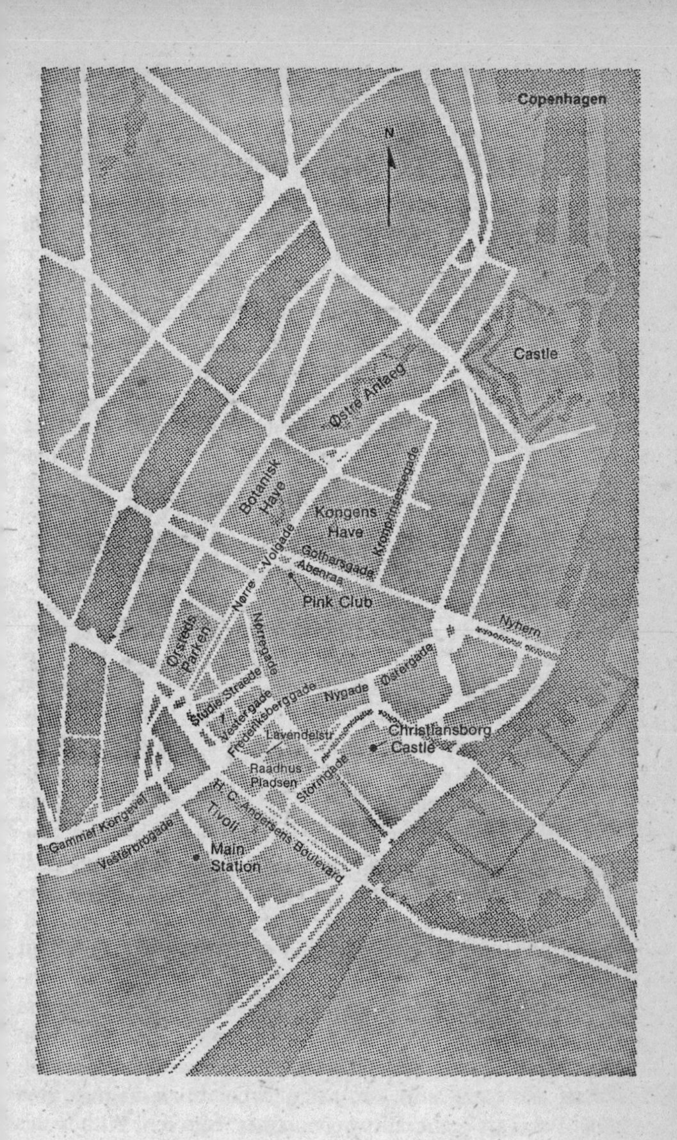
Copenhagen
N
Castle
Østre Anlaeg
Botanisk Have
Kongens Have
Kronprinsessegade
Volgade
Gothersgade
Abenraa
Pink Club
Nørre
Nørregade
Ørsteds Parken
Nyhern
Østergade
Studie Straede
Vestergade
Frederiksberggade
Nygade
Lavendelstr
Christiansborg Castle
Raadhus Pladsen
Stormgade
H. C. Andersens Boulevard
Tivoli
Gammel Kongevej
Vesterbrogade
Main Station

sexuals. This area runs off the main shopping street in Copenhagen, which is closed to vehicular traffic. In the daytime this is a very crowded thoroughfare, but at night it is relatively deserted. The streets off Frederiksberggade that contain the homosexual bars are narrow, ill lit, and often dirty; they are definitely not an area for tourist activity. The bars are interspersed with shops and warehouses. There are few residences, although there are some apartments above the shops. Unlike Amsterdam, the homosexual bars are not part of the general entertainment scene of dance halls, clubs, discotheques, movie theaters, and restaurants. (In Copenhagen this is centralized in Tivoli—the famous amusement park.) Thus, the streets are not crowded, and there is little traffic. Those who frequent these streets are young males who are often drunk, older people who are going to or from one of the neighborhood bars, and some female prostitutes. Later on in the evening, there are fights as well as public drunkenness and interference with passers-by. The area is depressing and potentially dangerous; its segregated character adds further to its general gloomy atmosphere.

The bars themselves are run-down. Generally, the decor is plain with old furniture and fittings. One bar has a sawdust floor and is generally raucous—when we visited it, two fights were observed on or about its premises. The "nicer" bars usually have doormen and a more subdued character. The most sociable bar we observed generally caters to the younger homosexual. One other bar toward the southeastern edge of the area is unique in that, as far as we know, it is the only homosexual bar that allows dancing. (It also has a rather high cover charge.)

Other bars are more active in the afternoon. They are generally "mixed," having homosexual and heterosexual clients, and seem more like neighborhood taverns than gay bars. Bars are generally open either between 9:00 P.M. and 5:00 A.M. or 5:00 A.M. and 12:00 P.M., so that it is possible to use a bar any hour of the day. Only two gay bars were found that stay open till 5:00 A.M. The clientele at one of them appeared to be mainly tourists and older males.

The only bar discovered outside of this area is one next to Club 48. Though small, it is one of Copenhagen's nicer gay bars, with a well-decorated interior and a clientele that is mainly professional and student. Nyhavn, the sailors' quarter, was reputed to have many bars; however, we found none that could be considered homosexual bars, and none were reported to us by Danish homosexuals.

There are only about half as many gay bars in Copenhagen as in Amsterdam, although the two cities are approximately equal in population. Also, few of the gay bars in Copenhagen are as nice as those in Amsterdam. The homosexual bars in Copenhagen, with few exceptions, are more like those in the United States than those in the Netherlands. As in the United States, they seem to be a place more for meeting sexual partners than for sociability. The American homosexual who comes to Copenhagen is likely to be disappointed, and we met some who expressed this feeling. We also met many Danish as well as other European homosexuals who were all agreed that Amsterdam is the "gay capital" of Europe and the best place to be.

CHAPTER 7

THE THREE SOCIETIES: CONCLUDING REMARKS

A Comparison of the Societies

The law and law enforcement policies on homosexuality most clearly distinguish the United States from the Netherlands and Denmark. In the latter countries, homosexuality is not a criminal offense. Dutch and Danish homosexuals are free from the sometimes arbitrary and unpredictable nature of law enforcement practices, which, as we have shown, create a built-in instability in the social situation of the American homosexual. While it is our contention that this difference has been somewhat overemphasized in accounting for the homosexual's difficulties, nonetheless, it is a persistent irritant for the majority of American homosexuals and the source of ruination for many of them. In addition, it symbolically buttresses a negative evaluation of their sexual orientation.

The negative evaluation of homosexuals is a problem shared in varying degrees by homosexuals in all three societies. The United States is the most negative, its anti-homosexuality being supported by religious traditions, legal statutes, and official practices. In the European countries, there is more tolerance. In addition to the survey data and field impressions previously discussed, the following survey comparisons further support these conclusions of differential response.

Samples of males from the general population in the United States, Amsterdam, and Copenhagen were acquired. Data for the United States are from an Institute for Sex Research study by Albert D. Klassen and Eugene Levitt. Data for that study, referred to on pages 34–35, were collected from a random sample in 1970. European data came from very small samples which we obtained from the names listed in telephone books. A more detailed description of this sampling and data collection is contained in Chapter 11.

As Table 1 (page 112) indicates, the general reaction toward homosexuality is more negative in the United States. Almost 50 per cent of respondents from large cities in the United States agree "very much" that homosexuality is obscene and vulgar, compared to 5.4 per cent in the Amsterdam sample and 11.8 per cent in the Copenhagen sample. Table 2 shows how respondents from the various countries anticipate reacting to knowledge that a male friend had been involved in homosexual acts. In the United States, 30.8 per cent would not want anything more to do with him, compared to only 3 per cent of the respondents in Amsterdam and Copenhagen. (Caution regarding these comparisons should be noted, however, because of the small European samples.)

Thus, Dutch and Danish homosexuals live in an environment that is more tolerant of homosexuality. In addition, they are not subject to many of the forms of institutionalized discrimination found in the United States.[1]

Comparing the three countries, the Dutch situation presents the fewest problems for the homosexual, due in part to the attitude of various official agencies. Government

TABLE 1

General Population's Evaluation of Homosexuality, by Society

Extent to Which General Population Agrees that Homosexuality is Obscene and Vulgar	United States (N = 239)*	Amsterdam (N = 37)†	Copenhagen (N = 34)
Very much	48.5%	5.4%	11.8%
Somewhat	23.0	18.9	26.5
Very little	17.1	21.6	23.5
Not at all	11.3	54.1	38.2

* Males from cities over 1,000,000; selected from the study's total sample in order to increase comparability with Amsterdam and Copenhagen. A more precise delimitation of city size was not possible from that study's code categories.

† One person in the Amsterdam sample and no one in the Copenhagen sample reports himself to be a homosexual on our sexual orientation item. The Klassen-Levitt sample (and the Kohn sample in Chapter 11) is taken to be representative of the general population with regard to sexual orientation.

intervention through the Ministry of Social Work established the Schorer Foundation, whose aim is to help homosexuals with their problems. Also, the Dutch government seems well disposed to attack other irritants to the homosexual's social situation, even though, as we have seen, they have not alleviated all such problems. Various religious bodies and law enforcement agencies, too, have taken a *positive* interest in alleviating the problems the homosexual confronts. Such liberalization from the top helps to sustain the tolerance of the general population toward homosexuals.

Nothing similar characterizes the situation of the homo-

TABLE 2

General Population's Response to a Male Friend's Homosexuality, by Society

How General Population Would Respond to Discovering a Male Friend's Homosexuality	United States (N = 240)*	Amsterdam (N = 37)†	Copenhagen (N = 33)
Not want to have any thing to do with him anymore	30.8%	2.7%	3.0%
Still be in touch with him, but no longer be friends	9.2	13.5	12.1
Stay friends, but it would be a problem	26.7	35.1	30.4
Still be friends, no problem	33.3	48.6	54.5

* See footnote to Table 1.
† See footnote to Table 1.

sexual in the United States and Denmark. In the United States, official assistance at the national level is completely absent. The National Institute of Mental Health Task Force on Homosexuality (the Hooker Report) did provide an admirable list of suggestions, but the national administration so far has given no indication of acting on any of them. Even on a more local level, for example, in New York, despite Lindsay's having been a somewhat sympathetic mayor, little has been done. In San Francisco, too, authorities have not shown any great concern for the homosexual's situation. In Denmark, official assistance to the homosexual is also lacking. True, liberalization from the top has occurred regarding other sex-related matters, such as birth control, abortion, and pornography, but the homosexual has not directly benefited from official intervention.

The Netherlands, and especially Amsterdam, therefore, would appear to be an especially favorable setting for the homosexual. In our conversations with homosexuals in Amsterdam we were told repeatedly that "there are no problems" when we asked how difficult it was to be a homosexual. In our conversations with C.O.C. counselors and the social workers at the Schorer Foundation we were told, however, that many Dutch homosexuals do have problems related to their homosexuality. Accepting their homosexuality is still a problem which many homosexuals face. Even in Amsterdam, to be homosexual is to be in a disvalued minority. It is interesting that in referring to heterosexuals and homosexuals, the Dutch use words which mean "normals" and "homos." Even Dutch homosexuals refer to heterosexuals as "normals"; thus, they appear to have taken over the view of themselves held by many members of the wider society. In this context it is difficult, according to a Catholic priest who counsels homosexuals, for the homosexual to talk to anyone about his problems. This, and its implications, also have been noted by a British observer: "Almost all Dutchmen I talked to told me that their parents did not know they were homosexual and would be scandalized if they did. But the fact that they wanted to go on concealing it from their parents meant they had to conceal it from almost everyone else."[2] In summary, therefore, despite tolerance, government intervention, and a lack of institutionalized discrimination and harassment, a lack of genuine social acceptance does cause problems even for the Dutch homosexual.

We have argued that a lack of social acceptance has in all three societies produced a subculture with its own bars, baths, and so forth, as well as homophile organizations and movements. It would appear, moreover, that the richer and more extensive the homosexual subculture, the greater the benefits for the homosexual. He can have more places to meet other homosexuals, a greater opportunity to develop a "we-feeling," and more organizations to help him with his specific problems. As has previously been pointed out, the nature and extent of the homosexual subculture vary among our settings, with New York and San Francisco evidencing a greater and more variegated collection of homosexual institutions. In the words of one commentator, Amsterdam and Copenhagen have "none of the polish, brilliance, or range of things to do and places to go that is now commonplace in most major American cities." [3] Compared with San Francisco, as we noted, Amsterdam (though roughly the same size) has fewer baths and bars, little variety in types of bars, no homosexual restaurants, shows, bookstores, coffee houses, or newspapers. It does, however, have an excellent homophile organization. Copenhagen is less well endowed. Not only are its bars not very appealing, but its homophile organization has yet to gain the influence and effectiveness of the Dutch C.O.C.[4]

The Homosexual and His Problems: Some General Remarks

Many of the homosexual's problems are obviously due to society's view of homosexuality. In addition, an important correlative source of problems for the homosexual is what we call "the social nature of homosexuality." For example, minor problems arise from situations where, *because of societal attitudes,* rules do not exist for successful interaction with persons of the same sex. A male homosexual may initially find himself at a loss for guidelines in relating to another male in certain ways—who should "lead" while dancing, cruising, engaging in sex, and running a household—without feeling like one is "not a man" for being subordinate. In addition, more serious problems involve searching for a permanent partner and maintaining stable relationships. Males, less socialized to being sexually inhibited, often find fidelity a strain. Where there are no social supports or rules for stable relationships, jealousy and "promiscuity" end many budding partnerships.

Other problems are more clearly rooted in the negative societal reaction toward homosexuality. Loneliness, for example, can result from a fear of being seen in a homosexual club or bar or a fear of approaching a strange male. The "one-night stand," which involves "sex without obligation or commitment" and thus precludes the development of more meaningful relationships, arises to some degree from the premium of anonymity which many homosexuals value lest their proclivity come to light.[5] Also, Martin Hoffman notes:

> . . . the reason that males who are homosexually inclined cannot form stable relations with each other is that society does not want them to. . . . How . . . is he expected to develop a warm, intimate relationship with a partner whom he unconsciously devalues as a person for engaging in acts with him which he defines as degraded? . . . The homosexual's own self-concept cannot easily commit him to being any more of a homosexual than is required by the sexual drive itself. . . . The problem of paired intimacy . . . is the central problem of the gay world. . . . Actually embedded in the individual's concept of himself is the idea that his homosexual proclivities are bad and that to establish a relationship with another man is carrying these proclivities to a worse extreme. Thus, the instability of relationships which is frequently used as grounds for condemnation of homosexuals is, in fact, the very product of this condemnation. There is, thus, to say the least, a strange irony in homosexuals being accused of not forming stable relationships, when it is the social prohibitions they suffer which largely prevent them from becoming involved in such relationships.[6]

Interestingly, the problems surrounding the social nature of homosexuality exist in all three societies, even though the countries vary in their degree of tolerance toward homosexuals.

Finally, one should examine combinations of the variables that we have discussed in this chapter. For example, legal repression combined with intolerance can make for a thriving homosexual subculture in which some of the homosexual's problems can be handled, but at the cost of segregating him from the wider society. More tolerance with no legal repression can, on the other hand, make for a relatively undeveloped homosexual subculture, where the homosexual is somewhat more integrated into society but does not enjoy the benefits of as extensive a subculture. Any attempts to help the homosexual should, therefore, consider the combination of factors involved.

Cautions

To end our concluding remarks, we offer the following cautions with regard to the ethnographies that comprise this second part of the book.

The time-bound nature of the descriptions/What we have said is restricted to the time the material was gathered (1965–70) and does not, therefore, provide an up-to-date description of the homosexual scene after 1970. Because the homosexual's social situation is changing, many issues are of necessity left open, and tentative generalizations may be dated by the time this work is published. Nonetheless, the specific events described were chosen to illustrate what we consider to be general processes surrounding the homosexual's life.

The range of the descriptions/In the main what we have described is the situation of those homosexuals who are involved in the homosexual subculture. Among the homosexuals who spoke on behalf of an organization, we found it difficult at times to disentangle personal views from views representative of the organization in question. In some cases, too, certain aspects of the homosexual world were excluded altogether. Females were not included; also, younger, militant American homosexuals were not studied in San Francisco (although they were in New York). Finally, there is the problem of nonhomosexual spokesmen. In Europe we had no problem getting police views on homosexual-police relations, but American policemen were reluctant to provide their perspective.

The negative focus/We have emphasized the problems faced by male homosexuals in managing their lives. This has directed us toward the negative aspects of the homosexual's life, such as police harassment and job discrimination. Although we do not treat the positive aspects of the homosexual's life, we are not unaware of the personal and social satisfactions that many experience in a homosexual way of life.

Documentary evidence/Some of our descriptions, especially in the United States, could be checked by recourse to studies by other social scientists, newspaper accounts, and the homosexual press. We are aware of possible biases in all these sources but found generally consistent interpretations of most of the situations we have described. We have gone beyond traditional ethnographic materials in using, for example, public opinion polls and historical material, and we feel these add to our descriptions. In Europe we were not able to make as much use of documentary materials due to language problems and also because of the smaller number of sociological studies of homosexuality and the less developed nature of the homophile press.

PART III

QUESTIONNAIRE STUDY—SAMPLES AND PROCEDURES

CHAPTER 8

METHODS AND DISTRIBUTIONS

On the basis of our field work we constructed an 11-page, 145-item questionnaire. Each draft of the questionnaire, or of any particular scale, was pretested with 20–30 homosexual respondents. The English questionnaire was later translated into Dutch and Danish in four steps: First, an initial translation was made of the English questionnaire. Then a second translator checked the initial translation and met with the first translator, resolving any disagreements between their translations. Next, the Dutch and Danish questionnaires were translated back into English by another translator and compared with the original (these back translations were generally very accurate). Finally, any changes warranted by the back translation were made.[1]

The Samples

Homosexual Samples

United States/Questionnaires were mailed to 2,700 persons on the mailing list of the Mattachine Society of New York.

Females on the mailing list were omitted. Approximately 950 of the addressees resided in New York City; 350 resided in New York State, Connecticut, and New Jersey. The remaining persons resided in 44 states. Two hundred additional questionnaires were mailed to San Francisco residents on the mailing list of the Mattachine Society of San Francisco.

Two hundred fifty-eight questionnaires were handed out at the Society for Individual Rights in San Francisco. A questionnaire was given to every other person at the club or at a club function (such as bowling and the weekly discussion group) during a ten-day period. Fifty questionnaires were also distributed among persons attending private homosexual clubs in Manhattan.

A questionnaire was handed to every seventh person in a random sample of 25 homosexual bars in San Francisco, resulting in the distribution of 234 questionnaires. Two hundred twenty-five questionnaires were similarly distributed in a random sample of 20 homosexual bars in Manhattan. Each of these distributions took place on two consecutive weekends.

Altogether, 3,667 questionnaires were distributed in the United States, of which 1,117 were completed and returned. The response rate, computed with a correction for the number of persons receiving more than one questionnaire and for undeliverable mailed questionnaires, was 38.7 per cent. Of the total respondents, 1,057 were male homosexuals.

Europe/European respondents were obtained in a similar way. Questionnaires were mailed to every other person on the mailing list of Amsterdam's C.O.C. and to every person on the mailing list of Copenhagen's Forbundet. Altogether, 1,859 questionnaires were sent out in the Netherlands and 962 questionnaires in Denmark. Females were excluded.

In Amsterdam, a questionnaire was handed to every male at the C.O.C. club over a period of nine days. In this way,

547 questionnaires were given out. In Copenhagen, a similar procedure was employed for handing out 558 questionnaires to males in attendance at Forbundet's two clubs: Club 48 and the Pink Club.

Next, all the homosexual bars in Amsterdam were visited, and a questionnaire was handed to every male there. As in the United States, the distribution was done on two consecutive weekends. This resulted in 388 questionnaires being distributed. The same procedure was utilized for handing out 396 questionnaires in Copenhagen's homosexual bars.[2] Of the 2,794 questionnaires distributed in the Netherlands, 1,077 were returned; the corrected response rate was 45.1 per cent. In Denmark, 303 were returned of the 1,916 which were estimated to have been distributed, providing an apparent corrected response rate of 24.2 per cent.[3] All these European respondents reported themselves to be homosexual.

Demographic Characteristics of the Homosexual Samples

Social class and education/Our homosexual samples appear to be skewed in the direction of higher social class and education. In the United States, for example, 82 per cent have at least some college education, 71 per cent are in the three highest-status occupation categories (census and Hollingshead categories), and 66 per cent place themselves in at least the upper-middle class. A similar skewing apparently occurs for the European homosexual samples, although the percentages in categories comparable to the above are not as high as for the United States.

Race and religious background/In all three countries the vast majority of respondents are white (96 per cent of the United States sample, 98 per cent of the Dutch sample, and all but one of the Danish respondents). With regard to religion, in the United States sample 53 per cent are Protestant, 29 per cent Catholic, 9 per cent Jewish, and

10 per cent other. In the Netherlands, 52 per cent of the respondents are Protestant, 44 per cent Catholic, 2 per cent Jewish, and 2 per cent other. In Denmark, 77 per cent of the respondents are of the Danish state church (Lutheran), 8 per cent Catholic, 6 per cent Protestant, 3 per cent Jewish, and 6 per cent other.

Age/The American homosexuals in our sample are generally older than the Europeans. The percentages of our samples in each age category are as follows: under age 26, in the United States 18 per cent, in the Netherlands 23 per cent, and in Denmark 32 per cent; between 26 and 35, 30 per cent, 39 per cent, and 45 per cent; between 36 and 45, 28 per cent, 24 per cent, and 15 per cent; and over 45, 24 per cent, 15 per cent, and 11 per cent.

Locale/In each country, most of our homosexual respondents live in cities with a population of at least 250,000. This includes 65 per cent of our sample in the United States, 59 per cent of those in the Netherlands, and 76 per cent of those in Denmark. The percentages living in communities with populations of less than 25,000 are 18 per cent in the United States, 14 per cent in the Netherlands, and 9 per cent in Denmark.

General Population Samples

For each country, we also obtained data from a general population sample. In Amsterdam and in Copenhagen, we selected a sample of 300 males from the phone book. They were sent that part of the questionnaire containing measures of psychological problems in order to get comparison samples on these items from the general population. In the United States, a comparison group from the general population (N = 3,101) which replied to these items was already available from a study by Melvin Kohn. These samples are described and compared with our homosexual samples in Chapter 11.

Concluding Remark

Our procedures obviously precluded our having obtained "representative" samples. Indeed, it is probably impossible to obtain such a sample of homosexuals (especially since so many persons feel that admitting their homosexuality involves extreme risk). However, representative samples are not necessary when the researcher's aim is neither to generalize specific quantitative values nor to generalize beyond a specific group or situation so much as to examine the validity of certain overall hypotheses and stereotypes.

Thus, in the present research we do not claim that our findings and conclusions can be generalized to the total population of homosexuals in each society. We do, however, claim that through the use of *reasonable criteria* our findings provide the basis for conclusions *about a significant number of homosexuals in these societies,* and further, can warrant the modification of a number of hitherto unexamined stereotypes and hypotheses.

Readers may wish to go directly to our results in Part IV (beginning on page 169) if they are not interested in the items which comprise our measures, response distributions on these items, an explanation of our analysis and presentation, and differences among respondents obtained from different sample sources.

Items and Percentage Distributions

In this section we present the items that comprise our most important measures. To describe the character of our main sample of 1,057 American homosexuals, we also present response distributions on these items. (Distributions for our European samples are not presented here, since the European data are specifically compared with United States data in Chapter 10.) In computing the response distribution, we omitted those respondents for whom the item was not applicable as well as those who did not respond to that item.

In constructing measures, consecutive numerical values were assigned to response categories so that a higher score indicates a higher value of the variable being measured (higher self-esteem, and so on). The score for any composite measure was obtained by adding the values attached to the subject's responses for all items in that scale. For composite measures, coefficient alpha is presented.[4]

Relating to the Heterosexual World

Extant data indicate that the American homosexual does cope fairly successfully with the heterosexual world. Simon and Gagnon, with an Institute for Sex Research sample of 550 white male homosexuals, found that between 75 and 80 per cent reported no trouble with the police, 90 per cent had no trouble at work, and 95 per cent had no trouble at school. They also report that, of those who had military experience, only one-fifth reported any difficulties[5]; similarly, a study by the present authors showed that the majority of homosexuals who have served obtained honorable discharges.[6] Also, in the present study, 84 per cent report they had never lost a job on account of their homosexuality, and 70 per cent report having few or no problems on any job they have had because people knew or suspected they were homosexual.[7]

Further data indicate also that the homosexuals in our sample are by no means cut off from the heterosexual world. For example, 59 per cent report a substantial number of *close* relationships with heterosexuals (other than family members), and 44 per cent say they are socially active in heterosexual circles. In fact, 46 per cent of our respondents indicate that the majority of their friends are heterosexual.

Nonetheless, the majority of our sample are covert in their homosexuality. Thirty per cent of the respondents report attempting to conceal their homosexuality from *all* heterosexuals, and an additional 38 per cent from *most* heterosexuals. On the other hand, 20 per cent claim they try to hide it from few or none. Thus, only a fifth of our sample could be considered overt.

This is consistent with our sample's perception of the reactions of heterosexuals toward homosexuals: 47 per cent feel that most or many people would break off social relationships with a person if they suspected he were homosexual, and nearly 38 per cent feel that most or many persons would make life difficult for someone they suspected to be homosexual. Sixty-seven per cent believe that most people are disgusted or repelled by or generally dislike homosexuals.

These data and other measures often referred to throughout the book subsumed under "relating to the heterosexual world" are presented at the end of this chapter to show the reader how our United States sample is distributed on various items. As such, they represent a description of the sample and provide data that are later obscured when composite measures and cross-tabulations are presented.

Relating to the Homosexual World

Certain items describe the relationship of our American respondents to the homosexual world. Regarding association with other homosexuals, for example, a bimodal distribution appears among the responses. For 49 per cent, over half their socializing is with other homosexuals; 27 per cent, on the other hand, indicate that only a small amount or none of their socializing is with other homosexuals. Sixteen per cent state that they are not really known among homosexuals and an additional 29 per cent that they are not part of any homosexual group. While 30 per cent attend homosexual bars and clubs once a week or more, 34 per cent never or almost never attend.

Our field work had indicated that acculturation to the homosexual world might be tapped by two questions concerning behaviors that homosexuals said took time to get used to (often more so than actual sexual practices) and which were thought to be engaged in less by homosexual persons who had infrequent contact with the homosexual world. The items, along with the percentage of respondents engaging in these practices, are: having "necked" with other men (96 per cent) and having danced slow dances with other men (75 per cent).

With regard to sexual relationships, a figure that appears quite high considering the image of "promiscuity" associated with homosexuality, is that 34 per cent of our respondents report at the time of questionnaire completion that they are limiting their sexual relationships primarily to one other person. Moreover, 23 per cent of the respondents report having sustained such a relationship for more than a year. With regard to having such an exclusive relationship at some time in the past, 69 per cent state they have, with 37 per cent of the respondents having sustained such a relationship for more than a year.

In terms of sexual behavior, 55 per cent report engaging in most of the various forms of homosexual practices. As for frequency, in the six months prior to completing the questionnaire, 50 per cent of the respondents report having homosexual relations about once a week or more; 24 per cent report having homosexual relations once a month or less. Finally, regarding the exclusiveness of their homosexuality, 56 per cent say they have engaged in sexual intercourse with a female, but only 11 per cent of the respondents report having done so within the six months prior to completing the questionnaire. Eighty-three per cent are single and have never been heterosexually married.[8]

In classifying their sexual orientation, 51 per cent state that they are exclusively homosexual, 30 per cent predominantly so (only being "insignificantly heterosexual"), and the remainder more bisexual.[9]

Finally, two sets of items indicate that a large percentage of our respondents do not feel they are responsible for their homosexuality and are disinclined to give it up even if this were possible. Fifty-six per cent say they are not responsible for being homosexual, 55 per cent that it is completely beyond one's control, and 20 per cent think people are born either heterosexual or homosexual. Forty-five per cent say they would not give up their homosexuality even if they could, 28 per cent that they would, and 27 per cent are not sure. Similarly, 54 per cent disagree with the statement, "I wish I were not homosexual," and only 22 per cent agree.

Measures referred to throughout the book subsumed under "relating to the homosexual world" may be found at the end of the chapter.

Psychological Problems

The distribution of the United States sample on items that were designed to reflect psychological problems shows that many homosexuals are neither as maladjusted as many psychiatrists have suggested nor as well adjusted as many homosexuals would like the public to think. Rather, a large variation appears, with a distribution in which the vast majority fit neither of these antithetical depictions. (In Chapter 11, we compare our homosexual respondents with general population samples with regard to psychological problems.)

The following eight dimensions comprise our major measures of psychological problems.

Self-acceptance/On the self-acceptance measure, items producing the greatest distribution are: "I certainly feel useless at times," with approximately 37 per cent of the respondents agreeing with this statement, and, of more direct relevance to our interests, the item, "I wish I could have more respect for myself," with 28 per cent of the sample agreeing with this statement.[10]

Stability of self-concept/This variable attempts to examine how stable self-evaluations are over time. Since the present research did not allow the researcher to determine stability by repeated testing at different times, items were used to get the respondent himself to evaluate the stability of his self-concept. There is a substantial dispersion across these items.

Depression/A more direct result of the failure to accept one's predilections and situation is a feeling of unhappiness. About 25 per cent of the respondents see themselves as depressed or unhappy, based upon their responses to the following items: "I am not as happy as others seem to be," and "I often feel downcast and dejected." To the question "Taking all things together how would you say things are these days—would you say you are: very happy, pretty happy, not too happy, very unhappy?" 24 per cent report being either "not too happy" or "very unhappy."

Anxiety/Three forms of anxiety are examined: psychosomatic symptoms considered indicative of anxiety, feelings of anxiety regarding one's homosexuality, and anticipations of pending nervous breakdown. Of most significance seems to be the fact that 42 per cent report that at some time or other they have been on the verge of a nervous breakdown.

Interpersonal awkwardness/A common belief is that acts of deviance will produce internal and external symptoms of shame. In addition to experiencing internal repercussions (self-degradation, depression, and anxiety), this belief implies that the transgressor will lose confidence in his ability to maintain poise. It is this element of social confidence that the items comprising this scale were intended to measure. It is probably true that for some persons interpersonal awkwardness is a consequence of shame. On the other hand, a homosexual's interpersonal awkwardness can result from the lack of social guidelines for certain situations. For other homosexuals it is quite possible that shyness and a lack of confidence contributed to their homosexuality due to a reluctance to engage in the heterosexual dating game.

With respect to our sample, a fair number of respondents describe themselves as interpersonally awkward, for example, 44 per cent report that they "often feel very self-conscious."

Faith in others/We were very interested in testing homosexuals' faith in others as a check on our field work impressions. Our impression was that many homosexuals demonstrated a surprisingly low degree of alienation, given the low status usually accorded the social category of "homosexual." Although a number of homosexuals, when they are together, show hostility toward heterosexuals (for example, those who might amble onto "their turf"), they seem to demonstrate less cynicism than members of other minorities. As the distribution of responses to the faith in others items shows, there is enough dispersion to cast doubt upon their typification as "cynical." This lack of cynicism may be due to the effectiveness with which many of these homosexuals pass as heterosexual.

Loneliness/Loneliness relates to psychological adjustment in that either objectively being alone or feeling alone because of a secret, unsharable differentness can lead to negative perceptions of self. (Both are situations many homosexuals often find themselves in.) The ramifications of loneliness are examined in some detail in Chapter 12.

Psychiatric experience/Psychiatric experience can be one indicator of a recognition of psychological problems. The respondents were asked a number of questions regarding past or present psychiatric treatment and whether or not that treatment was with regard to their homosexuality. While approximately 43 per cent have visited a psychiatrist with respect to their homosexuality, only 8 per cent of the respondents were receiving treatment in this regard at the time of questionnaire completion.

A full list of the items comprising the above measures and the response distribution of the United States sample is located at the end of this chapter.

Analysis and Presentation

These data have been presented to help describe the sample of United States homosexuals and to indicate the nature of our measures. As noted previously, of the European marginals only the demographic ones are presented, since the European data are compared with the United States data in Chapter 10.

We first compare in the next chapter the characteristics of male homosexuals obtained from various sample sources; then in Chapter 10 we examine, holding sample source constant, differences by society. For the remainder of the book (as well as the next chapter), we use the European data as replications to see if various features of the homosexual's situation have the same correlates in the different societies. (Because our conclusions were not meant to be restricted to the United States, in these chapters we consider as "findings" only those which were corroborated by data from the other societies.)

Each major variable of interest (that is, "independent"

variable) was run against all other variables, and findings are presented in tables of percentages at the end of each chapter. For simplicity, only one *row* of percentages from the complete table is provided. Only one residual row of percentages is omitted. The numbers in parentheses in the tables are the total number of respondents from which the adjacent percentage was computed. When the number is under 16, the data are not presented.

When we are interested in associations between variables irrespective of country (Chapters 9 and 11–21), *an association is assumed to exist, and data are presented, only where:*

1. for the United States data, the association is statistically significant, that is, the chi square obtained has a probability of equal to, or less than, .05;
2. for the United States data, the percentage difference has "substantive significance," that is, there is a difference between cells of at least 10 percentage points;
3. the relationship is replicated with the data from the European samples.

When we make comparisons among locales (Chapter 10), we interpret the data according to the same criteria of statistical significance, substantive significance, and replication. In these cases, however, we look for statistical and substantive significance within the "mail source" data and look at the other sample sources for replication.

In some instances, the association does not reach substantive and/or statistical significance in a replication. As a matter of course, therefore, we report for each table the "pooled" chi square and its associated probability. The probability associated with the pooled chi square is the probability for getting a particular relationship time after time.[11] Thus, in addition to having a probability for getting the observed results merely by chance in *each* sample, the pooled chi square indicates the similar probability for getting these relationships for *all three* samples.

All the relationships we regard as replicated have a pooled chi square probability of .05 or less. In the text, however, we do note where the trend is not replicated in one of the samples. *As it turns out, the replication rule does not eliminate any pattern of findings.*

Wherever appropriate, gammas are provided in the tables to indicate the strength of the association between the variables. Because the sign of the gamma refers to the direction of the data in the row presented (rather than to the complete table from which the row was taken), when percentages descend from high to low categories of the independent variable, gamma is given a positive sign; when they ascend from high to low categories, gamma is given a negative sign. Correlations do not, of course, imply causal direction. Our interpretations regarding the latter are based on field work and sociological theory. We point out in particular chapters where it seems probable that more than one interpretation and direction may explain the findings.

Being Known About—Scale I (Alpha Coefficient = .88)

Of the following people, check *how many* suspect or know that you are homosexual.

	All	Most	More than Half	About Half	Less than Half	Only a Few	None
Heterosexuals whom you know	3.3%	9.9%	5.5%	8.3%	9.9%	52.0%	11.3%
Male heterosexual friends	4.6	10.8	6.1	6.9	7.8	48.4	15.4
Female heterosexual friends	4.0	10.0	4.4	6.0	8.1	42.8	24.6
Aunts and uncles	4.9	3.9	1.7	2.1	2.3	16.2	68.9
Neighbors	2.6	5.8	3.0	3.7	3.3	30.4	51.3
Work associates	6.1	5.7	4.1	6.3	3.8	34.1	39.0
People whom *you* suspect or know are homosexual	12.0	29.0	9.0	8.0	9.3	28.0	4.9

Being Known About—Scale II (Alpha Coefficient = .70)

Do any of the following people know or suspect that you are homosexual? (If your mother or father is deceased, check whether they did know or suspect and put a "D" next to your check.) If a category does not pertain to you, check "Not Applicable."

	Definitely Know(s)	Definitely or Probably Suspect(s)	Do(es) Not Seem to Know or Suspect
Your mother	26.7%	23.6%	49.8%
Your father	20.0	17.8	62.3
Brother(s)	29.0	22.8	48.2
Sister(s)	25.5	26.7	47.6
Best heterosexual friend of same sex	43.6	17.3	39.0
Wife *	49.3	16.2	33.8
Best heterosexual friend of opposite sex	39.5	15.8	44.7
Your employer	14.0	13.2	72.8

* One hundred and forty-one of our 1,057 United States homosexuals are represented in these three response categories.

Putative Social Reactions (Alpha Coefficient = .85)

How do you think each of the following persons *would* react (or *has* reacted) to finding out that you are homosexual? (If a category does not pertain to you, check "Not Applicable.")

	Accepting (Or It Would Not Matter)	Understanding (But Not Accepting)	Tolerant (But Not Understanding)	Intolerant (But Not Rejecting)	Rejecting
Your mother	25.3%	18.5%	28.7%	19.4%	8.3%
Your father	14.0	14.1	29.7	22.6	19.5
Brother(s)	30.1	16.6	26.0	15.2	11.9
Sister(s)	31.0	20.5	28.3	12.7	7.6
Most of your aunts and uncles	10.2	9.0	30.4	28.7	21.8
Best heterosexual friend of same sex	52.9	14.8	16.7	8.7	6.9
Most other heterosexual friends of same sex	29.0	17.5	24.0	15.2	14.2
Wife	23.4	24.1	10.2	18.3	24.1
Best heterosexual friend of opposite sex	47.8	17.5	16.7	9.4	8.6
Most other heterosexual friends of opposite sex	24.1	18.1	28.3	14.6	14.9
Most of your work associates	22.9	11.2	25.5	16.4	24.1
Your employer	24.7	9.0	19.0	11.9	35.6

	Accepting (Or It Would Not Matter)	Under-standing (But Not Accept-ing)	Tolerant (But Not Under-standing)	Intol-erant (But Not Reject-ing)	Reject-ing
Most of your neighbors	15.5	7.7	28.0	18.2	30.6
Most heterosexuals in general	7.5	7.9	29.6	21.7	33.3

Anticipated Discrimination (Alpha Coefficient = .61)

Would there be problems at work if people found out [that you were homosexual]?

No	21.9%
Yes, but only to a very small degree	21.7
Yes, to some degree	22.1
Yes, very much so	32.2
Most people I work with already know	2.2

Do you think people are likely to break off social relationships with someone if they suspect he is homosexual?

Yes, most people would	13.5%
Yes, many would	33.7
Yes, a few would	44.5
No	8.3

Do you think people are likely to make life difficult for persons they suspect are homosexual?

Yes, most people would	10.6%
Yes, many would	27.0
Yes, a few would	52.7
No	9.8

Putative Attitude Toward Homosexuals

How do you think most people feel about homosexuals?

They feel disgusted or repelled by homosexuals ..	26.3%
They dislike homosexuals	40.4
They have a "live and let live" attitude toward homosexuals	28.8
They have some liking for homosexuals	4.6

Passing (Alpha Coefficient = .74)

	Strongly Agree	Agree	Not Sure	Disagree	Strongly Disagree
I do not care who knows about my homosexuality	5.5%	14.2%	8.6%	40.0%	32.2%
I do not like to associate with a person who has a reputation (among heterosexuals) of being homosexual *	6.9	22.5	11.8	42.7	16.1
I would not mind being seen in public with a person who has the reputation (among heterosexuals) of being homosexual *	11.3	45.4	12.3	23.7	7.4

From how many heterosexuals do you try to conceal your homosexuality?

All	29.9%
Most	37.7
More than half	5.2

* These two items were also run as a "Willingness to Associate with Known Homosexuals" scale (Alpha coefficient = .79).

About half	5.0
Less than half	2.3
Only a few	10.5
None	9.4

Labeling Experiences

Have you ever been labeled a homosexual on some official record (outside of homosexual or homophile organizational records)?

Yes, more than once	11.6%
Yes, once	30.0
No	58.3

If *yes:* Does this bother you?

Yes, a great deal	20.6%
Yes, somewhat	20.6
Yes, but not very much	20.8
No, not at all	37.8

If *no:* Would this bother you?

Yes, a great deal	39.9%
Yes, somewhat	26.1
Yes, but not very much	14.9
No, not at all	19.1

Have you ever been arrested on any charge related to your homosexuality?

Yes	24.6%
No	75.4

Have there been problems on any job you've had because people suspected or knew that you were homosexual?

No	69.7%
Yes, but only to a very small degree	15.7
Yes, to some degree	7.8
Yes, very much so	6.8

Have you ever lost a job because your homosexuality became known?

Yes, more than once	5.0%
Yes, once	11.2
No	83.8

Social Involvement with Heterosexuals
(Alpha Coefficient = .65)

Of all your friends, how many are (to your knowledge) heterosexual?

All	2.6%
Most	28.0
More than half	15.3
About half	17.3
Less than half	15.6
Only a few	19.2
None	2.1

At the present time, how many close relationships do you have with heterosexuals (other than family members)?

Many	22.3%
Some	36.3
Very few	33.6
None	7.8

At the present time, how socially active are you in heterosexual circles?

Very active	12.6%
Somewhat active	31.2
Not too active	38.7
Not active at all	17.5

Social Identification

	Strongly Agree	Agree	Not Sure	Disagree	Strongly Disagree
I feel "closer" to a heterosexual of my own social class than to a homosexual who is of a much lower social class	8.8%	36.2%	13.0%	31.0%	10.9%

Traditional Values

Check how important you personally think each of the following is:

	Very Important	Somewhat Important	Not Very Important	Not at All Important
Formal religion	18.1%	27.7%	21.0%	33.2%
Traditional morality	16.2	38.6	26.5	18.7
Conformity in general	7.9	40.4	30.2	21.6

Perceived Breach of Traditional Values

To what degree do you think homosexuality violates the following:

	Very Much	Somewhat	Not Too Much	Not at All
Formal religion	32.9%	24.4%	16.1%	26.5%
Traditional morality	36.0	30.8	15.4	17.9
Conformity in general	35.2	34.3	15.6	14.8

RELATING TO THE HOMOSEXUAL WORLD

Social Involvement with Homosexuals (Alpha Coefficient = .81)

What proportion of your leisure-time socializing is with homosexuals?

Most	30.6%
More than half	18.5
About half	13.8
Less than half	10.5
Only a small amount	21.8
None	5.0

How many of your friends are homosexuals?

All	4.5%
Most	33.1
More than half	13.4

About half	14.2
Less than half	11.9
Only a small amount	19.7
None	3.4

What proportion of your *close* friends are homosexual?
(This was computed from the replies to two questions: the first, which asked the respondent to specify the *number* of people he considered to be his close friends, was divided into the second, which asked, of these close friends write the number that are homosexual.)

81–100%	27.0%
61–80%	18.5
41–60%	20.6
21–40%	14.2
1–20%	7.2
None	12.4

Acculturation (Alpha Coefficient = .51)

	Yes, Often	Yes, a Few Times	Yes, Once	No, Never
Have you ever danced "slow" dances with another male?	29.7%	39.0%	6.0%	25.3%
Has "necking" (kissing) been a part of your sexual (homosexual) practices?	78.2	15.9	1.8	4.1

Sexual Practices

Which of the following homosexual practices have you engaged in at least three times? *

Mutual masturbation and/or received fellatio and/or performed anal intercourse	13.0%
Has in addition performed fellatio	20.9
Has in addition received anal intercourse	11.5
Has experienced all of the above	54.6

* The original response categories were coded into the form presented here.

Homosexual Frequency (Alpha Coefficient = .91)

In the last six months, how many times have you had sexual relations with males? (Our categorizing of respondent's frequencies)

Once a month or less	24.2%
More than once to three times a month	16.8
About every week to ten days	8.6
More than once a week	31.6
Three times a week or more	18.7

In the last month, how many times have you had sexual relations with males? (Our categorizing of respondent's frequencies)

Not at all	16.9%
Less than once a week	23.9
One up to two times a week	21.1
Two up to three times a week	15.3
Three times a week or more	22.7

Sexual Orientation

Exclusively homosexual	50.6%
Predominantly homosexual, only insignificantly heterosexual	29.8
Predominantly homosexual, but significantly heterosexual	13.1
Equally homosexual and heterosexual	4.4
Predominantly heterosexual, but significantly homosexual	2.1

Homosexual Social Situation

For how long have you had mostly homosexuals as friends?

I have never had mostly homosexuals as friends	34.9%
Only at some time in the past	5.0
For the past six months or less	0.9
For between six months and a year	1.4
For between one and two years	4.8
For longer than two years	53.1

How often do you ordinarily frequent homosexual bars or clubs?

More than once a week	14.5%
About once a week	15.9
About once every other week	7.4
About once a month	8.9
About once every few months	12.5
Less often	7.0
Almost never	21.3
Never	12.6

Exclusive Homosexual Relationships
(Alpha Coefficient = .22)

At the present time, are another homosexual and yourself limiting your sexual relationships primarily to each other?

No	66.5%
Yes, we have been for less than a month	2.5
Yes, we have been for one to six months	4.9
Yes, we have been for six months to a year	3.3
Yes, we have been for more than a year	22.9

At some time in the past, did another homosexual and yourself limit your sexual relationships primarily to each other? (This should refer to a different relationship than the one considered in the previous question.)

No	30.8%
Yes, for less than a month	6.4
Yes, for between one and six months	16.5
Yes, for between six months and a year	9.5
Yes, for more than a year	36.9

Homosexual Commitment (Alpha Coefficient = .78)

	Strongly Agree	Agree	Not Sure	Disagree	Strongly Disagree
I wish I were not homosexual	8.1%	13.5%	24.1%	30.6%	23.7%
I would not want to give up my homosexuality even if I could	17.7	27.5	27.0	17.7	10.3

Conception of Homosexuality—Normalization (Alpha Coefficient = .80)

	Strongly Agree	Agree	Not Sure	Dis-agree	Strongly Disagree
Homosexuality may be best described as an illness	3.1%	7.9%	16.5%	32.8%	39.7%
Homosexuality may be best described as a mental illness	2.2	8.2	16.3	30.2	43.2

Conception of Homosexuality—Responsibility

	Strongly Agree	Agree	Not Sure	Dis-agree	Strongly Disagree
Being a homosexual is something that is completely beyond one's control	28.5%	26.5%	26.9%	14.8%	3.3%
A person is born homosexual or heterosexual	9.4	10.3	33.8	26.1	20.4
I am probably responsible for the fact that I am a homosexual	4.2	14.6	25.1	31.3	24.8

PSYCHOLOGICAL PROBLEMS

Self-Acceptance (Alpha Coefficient = .86)

	Strongly Agree	Agree	Not Sure	Dis-agree	Strongly Disagree
I feel that I have a number of good qualities	62.1%	37.1%	0.7%	0.1%	0.1%

	Strongly Agree	Agree	Not Sure	Dis- agree	Strongly Disagree
I feel that I am a person of worth, at least on an equal plane with others	39.5	55.2	3.3	1.8	0.2
All in all, I am inclined to feel that I am a failure	1.8	7.1	7.8	38.8	44.5
I am able to do things as well as most other people	29.1	61.1	4.8	4.1	0.9
I feel I do not have much to be proud of	1.4	9.0	4.4	50.5	34.7
I take a positive attitude toward myself	28.5	49.7	12.3	8.2	1.3
On the whole, I am satisfied with myself	14.4	51.1	11.6	19.3	3.6
I wish I could have more respect for myself	4.3	23.2	12.2	44.7	15.6
At times I think I am no good at all	2.3	17.0	4.0	41.0	35.8
I certainly feel useless at times	4.6	32.7	7.1	38.4	17.2

Stability of Self-Concept (Alpha Coefficient = .79)

	Strongly Agree	Agree	Not Sure	Dis- agree	Strongly Disagree
I have noticed that my ideas about myself seem to change very quickly	2.4%	11.3%	9.4%	59.5%	17.5%
Some days I have a very good opinion of myself, other days I have a very poor opinion of myself	6.6	34.0	8.7	39.6	11.1

	Strongly Agree	Agree	Not Sure	Disagree	Strongly Disagree
I feel that nothing, or almost nothing, can change the opinion I currently hold of myself	10.3	31.9	20.0	32.2	5.6

	Changes a Great Deal	Changes Somewhat	Changes Very Little	Does Not Change
Does the opinion you have of yourself tend to change a good deal?	6.9%	21.6%	48.9%	22.5%

	Yes, Happens Often	Yes, Happens Sometimes	Yes, But Rarely	No, Never Happens
Do you ever find that on one day you have one opinion of yourself and on another day you have a different opinion?	10.2%	24.3%	31.6%	27.9%

Depression (Alpha Coefficient = .88)

	Strongly Agree	Agree	Not Sure	Disagree	Strongly Disagree
On the whole, I think I am quite a happy person	15.7%	52.4%	12.7%	16.4%	2.8%
I get a lot of fun out of life	20.2	48.7	12.5	15.6	2.9
I am not as happy as others seem to be	4.4	20.9	10.4	46.4	17.9
In general, I feel in low spirits most of the time	2.1	9.3	5.6	54.0	29.0

	Strongly Agree	Agree	Not Sure	Disagree	Strongly Disagree
I often feel downcast and dejected	3.6	23.0	5.7	51.6	16.1

	Very Happy	Pretty Happy	Not Too Happy	Very Unhappy
Taking all things together, how would you say things are these days—would you say you are:	16.9%	59.1%	20.4%	3.6%

Psychosomatic Symptoms (Alpha Coefficient = .85)

How often do the following things happen to you?

	Never	Not Very Much	Pretty Often	Nearly All the Time
Do you ever have any trouble getting to sleep or staying asleep?	22.7%	54.2%	19.0%	4.1%
Have you ever been bothered by nervousness, feeling fidgety and tense?	13.0	50.1	30.7	6.2
Are you ever troubled by headaches or pains in the head?	39.2	46.7	11.9	2.2
Do you have loss of appetite?	56.8	36.3	5.9	1.1
How often are you bothered by having an upset stomach?	33.8	51.1	13.6	1.5
Do you find it difficult to get up in the morning?	20.7	42.2	20.6	16.6

	Never	Hardly Ever	Sometimes	Many Times
Have you ever been bothered by shortness of breath when you were not exercising or working hard?	48.8%	31.1%	15.9%	4.2%
Have you ever been bothered by your heart beating hard?	40.5	34.0	21.9	3.5
Do you drink more than you should?	29.4	31.3	27.9	11.4
Have you ever had spells of dizziness?	54.8	31.1	12.3	1.8
Are you ever bothered by nightmares?	44.5	40.0	13.2	2.3
Do you tend to lose weight when you have something important bothering you?	59.7	24.3	13.3	2.7
Do your hands ever tremble enough to bother you?	65.8	21.7	10.3	2.3
Are you troubled by your hands sweating so that you feel damp and clammy?	59.5	26.7	10.2	3.7
Have there ever been times when you couldn't take care of things because you just couldn't get going?	32.7	41.3	20.7	5.4

Anxiety Regarding Homosexuality (Alpha Coefficient = .78)

	A Great Deal	Somewhat	Not Very Much	Not at All
Does knowing you are a homosexual "weigh on your mind" (make you feel guilty, depressed, anxious, or ashamed)?	7.6%	15.0%	30.4%	47.1%

	Nearly Always	Pretty Often	Not Very Much	Never
At the present time do you ever experience shame, guilt, or anxiety after having sexual (homosexual) relations?	3.6%	5.2%	25.1%	66.2%

Nervous Breakdown

	Strongly Agree	Agree	Not Sure	Dis-agree	Strongly Disagree
There have been times when I felt I was going to have a nervous breakdown.	9.7%	32.3%	5.1%	35.1%	17.8%

Interpersonal Awkwardness (Alpha Coefficient = .84)

	Strongly Agree	Agree	Not Sure	Dis-agree	Strongly Disagree
I often feel very self-conscious	8.1%	35.6%	8.1%	39.8%	8.4%
I have a harder time than other people in gaining friends	6.1	21.1	8.0	43.3	21.5
I tend to be a rather shy person	5.9	34.2	8.7	38.7	12.6
I am easily embarrassed	4.6	28.2	8.7	47.6	10.9
I often feel ill at ease when I'm in the presence of others	4.3	24.2	7.8	47.3	16.5
I prefer to pass by friends or people I know but have not seen for a long time unless they speak to me first	3.1	18.2	5.6	53.1	20.1

	Strongly Agree	Agree	Not Sure	Disagree	Strongly Disagree
I have a harder time than other people in making conversation	4.8	17.4	6.4	45.6	25.9

Faith in Others (Alpha Coefficient = .63)

	Strongly Agree	Agree	Not Sure	Dis-agree	Strongly Disagree
No one is going to care much what happens to you, when you get right down to it	9.5%	22.9%	9.5%	44.1%	14.0%
Human nature is really cooperative	6.8	46.4	26.2	17.3	3.3
Most people can be trusted	3.3	54.0	15.0	20.6	7.0
Most people are inclined to look out for themselves	17.1	70.3	6.4	5.7	0.5
If you don't watch out for yourself, people will take advantage of you	18.6	45.1	12.5	22.4	1.4

Loneliness (Alpha Coefficient = .60)

	Strongly Agree	Agree	Not Sure	Dis-agree	Strongly Disagree
I feel that I don't have enough friends	9.5%	30.5%	8.6%	39.1%	12.3%

	Very Often	Often	Seldom	Never
Do you feel lonely?	12.3%	28.7%	49.6%	9.4%

Psychiatric Experience

Regarding your homosexuality:

	Yes	No
Have you ever visited a psychiatrist?	42.7%	57.3%
Have you received psychiatric treatment?	32.3	67.7
Are you presently receiving psychiatric treatment?	7.6	92.3
If *no*:		
Would you like to obtain psychiatric treatment regarding your homosexuality?	14.1	86.0
Have you ever had (or are you presently receiving) psychiatric treatment for reasons other than your homosexuality?	17.9	81.9

CHAPTER 9

SOURCE-RESPONDENT VARIATION

We have described the sources from which the members of our sample were drawn: mail organizations (respondents from the mailing lists of the Mattachine Societies of New York and San Francisco, Amsterdam's C.O.C., and Copenhagen's Forbundet); clubs (respondents attending private homosexual clubs in Manhattan, club functions of S.I.R. and C.O.C., and Forbundet's two clubs); and bars (respondents given questionnaires in homosexual bars in each city).[1]

During the field work it became evident that each particular source attracts a particular type of homosexual. This has to be taken into account in making cross-cultural comparisons, since the proportion of the sample from each source differs among societies. We thus examine *within* each city the type of homosexual obtained from the various sources. In doing so, we compare the respondents obtained through clubs and bars in each city with those reached by mail who *live in the same city,* that is, we delete mail sample respondents who live outside of these cities.

These source comparisons are complicated somewhat by problems we encountered in trying to get comparable *club* samples in the four cities. In San Francisco, it will be remembered, our club sample consists of males attending a wide range of social activities at S.I.R. For our New York sample we were unable to obtain a similar club and had to rely instead on a discussion club and two bars which had been converted into private bar-clubs. In Amsterdam and Copenhagen, our samples are made up of males attending dancing and drinking clubs, in contrast to the more diversified club from which the San Francisco sample is obtained.

Thus, the type of club sampled varies so much from city to city that these clubs do not form a homogeneous category. For this reason, it is difficult to generalize about the club sample or to compare it with the mail and bar samples. Also, because of the diversity within the club sample, generalizations about the mail and bar samples have to be based primarily on comparisons between these two samples rather than comparisons with the club sample.

Mail Sample

As we have pointed out, organizations like Mattachine keep social functions to a minimum, maintaining contact with their membership primarily by mail. Their major concern is with the betterment of the homosexual's total situation by acting as a pressure group rather than by trying to meet the personal needs of individual homosexuals. Their political style is "respectable," working within the establishment and its rules to accomplish these goals. This is true of C.O.C. and Forbundet as well, but these organizations also provide social facilities for their members. One might expect homosexuals reached through these organizations to have many of the characteristics which we associate with "respectability." In general, this is what we find, regardless of the society. For example, mail source respondents are the most stable in terms of residence and employment.[2] They are also older than respondents from bars and clubs (Table 1).

Nonetheless, despite this interpretation of "respectability," mail source respondents (in New York, Amsterdam, and Copenhagen, but not in San Francisco) are the most likely to have been officially labeled homosexual on records other than the listings of homophile organizations (Table 2).

At the same time, in their relation to the homosexual world, these respondents attend homosexual bars and clubs less frequently. They also report less frequent sexual relations (Table 3).

None of these findings is explained by age—that is, they are not due to differences in the age distributions found for the different sources—or by extent of association with other homosexuals. Furthermore, there are no significant differences in the class composition of the sample sources, so the findings cannot be explained by social class.

Thus, it appears that the structural character and operations of mail organizations appeal most to homosexuals with particular social characteristics. Generally, these are older, more stable persons who are not as actively involved in the public and visible environment of the homosexual world. Mail organizations such as we have described seem to provide a surrogate means of support and identification for this type of homosexual.

Club Sample

Sampling from New York homosexual clubs proved to be the weakest point in the sampling strategy. Initially, the private club most similar to the club used in San Francisco (yet much more limited in size, facilities, and functions) was chosen. The owner of the club refused, however, to allow research assistants on the premises. He did agree to distribute the questionnaires himself, but none of these questionnaires was returned. When the owner was contacted about this, he replied that he did not know what had happened, but agreed to see that questionnaires would be distributed if additional ones were provided. A large number of questionnaires was sent, but the club maintained that these were never received.

When it became clear that the members of the club were unwilling to cooperate, the small number of questionnaires that remained for distribution was given to other private clubs. These clubs would not allow research assistants on the premises either. Moreover, these clubs were bars that had been converted into private clubs and thus were less like the type of social club in San Francisco. In addition, a homosexual discussion club was contacted. Fifty questionnaires (all that remained) were provided, and fifteen were completed and returned. Since the number of respondents is so low—often as low as eleven for a particular measure—their percentages are omitted from the tables. While nothing can be said about the special character of the club respondents in New York because of their small number, it is interesting that they do not produce any divergent distributions in comparison with the other sources.

As previously described, the club source in San Francisco is S.I.R. While this organization is engaged in many of the same activities as M.S.N.Y., it functions more as a social club than M.S.N.Y. (As mentioned previously, its premises are used for dances, relaxation, shows, and discussion groups. Also it provides for various athletic activities and participation in various community programs.) Sampling occurred over different nights and across various activities so that those members who used the organization as a social club would be reached.

In Amsterdam, members who used C.O.C. as a social club were sampled in a similar way—questionnaires being systematically distributed to respondents who attended the club. But here we obtain, almost exclusively, a sample of those who attend a "dancing and drinking club" rather than a more diversified type of club like S.I.R. In Copenhagen also, the club sample is comprised of persons attending dancing and drinking clubs (Club 48 and the Pink Club).

Thus, the heterogeneity of the club sample minimizes any possibility of obtaining a consistent differentiation of club respondents across cities. The only results are the idiosyncratic results obtained in San Francisco. Compared to respondents from other San Francisco sources, the San Francisco club respondents have the highest social involvement with other homosexuals and the lowest social involvement with heterosexuals. They also anticipate the least discrimination from heterosexuals, score the lowest in passing, are the most known about, and are the most likely to be highly acculturated and to not see homosexuality as immoral or as an illness (Table 4). None of these differences is explained by age or extent of association with other homosexuals. Rather, these differences appear to be those that would be almost necessarily related to participation in this type of homosexual club. While it could be claimed that many of these differences were a consequence of participation in this organization, the cross-sectional questionnaire data do not, of course, allow for such a directional interpretation. Thus, while the data may indicate the differential character of those choosing to join the organization, anyone who sees this organization in operation is bound to conclude that in addition to any differential selection, many members are so affected by the form of participation provided by the organization.

Bar Sample

One main feature that seemed to characterize our respondents from homosexual bars is their covertness. In general, they are higher in passing than respondents from other sources. There is a tendency also for bar respondents to be less known about than respondents from other sources, which is in accord with such secrecy (Table 2). Further comparisons show the bar respondents to be the least stable residentially and less likely than mail respondents to have been officially labeled as homosexual (Tables 1 and 2). Neither age nor extent of association with other homosexuals explains these findings. Rather, they seem to reflect the anonymity and opportunity which the bar scene fosters. Although homosexual bars are not as anonymous as public toilets, parks, or steam baths as places to find sexual partners, they are relatively anonymous when compared to formal organizations which require one's name and address.

Summary

The data show systematic differences for respondents obtained from different sources. Since these differences are generally replicated in the various societies studied, it seems safe to say that they are a function of the structural and functional character of the different sources examined.

Differences by sample source which are not explained by age, association with other homosexuals, or social class may be summarized briefly.[3] (a) Mail source respondents are, on the average, older, more socially stable, participate less in those activities collectively referred to as the homosexual subculture, and have lower frequencies of sexual relations. (b) Respondents from bars are, on the average, less socially stable and more secretive and discreet with regard to their homosexuality. (c) Respondents from clubs are difficult to generalize about because of the sampling problems mentioned above and the different types of clubs sampled. Only in San Francisco do the club respondents stand out. S.I.R. respondents report having the most to do with the homosexual world and the least to do with the heterosexual world.

They are the least secretive, are least likely to anticipate discrimination from heterosexuals, and are the most likely to have normalized their homosexuality.

Even more important than the differences enumerated above is the lack of differences among sample sources on our various measures of *psychological* problems. While these scales (self-acceptance, stability of self-concept, depression, and so forth) prove useful in distinguishing respondents with respect to the variables of other chapters, no significant differences are found between respondents from the different sample sources. This suggests that if the psychological adjustment of the homosexual is the major concern of a study—and many of the studies in progress seem most concerned with this—then any of the sample sources which have been discussed may be as representative as any of the others. This is not to say that the sample would provide distributions on such scales that are representative of the homosexual population as a whole, but they are representative of those male homosexuals whom the researcher would be likely to obtain from nonclinical and noninstitutional sources.

The differences that we do obtain also seem to suggest that the common typology of homosexuals as ranging along an overt-covert dimension does not do justice to the multiple aspects of the life style of the homosexual as he relates to the homosexual and the heterosexual world. Thus, covertness should not be taken as synonymous with low participation in the public and visible aspects of the homosexual subculture. The bar respondents, for example, appear to be the most secretive regarding their homosexuality. Respondents from mail organizations, on the other hand, though having less to do with the public and visible aspects of the homosexual subculture, are not as covert in other aspects of their lives. Homosexuals who are very covert and who have little to do with the homosexual subculture are another variation. For obvious reasons, these persons are not as likely to be in our sample.

Demographic Correlates of Sample Source

	Source								
	Mail		Club		Bar		x^2	df	p
Has been living at present address more than two years									
New York	65.9%	(314)	—		38.9%	(72)	19.108	2	.001
San Francisco	52.8	(53)	34.0%	(47)	29.5	(78)	7.678	2	.05
Amsterdam	57.6	(238)	48.3	(143)	39.1	(46)	6.778	2	.05
Copenhagen	57.1	(84)	42.7	(75)	38.5	(26)	4.580	2	.20
							Pooled $x^2 = 38.144$, $df = 8$, $p < .001$		
Has been in present job longer than three years									
New York	54.4	(283)	—		29.6	(71)	19.019	2	.001
San Francisco	55.8	(52)	34.8	(46)	32.4	(74)	7.667	2	.05
Amsterdam	49.3	(209)	49.2	(124)	41.9	(43)	.833	2	.70
Copenhagen	60.8	(79)	42.0	(69)	54.2	(24)	5.218	2	.10
							Pooled $x^2 = 32.737$, $df = 8$, $p < .001$		
Is under 35 years of age									
New York	42.1	(318)	—		68.9	(74)	23.465	2	.001
San Francisco	30.2	(53)	75.5	(49)	64.9	(77)	24.429	2	.001
Amsterdam	64.7	(238)	68.5	(143)	86.7	(45)	8.436	2	.02
Copenhagen	61.9	(84)	89.2	(74)	76.9	(26)	15.680	2	.001
							Pooled $x^2 = 72.010$, $df = 8$, $p < .001$		

TABLE 2

Relating to the Heterosexual World, by Source

	Source								
	Mail		Club		Bar		x^2	df	p
Is officially labeled as homosexual									
New York	51.4%	(317)	—		34.7%	(75)	7.211	2	.05
San Francisco	40.7	(54)	54.0%	(50)	32.1	(78)	6.084	2	.05
Amsterdam	40.4	(235)	29.5	(139)	26.7	(45)	6.220	2	.05
Copenhagen	32.1	(84)	15.6	(77)	23.1	(26)	6.044	2	.05
							Pooled $x^2 = 25.559$, df = 8, $p < .01$		
Is high in passing									
New York	57.5	(299)	—		64.7	(68)	1.359	2	.70
San Francisco	59.2	(49)	33.3	(48)	71.4	(70)	16.998	2	.001
Amsterdam	24.2	(236)	24.6	(134)	40.0	(45)	5.131	2	.10
Copenhagen	28.9	(76)	41.3	(75)	36.0	(25)	2.546	2	.30
							Pooled $x^2 = 26.034$, df = 8, $p < .001$		
Reports best male heterosexual friend knows or suspects his homosexuality									
New York	70.3	(297)	—		56.1	(66)	6.167	2	.05

San Francisco	56.9	(51)	76.9	(39)	48.6	(72)	8.367	2	.02
Amsterdam	89.6	(192)	80.0	(120)	80.0	(40)	6.366	2	.05
Copenhagen	82.7	(75)	77.9	(68)	59.1	(22)	5.444	2	.10
							Pooled $x^2 = 27.344$, $df = 8$, $p < .001$		
Reports best female heterosexual friend knows or suspects his homosexuality									
New York	67.3	(281)	—		56.1	(66)	3.463	2	.20
San Francisco	46.9	(49)	77.5	(40)	51.4	(70)	9.737	2	.01
Amsterdam	92.1	(189)	85.3	(109)	73.7	(38)	10.899	2	.01
Copenhagen	84.7	(72)	74.2	(62)	60.0	(20)	6.008	2	.05
							Pooled $x^2 = 30.107$, $df = 8$, $p < .001$		
Reports half or more of people he knows or suspects to be homosexual know or suspect his homosexuality									
New York	65.4	(309)	—		56.8	(74)	3.601	2	.20
San Francisco	64.2	(53)	88.0	(50)	59.2	(76)	12.357	2	.01
Amsterdam	79.0	(224)	67.7	(133)	59.5	(42)	9.939	2	.01
Copenhagen	74.3	(74)	75.7	(74)	68.0	(25)	.580	2	.80
							Pooled $x^2 = 26.477$, $df = 8$, $p < .001$		

TABLE 3

Relating to the Homosexual World, by Source

	Source								
	Mail		Club		Bar		x^2	df	p
Attends homosexual bars and clubs more than once a month									
New York	38.4%	(318)	—		85.1%	(74)	54.813	2	.001
San Francisco	44.4	(54)	88.0%	(50)	85.9	(78)	35.502	2	.001
Amsterdam	66.0	(238)	93.7	(143)	97.8	(45)	51.891	2	.001
Copenhagen	67.1	(85)	90.9	(77)	81.5	(27)	13.906	2	.001
							Pooled $x^2 = 156.112$, $df = 8$, $p < .01$		

Has homosexual sex less than once a month *									
New York	12.0	(299)	—		2.8	(72)	11.234	2	.01
San Francisco	19.2	(52)	6.1	(49)	1.4	(74)	13.351	2	.01
Amsterdam	8.1	(221)	4.4	(136)	4.5	(44)	18.196 †	2	.001
Copenhagen	6.3	(79)	0.0	(70)	0.0	(26)	6.068	2	.05
							Pooled $x^2 = 48.849$, $df = 8$, $p < .001$		

* While we usually cut this composite measure at the median, in the present instance differences of any magnitude were obtained only at this more polar point (namely, sex less than once a month).

† Throughout the book we have examined the expected frequencies involved in the computation of our x^2's to see that they meet Cochran's recommendations (William G. Cochran, "Some Methods for Strengthening the Common x^2 Tests," *Biometrics* 10 [1954], pp. 417–51). They are not met in this table, as well as in two others (Chapter 20). Here they are not met for the Amsterdam and Copenhagen distributions. For Copenhagen, the expected frequency in question does not inflate the significance level (which is the condition against which he cautions). The significance level for Amsterdam may be inflated, but the pooled x^2 is high enough that it would be significant at the .001 level even if the x^2 for Amsterdam were near zero. Thus, although the probability for the x^2 for Amsterdam could be computed more exactly, we did not feel it necessary in light of the very high pooled x^2.

TABLE 4

Differences Between Club and Other Sample Sources in San Francisco

Measures	Source								
	Mail		Club		Bar		x^2	df	p
Is high in social involvement with homosexuals	66.7%	(51)	97.9%	(47)	84.9%	(73)	17.236	2	.001
Is high in social involvement with heterosexuals	44.4	(54)	14.3	(49)	34.6	(78)	11.146	2	.01
Anticipates a great deal of discrimination	57.7	(52)	30.4	(46)	51.3	(78)	7.978	2	.02
Is high in passing	59.2	(49)	33.3	(48)	71.4	(70)	17.998	2	.001
Reports best male heterosexual friend knows or suspects his homosexuality	56.9	(51)	76.9	(39)	48.6	(72)	8.367	2	.02

Reports best female heterosexual friend knows or suspects his homosexuality	46.9	(49)	77.5	(40)	51.4	(70)	9.737	2	.01
Reports half or more of people he knows or suspects to be homosexual know or suspect his homosexuality	64.2	(53)	88.0	(50)	59.2	(76)	12.357	2	.01
Is high in acculturation	57.4	(54)	92.0	(50)	76.9	(78)	16.891	2	.001
Believes homosexuality is immoral	13.0	(54)	0.0	(50)	16.7	(78)	8.959	2	.02
Believes homosexuality is not an illness	77.8	(54)	91.8	(49)	74.0	(77)	6.175	2	.05

PART IV

QUESTIONNAIRE STUDY—RESULTS

CHAPTER 10

LOCALE

We have shown that homosexual respondents differ according to the source from which they were derived. In this chapter, we compare respondents from the *same* source, but from *different* locales. As we have discussed previously, societal reaction theory suggests that homosexuals in the United States would experience more social and psychological problems than would homosexuals in the Netherlands and Denmark, where there is more tolerance of homosexuality and of the homosexual.

In this chapter we present two sets of findings: (1) differences among respondents living *in* the four major cities studied, and (2) differences among respondents living *outside* the major cities in the three countries. In comparing homosexuals from the major cities, we rely primarily on differences in the mail samples, using the club and bar samples for replication. For homosexuals outside the major cities, we rely exclusively on the mail samples. The mail sample questionnaires were precoded as to whether the mailing address was inside or outside the major cities. (By contrast, it is difficult to know whether members of the club and bar samples live inside or outside our major cities.)

Originally, we also expected to find and discuss an

"urbanism effect," for example, that in large cities the respondent worries less about discovery. Within each country, therefore, we examined the relation between the size of the city where the respondent lives and our other variables with the following results.

(1) *Outside* each of the major metropolises, city size is *not* associated with any other variable. (Thus, we collapse the locales outside *each* major city into the unit "outlying areas." Moreover, respondents from locales outside of New York and San Francisco are also combined, since no significant differences are found between them. Thus, we have three "outlying areas," one for each country.[1])

(2) Even when we compare respondents living in the *major cities versus the outlying areas* in each country, we do not find a marked urbanism effect. No differences appear in psychological problems. For the United States, we do find other differences which meet our 10 per cent criterion (and are statistically significant); however, the percentage difference is usually small, between 10 and 13 per cent. Also, the Dutch replication is often very weak (60 per cent of the time the difference being less than 10 per cent and only once over 12 per cent), and no differences replicate in Denmark. For these reasons, we have omitted any detailed comparison of respondents living in our major cities with those living in outlying areas. The differences for the United States are that in outlying areas respondents are less known about, worry more about exposure of their homosexuality, pass more, and anticipate more intolerance and discrimination. Americans in outlying areas also report fewer exclusive homosexual relationships, less frequent homosexual sex and more restricted sex practices, less acculturation and dressing in women's clothing, and less social involvement with other homosexuals and more with heterosexuals.[2]

The lack of findings in Denmark may be due in part to a sampling problem.[3] Nonetheless, the small differences found for the United States and the Netherlands do suggest some further thoughts regarding the urbanism hypothesis.

This hypothesis proposes that the "deviant" adapts much more easily in the city where anonymity protects him somewhat from social rejection and where heterogeneity and differentiation allow him to find his own supportive milieu (for example, through involvement in a deviant subculture). By contrast, this hypothesis implies, the smaller town is a "folk community," in which everyone knows and interacts with everyone else and in which knowledge of "deviance" spreads throughout the community and moral indignation is more effectively communicated to the "deviant." Our weak findings suggest, however, that adaptations may be made more easily than we expected by homosexuals in areas that we usually consider small in population size, for example, 25,000. It may be that a "folk community" is not at present approximated until a locale reaches a much smaller size, perhaps 5,000. (Unfortunately, we do not have enough respondents from such small towns to allow us to test this notion.) Also, it is often overlooked that communities of the same size differ in terms of isolation, homogeneity, and migration, and nowadays even in a small and homogeneous town the homosexual can often drive easily to a city where there is some established homosexual activity.

In our cross-cultural comparisons, we retain the distinction between living in a major city or outside for the following reasons. First, even though the differences between respondents from major cities and those from outlying areas are small, we do not wish to obscure them. Second, although generally the same cross-cultural differences are found in comparing (a) our major cities and (b) our outlying areas, there are a few differences which appear for only one of the comparisons. The findings are described below.

Relating to the Heterosexual World (Table 1)

Both in the major cities and in the outlying areas, we generally find the European homosexual to be more at ease with, and less threatened by, the heterosexual world than is his American counterpart.[4] For example, European respondents are less likely to state that they anticipate or have experienced intolerance or rejection because of their homosexuality, or to anticipate discrimination by heterosexuals.

A less stressful relationship with heterosexuals on the part of European homosexuals is also evident in their responses to those items that relate to being known about. Compared with homosexuals in the United States, they care less about who knows they are homosexual and are less worried about being exposed as such. (Generally, the club findings do not replicate here, probably due to the problem of the heterogeneity of clubs discussed earlier.) European homosexuals are also lower in passing, are more known about, and in outlying areas are lower in social involvement with heterosexuals.

Finally, compared with homosexuals in the United States, European homosexuals report formal religion, traditional morality, and conformity to be less important to them. Moreover, they tend to be less likely to see homosexuality as violating the precepts of these codes. (Again, the club sample does not replicate.)

A more tolerant climate toward homosexuals on the part of the Dutch and Danish populations and a general lack of condemnation by church and state, therefore, seem to make the European homosexual less apt to hide his sexual proclivity or to fear negative reactions from heterosexuals.

Relating to the Homosexual World (Table 2)

While in outlying areas our Americans are more likely than our Europeans to consider homosexuals as a very important reference group, the Europeans in outlying areas score higher in association with other homosexuals (and lower in association with heterosexuals—see above) than do similarly located homosexuals in the United States (Table 2). No such differences are found between the four major cities. This suggests that it is easier for European homosexuals residing in smaller cities and towns than for American homosexuals so situated to live a life more circumscribed by other homosexuals.

In the major cities, however, we find that compared with European homosexuals, American homosexuals are more likely to report having mainly homosexuals as friends. At the same time, European homosexuals are more likely to attend homosexual bars and clubs and generally appear to be more highly acculturated (although this is not replicated for the bar sample).

Thus, it appears that the European homosexual is, on the average, more involved with the public aspects of homosexual life (namely, bars and clubs) than is the American homosexual. This is interesting in that from our field work we concluded that the homosexual subculture in Europe is developed less extensively than in the United States. On that basis one might have expected to find less public involvement by European homosexuals simply because there is less to get involved in.

It would seem that the gay bar, the central institution of the homosexual world, is sufficient (along perhaps with a few private clubs) to provide for the needs of many homosexuals. Along this line, a more elaborate argument is also proposed. The more repressive a culture is toward homosexuals, it would seem, the more they set themselves apart to form a subculture. However, because of the greater fear of exposure, less of the homosexual population use the public institutions of that subculture. Those who do, however, may extend its forms and functions because, less concerned about exposure, they choose to live a homosexual life style. On the other hand, in a less repressive culture, the homosexual has less need to set himself as completely apart, and the homosexual subculture is less developed.

However, because they are less fearful of exposure, perhaps more of the homosexual population use the public institutions that do exist.

A final set of related findings is that the European homosexuals neutralize responsibility for their homosexuality to a greater extent than do the American homosexuals. They are more likely to believe they were born homosexual and to agree that their homosexuality is beyond their control. Also, while few homosexuals believe they are responsible for being homosexual, in our city comparison even fewer do in Europe. The reason for these striking differences is not very clear, although they do provide an interesting cultural difference. With regard to being born homosexual, biological theories of human behavior, especially of "deviant behavior," generally are more prevalent in Europe than in the United States.[5] Sociology is relatively undeveloped in Europe, and both psychology and anthropology in Europe have a more biological perspective than in the United States. (There is, for example, little *social* psychology in Europe, and *cultural* anthropology is an American innovation.) It might be, therefore, that what we label as neutralization is associated with commonsense theories of human behavior held by the general public in the Netherlands and Denmark.

Psychological Problems (Table 3)

In our cross-cultural comparisons, the model we employ points to different homosexual life-styles and differences in the degree and kind of problems homosexuals face as the result of differences in the societal reaction to homosexuality. Due to more rejection, in general, one would expect American homosexuals to have more psychological problems than their European counterparts.

Our data, however, provide no support for such reasoning. Generally, our European samples are no different from our American samples on our psychological dimensions.

The only difference we find is that European homosexuals in outlying areas feel somewhat less guilt, shame, or anxiety regarding their homosexuality. Perhaps the societal reaction model we have employed is too simple to do justice to the complexity of the situation. We argue (and the data suggest) that there are no major differences among the three societies with regard to our respondents' psychological problems, despite differences in the socio-cultural reactions to homosexuals. (Differences between our homosexual and general population samples within each society—which are meaningful with respect to this question—are examined in Chapter 11; these results also support the present argument.)

We offer four points with regard to this model and our research. First, this model implies that societal rejection and psychological problems are related in a linear manner, with increasing "amounts" of rejection followed by a similar monotonic increase in psychological problems. It may be, instead, that after a certain degree of rejection is reached—be it official reactions in the United States or the more personal lack of acceptance in Europe—further increments of rejection may not increase the number or severity of noticeable negative effects. (Of course, we exclude the most extreme forms of persecution of homosexuals, for example, as practiced in Nazi Germany, where homosexuals were placed in concentration camps.) Thus, the mere fact that there is rejection in both Europe and America, of whatever type, may be enough to account for the lack of difference we find among the samples.

Second, perhaps rejection itself is not *directly* the major cause of the homosexual's stress. We discussed previously the social features of homosexuality itself, as practiced in these three societies, which produce stress. Also, different combinations of factors can produce similar scores on our psychological measures. That is, it need not be societal rejection alone, but societal rejection in combination with one or more other factors that produces psychological problems.

Third, even if negative societal reactions do produce stress, it may also be that in each country homosexuals have worked out ways of adapting to these problems, perhaps with equal success, which again would account for a lack of difference in psychological problems. Homosexuals in the United States, due to a broad-based rejection, make more use of subcultural solutions. Homosexuals in Europe, due to a less pervasive rejection, rely perhaps on other modes of solution, for example, official intervention. Both modes may be effective (or both may be ineffective), given the particular problem; the results in either case could be a lack of cross-cultural differences in psychological problems.

Finally, the character of our samples might preclude a fair test of the model. The samples are, most likely, not representative of those homosexuals who are the most covert and who are inactive in the subculture. And it could be precisely among these homosexuals that the greatest cross-cultural differences in psychological problems exist. These are the homosexuals who are perhaps the most affected by societal reactions, since they lack the mitigating elements the homosexual subculture might provide. With our own respondents we reran indices of psychological problems by country, holding constant the extent of involvement with other homosexuals. We still find no differences among countries, however. (Since there is a difference in the age composition of the European and American samples, all the findings in the chapter were also checked holding age constant. None of the findings is affected.)

The findings in this chapter suggest that the Dutch and Danish homosexuals enjoy certain advantages over the American homosexual living in a comparable locale. Insofar as our samples and measures permit us to estimate, the extent to which our European respondents face fewer problems seems to be basically the same regardless of the size of their locale. That is, the magnitudes of the European-American percentage differences found among the major cities are similar to those found among outlying areas.

It would appear from these findings, however, that from country to country there is slightly more similarity among the large cities than among outlying areas, probably due to the similar structural factors that accompany urbanism. That is, it may be that the anonymity, opportunity, and subcultural support which the city provides do not vary significantly among these cities.

Comparing homosexuals in outlying areas, Europeans are *further* differentiated in that they report greater association with other homosexuals and less guilt, shame, or anxiety over their homosexuality. The additional differences we find among outlying areas may be accounted for by the fact that the United States, unlike the Netherlands and Denmark, has neither (a) the liberal *societal* ethos (that is, one which extends beyond the cosmopolitan cities) nor (b) the proximity between the "outside locales" and the major urban areas. Not only may geography permit a greater proportion of Dutch and Danish homosexuals to be closer to a major city with all its benefits for homosexuals; it may also provide somewhat greater similarity between cities and outlying areas with regard to liberal ideas.

Summary

The chapter compared American, Dutch, and Danish homosexuals in order to determine the effects of locale on social and psychological dimensions. We compared homosexuals in the four major cities that we studied—New York, San Francisco, Amsterdam, and Copenhagen—and those in outlying areas as well. We found European homosexuals to be more at ease with, and less threatened by, the heterosexual world than are American homosexuals. The

European homosexuals are less secretive about their homosexuality and more known about, and they anticipate less discrimination and rejection from heterosexuals.

European homosexuals are also more involved in the public aspects of homosexual life—for example, in attending homosexual clubs and bars—and are higher in acculturation. In outlying areas, while homosexuals are a more important reference group for American homosexuals, European homosexuals have more association with other homosexuals and less with heterosexuals. Moreover, more European homosexuals neutralize any responsibility for their homosexuality. This is perhaps best viewed as a cultural phenomenon, reflecting European theories of human behavior rather than being specifically related to the homosexual milieu.

The most unexpected result is that, contrary to the widely held belief that greater societal rejection leads to greater psychological problems, virtually no such differences appeared between American and European homosexuals. The only exception was that homosexuals living outside the major cities feel somewhat less guilt, shame, or anxiety regarding their homosexuality in Europe than in America. An explanation for the general lack of differences in psychological problems reported was offered centering around the oversimplicity and reified nature of the societal reaction model and/or the limitations of our sample.

The findings in this chapter were interpreted as suggesting that (a) the cultural ethos is more congenial to homosexuals in the Netherlands and Denmark than in the United States, not only in the major cities but also in the outlying areas, and (b) except for association with other homosexuals and feelings of guilt, shame, or anxiety over their homosexuality, the contrast between the United States and Europe is of approximately the same magnitude outside the major cities as in them.

TABLE 1

Relating to the Heterosexual World, by Locale

1A. Anticipates or Has Experienced Intolerance or Rejection Because of His Homosexuality

	City						
	New York	San Francisco	Amsterdam	Copenhagen	x^2	df	p
Mail	42.8% (311)	52.8% (53)	8.2% (219)	11.3% (80)	102.646	3	.001
Club	—	35.4 (48)	12.5 (136)	11.0 (73)	20.312	3	.001
Bar	49.3 (73)	47.8 (77)	14.0 (43)	21.7 (23)	19.506	3	.001
					Pooled $x^2 = 142.464$, $df = 9$, $p < .001$		
		Other Areas					
		United States	Netherlands	Denmark			
Mail		51.6% (446)	14.0% (579)	9.1% (55)	253.556	2	.001

TABLE 1—Continued

1B. Anticipates a Great Deal of Discrimination

	City										
	New York		San Francisco		Amsterdam		Copenhagen		x^2	df	p
Mail	33.8%	(275)	57.7%	(52)	16.9%	(207)	18.9%	(74)	42.724	3	.001
Club	—		30.4	(46)	17.7	(124)	29.6	(71)	5.592	3	.20
Bar	39.4	(71)	51.3	(78)	21.1	(38)	26.9	(26)	11.694	3	.01
									Pooled $x^2 = 60.010$, $df = 9$, $p < .001$		

	Other Areas							
	United States		Netherlands		Denmark			
Mail	62.5%	(461)	26.5%	(558)	16.4%	(55)	149.460	2	.001

1C. Does Not Care Who Knows about His Homosexuality

	City								x^2	df	p
	New York		San Francisco		Amsterdam		Copenhagen				
Mail	22.1%	(294)	24.1%	(54)	52.7%	(237)	43.4%	(83)	58.895	3	.001
Club	—		40.0	(50)	43.4	(143)	40.8	(76)	3.086	3	.50
Bar	12.3	(73)	12.8	(78)	46.7	(45)	44.4	(27)	30.197	3	.001

Pooled $x^2 = 92.178$, $df = 9$, $p < .001$

	Other Areas								
	United States		Netherlands		Denmark				
Mail	17.9%	(486)	37.0%	(619)	34.3%	(67)	49.289	2	.001

1D. Worries about Exposure of His Homosexuality

	City								x^2	df	p
	New York		San Francisco		Amsterdam		Copenhagen				
Mail	61.8%	(295)	69.2%	(52)	46.0%	(237)	51.2%	(82)	30.745	3	.001
Club	—		59.2	(49)	52.4	(143)	65.3	(75)	3.471	3	.50
Bar	80.8	(73)	85.5	(76)	50.0	(46)	65.4	(26)	21.897	3	.001

Pooled $x^2 = 49.171$, $df = 9$, $p < .001$

TABLE 1—Continued

	United States	Other Areas Netherlands	Denmark	x^2	df	p
Mail	80.0% (475)	56.8% (620)	59.7% (67)	66.511	2	.001

1E. Is High in Passing

	City						
	New York	San Francisco	Amsterdam	Copenhagen	x^2	df	p
Mail	57.2% (276)	59.2% (49)	24.2% (236)	28.9% (76)	68.546	3	.001
Club	—	33.3 (48)	24.6 (134)	41.3 (75)	9.456	3	.05
Bar	64.7 (68)	71.4 (70)	40.0 (45)	36.0 (25)	17.407	3	.001

Pooled $x^2 = 76.497$, $df = 9$, $p < .001$

	United States	Other Areas Netherlands	Denmark	x^2	df	p
Mail	67.5% (452)	35.5% (611)	33.3% (63)	112.226	2	.001

1F. Is High in Being Known About (Scale I)

	Other Areas					
	United States	Netherlands	Denmark	x^2	df	p
Mail	20.9% (454)	49.4% (498)	46.2% (52)	85.485	2	.001

1G. Is High in Being Known About (Scale II)

	City						
	New York	San Francisco	Amsterdam	Copenhagen	x^2	df	p
Mail	42.1% (209)	37.9% (29)	88.8% (206)	80.5% (77)	118.506	3	.001
Club	—	53.7 (41)	80.6 (124)	74.6 (71)	14.294	3	.01
Bar	25.6 (39)	29.8 (47)	85.0 (40)	65.0 (20)	38.256	3	.001
					Pooled $x^2 = 171.056$, $df = 9$, $p < .001$		

	Other Areas					
	United States	Netherlands	Denmark			
Mail	37.3% (255)	80.5% (529)	81.4% (59)	152.424	2	.001

TABLE 1—Continued

1H. Is High in Social Involvement with Heterosexuals

	Other Areas					
	United States	Netherlands	Denmark	x^2	df	p
Mail	59.1% (437)	45.9% (619)	46.9% (64)	19.745	2	.001

1I. Thinks Formal Religion Is Important

	City						
	New York	San Francisco	Amsterdam	Copenhagen	x^2	df	p
Mail	35.3% (292)	49.1% (53)	16.0% (237)	23.8% (84)	36.820	3	.001
Club	—	43.8 (48)	30.8 (143)	22.7 (75)	7.658	3	.10
Bar	41.3 (75)	48.1 (77)	30.4 (46)	20.0 (25)	8.035	3	.05

Pooled $x^2 = 52.513$, df $= 9$, $p < .001$

	Other Areas					
	United States	Netherlands	Denmark			
Mail	52.2% (490)	26.2% (615)	19.4% (67)	88.912	2	.001

1J. Thinks Traditional Morality Is Important

	City										
	New York		San Francisco		Amsterdam		Copenhagen		x^2	df	p
Mail	50.9%	(291)	54.7%	(53)	19.3%	(238)	34.9%	(83)	62.325	3	.001
Club	—		36.7	(49)	30.3	(142)	40.5	(74)	3.350	3	.50
Bar	53.3	(75)	61.8	(76)	34.8	(46)	33.3	(24)	11.520	3	.01
									Pooled $x^2 = 70.495$, $df = 9$, $p < .001$		

	Other Areas								
	United States		Netherlands		Denmark				
Mail	58.4%	(408)	28.6%	(612)	32.8%	(67)	101.600	2	.001

1K. Thinks Conformity Is Important

	City										
	New York		San Francisco		Amsterdam		Copenhagen		x^2	df	p
Mail	45.2%	(292)	50.9%	(53)	25.6%	(238)	27.5%	(80)	29.246	3	.001
Club	—		40.8	(49)	29.6	(142)	36.6	(71)	2.465	3	.50
Bar	53.3	(75)	48.1	(77)	37.0	(46)	24.0	(25)	8.054	3	.05
									Pooled $x^2 = 39.765$, $df = 9$, $p < .001$		

TABLE 1—Continued

		Other Areas				
	United States	Netherlands	Denmark			
Mail	50.3% (487)	26.3% (608)	36.9% (65)	66.788	2	.001

1L. Thinks Homosexuality Violates Formal Religion

	City						
	New York	San Francisco	Amsterdam	Copenhagen	x^2	df	p
Mail	58.2% (287)	55.6% (54)	49.8% (235)	43.8% (80)	6.957	3	.10
Club	—	56.3 (48)	40.4 (141)	38.0 (71)	5.173	3	.20
Bar	56.8 (74)	59.2 (76)	40.0 (45)	48.0 (25)	4.899	3	.20
					Pooled $x^2 = 17.029$, $df = 9$, $p < .05$		

		Other Areas				
	United States	Netherlands	Denmark			
Mail	57.1% (482)	45.6% (601)	48.4% (64)	14.184	2	.001

1M. Thinks Homosexuality Violates Traditional Morality

	City						
	New York	San Francisco	Amsterdam	Copenhagen	x^2	df	p
Mail	68.9% (289)	66.0% (53)	60.3% (234)	50.6% (81)	10.558	3	.02
Club	—	68.8 (48)	52.1 (140)	60.6 (71)	4.499	3	.30
Bar	67.6 (74)	64.0 (75)	57.8 (45)	33.3 (45)	9.487	3	.05
					Pooled $x^2 = 24.544$, $df = 9$, $p < .01$		

	Other Areas					
	United States	Netherlands	Denmark			
Mail	66.0% (486)	56.3% (599)	52.4% (63)	12.427	2	.01

TABLE 1—Continued

1N. Thinks Homosexuality Violates Conformity

	City										
	New York		San Francisco		Amsterdam		Copenhagen		x^2	df	p
Mail	71.4%	(290)	61.1%	(54)	56.6%	(235)	47.4%	(78)	20.824	3	.001
Club	—		62.5	(48)	48.9	(141)	63.8	(69)	5.446	3	.20
Bar	71.6	(74)	64.0	(75)	55.6	(45)	37.5	(24)	9.935	3	.02
									Pooled $x^2 = 25.313$, $df = 9$, $p < .01$		

	Other Areas								
	United States		Netherlands		Denmark				
Mail	71.0%	(486)	53.4%	(594)	52.5%	(61)	36.722	2	.001

TABLE 2

Relating to the Homosexual World, by Locale

2A. Homosexuals Are Important Reference Group

		Other Areas				
	United States	Netherlands	Denmark	x^2	df	p
Mail	65.9% (458)	45.9% (599)	46.8% (62)	43.378	2	.001

2B. Is High in Social Involvement with Homosexuals

		Other Areas				
	United States	Netherlands	Denmark	x^2	df	p
Mail	50.1% (457)	67.5% (590)	74.6% (59)	37.533	2	.001

TABLE 2—Continued

2C. Most Friends Are Homosexual

	City						
	New York	San Francisco	Amsterdam	Copenhagen	x^2	df	p
Mail	72.6% (288)	70.4% (54)	55.0% (238)	64.7% (85)	28.613	3	.01
Club	—	86.0 (50)	67.6 (142)	68.4 (76)	22.229	3	.01
Bar	70.7 (75)	82.3 (78)	57.8 (45)	69.2 (26)	23.291	3	.01
					Pooled $x^2 = 74.133$, $df = 9$, $p < .001$		

2D. Attends Homosexual Bars and Clubs More than Once a Month

	City						
	New York	San Francisco	Amsterdam	Copenhagen	x^2	df	p
Mail	38.4% (294)	44.4% (54)	65.0% (238)	67.1% (85)	49.230	3	.001
Club	—	87.0 (50)	93.7 (143)	90.9 (77)	12.028	3	.01
Bar	85.1 (74)	85.9 (78)	97.8 (45)	81.5 (27)	5.802	3	.20
					Pooled $x^2 = 67.060$, $df = 9$, $p < .001$		

		Other Areas				
	United States	Netherlands	Denmark			
Mail	34.9% (487)	61.5% (621)	57.6% (66)	78.787	2	.001

2E. Is High in Acculturation

	City						
	New York	San Francisco	Amsterdam	Copenhagen	x^2	df	p
Mail	50.2% (293)	35.2% (54)	63.7% (237)	74.1% (85)	30.534	3	.001
Club	—	66.0 (50)	71.1 (142)	83.1 (77)	5.824	3	.20
Bar	65.3 (75)	53.8 (78)	50.0 (46)	63.0 (27)	3.689	3	.30
					Pooled $x^2 = 32.669$, $df = 9$, $p < .001$		

		Other Areas				
	United States	Netherlands	Denmark			
Mail	46.2% (483)	71.0% (618)	88.1% (67)	91.816	2	.001

TABLE 2—Continued

2F. Believes Homosexuals Are Born Homosexual

	City				x^2	df	p
	New York	San Francisco	Amsterdam	Copenhagen			
Mail	20.3% (291)	22.2% (54)	42.2% (237)	39.5% (81)	34.408	3	.001
Club	—	14.0 (50)	40.6 (143)	32.9 (76)	13.050	3	.01
Bar	13.3 (75)	7.7 (78)	32.6 (46)	38.5 (26)	20.543	3	.001
					Pooled $x^2 = 68.001$, $df = 9$, $p < .001$		

	Other Areas			x^2	df	p
	United States	Netherlands	Denmark			
Mail	22.5% (489)	55.0% (620)	42.4% (66)	119.700	2	.001

2G. Believes Homosexuality Is Beyond One's Control

	City					
	New York	San Francisco	Amsterdam	Copenhagen	x^2	df	p
Mail	59.5% (294)	51.9% (54)	81.9% (238)	87.1% (85)	52.056	3	.001
Club	—	57.1 (49)	82.4 (142)	88.2 (76)	21.662	3	.001
Bar	50.0 (74)	42.3 (78)	69.6 (46)	88.9 (27)	22.304	3	.001
					Pooled $x^2 = 96.022$, $df = 9$, $p < .001$		

	Other Areas					
	United States	Netherlands	Denmark	x^2	df	p
Mail	54.9% (490)	86.6% (619)	89.6% (67)	150.578	2	.001

TABLE 2—Continued

2H. Accepts Responsibility for His Homosexuality

	City								x^2	df	p
	New York		San Francisco		Amsterdam		Copenhagen				
Mail	14.0%	(292)	27.8%	(54)	4.2%	(238)	7.1%	(84)	31.318	3	.001
Club	—		16.0	(50)	4.2	(143)	9.2	(76)	23.359	3	.001
Bar	18.7	(75)	17.9	(78)	8.7	(46)	3.8	(26)	5.373	3	.20

Pooled $x^2 = 60.050$, $df = 9$, $p < .001$

TABLE 3

Psychological Problems, by Locale

3A. Is High in Guilt, Shame, or Anxiety Regarding Homosexuality

		Other Areas				
	United States	Netherlands	Denmark	x^2	df	p
Mail	23.7% (476)	10.4% (617)	11.9% (67)	36.667	2	.001

CHAPTER 11

HOMOSEXUAL–GENERAL POPULATION COMPARISONS

In the previous chapter, we looked at the differences among homosexuals living in societies that vary in their attitudes toward homosexuality in order to examine some of the implications of societal reaction theory. In this chapter, we evaluate the implications of societal reaction theory further by comparing male homosexuals with a sample of the general male population in each country. If, for example, psychological problems are a function of societal reaction toward homosexuals rather than homosexuality being psychopathological per se, then we would expect to find not only that homosexuals show greater psychological problems than the general population in our three societies, but also that the more tolerant the society, the less this difference is between homosexuals and the general male population. Specifically, we would expect greater differences to appear between homosexuals and the general male population in the United States than in the Netherlands and Denmark.

For the general male population of the United States, Melvin Kohn's sample of 3,101 men, selected in 1964 to be representative of all those employed in civilian occupations in the United States, was utilized.[1] There are four sets of items that were used in both Kohn's and our studies: six self-acceptance items, five psychosomatic symptom items, two depression items, and four faith-in-others items.[2] We compare our homosexuals with Kohn's respondents on each of these items. (We standardized our homosexual response distributions according to age and education to make them comparable to Kohn's sample.)

For the European countries, no prior samples of their general male populations were available. We obtained small samples of the general male populations of Amsterdam and Copenhagen by the following method. Three hundred men from each city were randomly selected from the telephone book and sent that part of the questionnaire containing items regarding psychological problems and reactions to homosexuals and homosexuality. (The latter results were reported in Chapter 7.) Although using telephone books as a sampling frame can be criticized, Phillips and Clancy obtained findings on psychological items from subjects whom they selected from telephone books in the United States that are similar to those found by studies employing other procedures.[3] As to the possible biasing effect of only using men who can afford telephones, no significant differences were found in occupational status, education, or income between the European general male population samples and our homosexual samples. Since the general population response rate was low (approximately 12 per cent for each city) and the samples very small (Amsterdam N = 37; Copenhagen N = 35), we offer data from these samples only in a suggestive way.[4] Finally, for the European comparisons, we compare the general samples for Amsterdam and Copenhagen with the entire Dutch and Danish homosexual samples, respectively—rather than comparing them just to homosexuals from Amsterdam and Copenhagen—since, as noted in Chapter 10, no significant differences were found on psychological dimensions between homosexuals from inside and outside these cities.

Our findings for the homosexual–general population comparisons are as follows. In all three countries, homosexuals report less happiness and less faith in others than the general sample (Table 1). However, despite the negative societal reaction toward homosexuals, there is little difference in self-acceptance and psychosomatic symptoms reported by our homosexuals and the general male population samples. (A number of other studies of American homosexuals have obtained similar findings.[5]) *Regardless* of the representativeness of our homosexual samples, this is important.[6] We may conclude that *for many homosexuals,* problems of self-acceptance and psychosomatic symptoms may not be any more prevalent than for the population at large.

We cannot say that differences would not be found between *representative* samples of homosexuals and of the general male population. If such differences were found (namely, homosexuals being less adjusted), they might be produced by those homosexuals who are most isolated from the homosexual world and therefore least likely to be in our sample. (However, with age and education standardized, no additional findings are obtained by comparing the general male population with only our homosexual respondents who are least socially involved with other homosexuals.) Moreover, we also did not reach very young homosexuals, for whom identity crises may sometimes be quite severe. (Examining our data by age, with education standardized, on some dimensions younger homosexuals report somewhat more psychological problems than do younger heterosexuals, but the differences are not large enough to meet our criteria for "findings.")

Because of the overall paucity of our findings (as well as the small European samples), we cannot make conclusions regarding cross-cultural variations in the magnitude of differences between homosexuals and the general male population. For the two sets of items for which we find differences, however, we find little variation in the magnitude of differences found in the United States and those found in the Netherlands and Denmark; that is, we do not find, as societal reaction theory implies, smaller differences between the homosexual and general population samples in the more tolerant societies.

The general lack of differences in psychological problems between our homosexual and general samples parallels the lack of cross-cultural differences in psychological problems when only homosexuals were considered. This chapter, too, suggests that societal reaction theory needs further amplification. Some points have already been detailed in Chapter 10. We would like to add the following.

First, sexual orientation is not necessarily strongly correlated with psychological problems, even in a society generally rejecting of homosexuality. Both heterosexuals and homosexuals engage in a nonsexual, daily round of life and face a multitude of nonsexual situations that affect their psychological well-being. For example, the extent to which a man has psychological problems may be affected by job frustrations. Moreover, even in the sexual realm, there are heterosexual behaviors—for example, extramarital sex—that may be as guilt- and anxiety-producing as being homosexual.

Second, social scientists often seem to forget the tremendous human potential for adaptation, even to the most strained situations. People commonly use techniques such as compartmentalization to divert attention from conflicts and thus to facilitate adaptation.[7] Homosexuals are no exception. The evidence presented in this book suggests that many homosexuals do become routinized to "being homosexual" so that occupying a "deviant status" need not necessarily intrude upon their day-to-day functioning.

Finally, the whole question of the homosexual's psychological status is typically raised from a heterosexual point of view. Commentators on homosexuals' psychological problems usually attribute powers to both sexual orientation and societal reaction that are universalized and exaggerated.[8] Oversimplifying and thus dehumanizing the homosexual, they deny him the recuperative strategies that most people use in dealing with "problems." In terms of this logic, then, it follows that the homosexual *must* be psychologically maladjusted. (Here we are talking about those commentators who naïvely employ the societal reaction perspective; for those employing a "pathology perspective," such maladjustment is, of course, antecedent to and inherent in homosexuality. See Chapter 1.)

Also, such commentators treat homosexuals as a unitary and homogeneous type. We believe, instead, that there are some types of male homosexuals who are on the average better adjusted than the general male population as well as some who are less well adjusted.[9]

At the same time, the homosexual samples in our three societies are found to be less happy and to have less faith in others, which is in line with societal reaction theory. The fact that unhappiness and lower faith in others may not generate greater reported problems of self-acceptance and psychosomatic symptoms for members of our homosexual samples may attest to the human flexibility we have discussed—the ability to compartmentalize and effectively neutralize various problems.[10] Further investigation is needed, however, concerning the multidimensionality of psychological problems and the extent to which various facets can be tapped by survey research, be the subjects homosexual or heterosexual.

Summary

To further examine societal reaction theory, samples of homosexuals and of the general male population were compared in terms of psychological problems. Our expectation was that the former would have more problems, but that the magnitude of the differences between the two groups would be less in Europe, where there is more tolerance of homosexuality. Generally, these notions were not supported. On the basis of these findings, even though they are only suggestive (due to the small size of our European general samples), we proposed that societal reaction theory be further amplified to (a) recognize other factors affecting well-being, in addition to a "deviant proclivity" and the "societal reaction" to it, and (b) pay more attention to the human capacity for adaptation. We further suggested that, in considering the psychological problems of homosexuals and of the general male population, the adoption of an oversimplified heterosexual perspective exacerbates the failure to take the above two factors into account.

In all three countries homosexuals do score lower in happiness and faith in others. This was interpreted as being congruent with societal reaction theory without invalidating our points about the abilities of humans to adjust.

TABLE 1

Psychological Differences Between Homosexuals and the General Male Population Samples

	Sample							
	Homosexual		General Population		x^2	df	p	γ
Depression item								
Feels he is a happy person								
United States	68.8%	(1057)	92.8%	(3101)	446.631	1	.001	.71
Netherlands	52.3	(1064)	67.6	(37)	2.777	1	.10	.31
Denmark	68.7	(252)	80.0	(35)	1.384	1	.30	.29
					Pooled $x^2 = 450.792$, $df = 3$, $p < .001$			
Faith in others items								
No one cares what happens to you								
United States	34.0%	(1057)	23.0%	(3101)	49.591	1	.001	.27
Netherlands	16.5	(1062)	5.4	(37)	2.477	1	.20	.55
Denmark	41.1	(253)	20.0	(35)	4.926	1	.05	.47
					Pooled $x^2 = 56.994$, $df = 3$, $p < .001$			

Human nature is cooperative								
United States	51.6	(1057)	72.9	(3101)	163.212	1	.001	.43
Netherlands	43.5	(1054)	21.6	(37)	6.099	1	.02	.63
Denmark	60.9	(253)	74.3	(35)	1.824	1	.20	.30
					Pooled $x^2 = 158.937$, $df = 3$, $p < .001$			
Most people can be trusted								
United States	47.0	(1057)	76.8	(3101)	329.646	1	.001	.58
Netherlands	34.5	(1062)	40.5	(37)	0.346	1	.90	.13
Denmark	31.0	(252)	48.6	(35)	3.549	1	.10	.36
					Pooled $x^2 = 333.541$, $df = 3$, $p < .001$			

CHAPTER 12

SELF-OTHER PROCESSES

"Self-acceptance is the first step to happiness." [1]

In previous chapters we have examined some of the implications of societal reaction theory. In this chapter, we consider other implications of the theory, which have their source in earlier formulations of symbolic interactionist theory and which center around and extend the notion of the "looking glass self." This notion suggests that a person's feelings about himself are derived from imagining how others regard him. Thus, a person's evaluations and image of himself, as well as his general psychological state, are affected by how he imagines other people react to him, regardless of whether these imputations are accurate or not. It is further suggested that such perceptions are more consequential when the reactors are more important or "significant" to the person.

Other aspects of a person's looking glass self are his general feelings of social competence—feelings which are derived from experiences the person has had in his social relations with others—and how he feels about his personal identities. These considerations should be of particular importance in understanding the psychological problems of the homosexual. In this chapter we examine the association between the homosexual's psychological problems and these facets of his looking glass self: (1) how he thinks others appraise him, (2) how he appraises his social competence, and (3) how he appraises his homosexuality. None of the findings is accounted for by degree of involvement with other homosexuals.

Perceived Appraisals of Others

Heterosexual Appraisals

The homosexual can encounter a variety of reponses from the heterosexual world. Some may accept him or even regard him as something of a celebrity because of his "difference." Others, however, are likely to sanction him in ways which may range from subtle rejection, a smirk or double entendre, to violence, assaulting the homosexual. Fear of sanctions often inhibits persons from more fully embracing a homosexual role and the identity it implies. Indeed, imagining others' reactions is often as punishing as actual sanctions. Even if the homosexual himself has not actually been sanctioned because of his sexual orientation, the way he feels about himself can be damaged by his *imputing* negative reactions to the heterosexuals he knows and to people in general. And there are a number of factors which the homosexual is likely to encounter that reinforce such imputations. For instance, he is surrounded by a culture in which antihomosexual meanings proliferate. The mass media alone provide ample evidence that the homosexual is regarded by many in very negative terms—as immoral, criminal, or sick. Also, other homosexuals may supply him with lugubrious accounts of their own misfortunes. The homosexual, then, may build his expectations for the future around these accounts.

Turning to our data, we examine three indicators of the homosexual's perception of how heterosexuals appraise him.

First, how do our respondents think most people feel about homosexuals? Those who check the more negative categories (disgust, repulsion, dislike) report less psychological well-being on six of our eight measures of psychological problems (and less homosexual commitment) than do those who check more positive categories (Table 1). Second, when questioned about the sanctions they felt would accompany discovery of their homosexuality, those who anticipate the most discrimination from heterosexuals fare worse on seven out of the eight measures than do those anticipating little discrimination (Table 2). Finally, when the putative reactions of others (rejection to acceptance) are considered, those who anticipate the most negative responses from others show more problems on five of the measures than do those anticipating less negative responses (Table 3). These relationships are in accord with the notion of the looking glass self, and they indicate that others' reactions are associated with a number of psychological problems even when the reactions are only expected rather than actually incurred.

Where we found a significant relationship between psychological problems and the imagined appraisals of heterosexuals, we examined the effect of the "significance of the other." We expected that the association between such appraisals and psychological problems would be weaker when the respondent rates the opinion various heterosexuals have of him as relatively *unimportant*. This trend appears but is not strong, with heterosexuals' appraisals being related to the homosexual's well-being, regardless of the significance of the heterosexuals. We offer the following as an explanation. The homosexual generally perceives that societal reactions toward him are negative. Thus, the consequences of *any* negative response can be serious enough to override the significance of the other. If a person is negative toward homosexuals and his opinions are held in great esteem by a particular homosexual, he is in a position, by slight and innuendo, to cause great misery. This may also be the case, however, for a person whose opinions the homosexual may not regard as important. This is so because any negative reactions which the homosexual perceives may symbolize the rejection of the homosexual in the larger society.

Heterosexual Acceptance

The extent to which the homosexual feels he is genuinely accepted and not merely tolerated by heterosexuals is examined more closely here. Two questions comprise this measure: At the present time how popular are you in heterosexual circles? What do you think that most heterosexuals that know you think of you? Those homosexuals who feel more accepted by heterosexuals show better psychological adjustment on seven of the eight measures when compared with those who feel less accepted by heterosexuals (Table 4).[2] We suspected that these relationships might be stronger for homosexuals who attach more importance to heterosexuals' opinions. Controlling for the reported significance of heterosexual opinions, however, did not affect the relationship; thus, perceived acceptance by heterosexuals is inversely related to the homosexual's psychological problems, regardless of how much importance he attributes to heterosexuals' opinions. The rationale at the end of the preceding section is also applicable here.

Homosexual Acceptance

Heterosexual reaction in the main is an important source of insecurity for the homosexual. The reaction from other homosexuals, however, is also tremendously important. The homosexual is not automatically accepted as a person by other homosexuals. If he is young and attractive, the male homosexual can enjoy considerable popularity. If he is old, or too flamboyant, or not radical enough, or not conservative enough, however, he learns that heterosexuals do not have a monopoly on prejudice and rejection. Not to feel accepted by other homosexuals can produce an acute sense of isolation, marginality, and psychological strain. On the other hand, acceptance can create a feeling of identity and a sense of belonging which operate as a shield against perceived rejection by the heterosexual world.

Two questions comprise our measure of homosexual acceptance: Which category best describes your social situation among homosexuals? . . . What do you think most homosexuals that know you think of you? Compared with those who do not feel accepted by other homosexuals, those who feel accepted are higher in self-acceptance and stability of self-concept and lower in depression, interpersonal awkwardness, and loneliness (Table 5).

We held constant the reported importance of other homosexuals' opinions to the respondent. Again, this does not change the above relationships; perceived acceptance by other homosexuals is inversely related to psychological problems, regardless of the importance of other homosexuals' opinions. The explanation offered for this is similar to the preceding—acceptance and rejection by other homosexuals is important in that it symbolizes a more prevasive situation of acceptance or rejection.

Appraisals of One's Social Competence

In the preceding section we examined the perceived responses of various others which *directly* reflect how accepted or rejected the homosexual feels. In this section, we examine more subtle indicators of acceptance. Here we look at indicators of how successful and at ease the homosexual feels in his social interaction. These factors were expected to be associated with the way the homosexual regards himself, and thus his psychological well-being, because they *indirectly* reflect how accepted he feels.

Sex and Exclusive Relationships

Just as popularity in heterosexual dating or "going steady" can make a heterosexual feel socially valued, a high frequency of homosexual sex and having sustained an exclusive homosexual relationship may indicate to the homosexual that other homosexuals appraise him positively. Moreover, their absence may lead a homosexual to regard himself as unworthy or inadequate. Thus, we expected that a high frequency of homosexual sex and having had an exclusive homosexual relationship would be related to psychological well-being.[3]

Our data support this reasoning. First, compared with those low in frequency of homosexual sex, those high in frequency show fewer psychological problems on six of the eight measures and show higher commitment to their homosexuality (Table 6). We also find support for the association between having (or having had in the past) an exclusive homosexual relationship and psychological well-being. Those who have more experience with an exclusive relationship, compared with those having less experience, report more self-acceptance, stability of self-concept, and less depression, interpersonal awkwardness, and loneliness (Table 7).

We recognize, of course, that psychological problems can make certain homosexuals less attractive and thus decrease their likelihood of obtaining sexual activity or an exclusive relationship.

Loneliness

Another important indirect indicator of feeling accepted is freedom from loneliness. We saw loneliness as comprised of two aspects: objective, the fact of being alone; and subjective, the sense of feeling alone.

Loneliness is a crucial problem for many homosexuals. Objectively, the homosexual may find himself alone quite often. First of all, those who score 5 or 6 on the Kinsey Scale (as most of our respondents do) are usually bachelors. Second, liaisons with other homosexuals are often unstable. Our field impression was that there is often little talk between homosexuals once they have implicitly agreed to engage in sex. The sex may be directly attended to and consummated, and the participants may separate and not sustain any form of relationship. This is generally unlike heterosexual dating, which usually requires some development of the relationship and a much greater amount of time spent together. Moreover, homosexuals "cruise," or look for a sexual partner, alone. Cruising is a competitive activity, and the homosexual may often experience rejection in his attempts at engaging a partner. In this sense, he is often left alone.

Subjectively, even when the homosexual is with others, he may feel alone. He often feels separate from heterosexuals because he is different. When he associates with heterosexuals, he may also feel alone because he is not a part of a couple, which he has been socialized to view as the normal and expected state of affairs. Even with family and associates, he may feel alone because they do not share an encompassing part of his life.

Whether or not it is apt, loneliness can be used by a person as an indicant of a lack of social success. Even though the person may not really be a social failure (and many homosexuals are not, since their isolation from heterosexual society is by their own choice), loneliness can still have consequences for the looking glass self. Aloneness can signify failure to achieve what others in the society supposedly have achieved. Thus, homosexuals who report more loneliness also report more psychological problems on seven of the eight measures reflecting psychological well-being as well as less normalization and commitment (Table 8). Of course, this is not to say that psychological problems do not contribute to social failure.

Interpersonal Awkwardness and Effeminacy

As we have suggested, one consequence of being labeled homosexual by others or by the homosexual himself can be low social confidence and feelings of awkwardness and uneasiness in social interaction. It is these feelings which our interpersonal awkwardness scale taps. As Table 9 shows, interpersonal awkwardness is positively associated with every other problem considered here. Homosexuals who score high on interpersonal awkwardness also report less normalization of homosexuality and homosexual commitment.

Effeminacy may also be associated with psychological well-being. A man's natural body build or manner may be regarded as less than masculine, and this may initially contribute to problems of sexual identity. Also, effeminacy may follow from the homosexual's efforts to establish a sense of identity. In searching for an identity, many homosexuals acquire the same stereotypes of homosexuals that many heterosexuals hold, or they are influenced by what in the past have been the most visible types of homosexuals. The result can be their "acting out" being homosexual in an effeminate manner. Whatever the case, heterosexuals in general, as well as many homosexuals themselves, react negatively to effeminacy. Thus, we expected that effeminacy may be associated with a number of psychological problems.

The following items comprise a composite measure of effeminacy: I look effeminate; I tend to behave effeminately when in the heterosexual world; and, I tend to behave effeminately when I'm with other homosexuals. We find that those homosexuals who score higher in effeminacy are lower in psychological well-being on six of the eight measures (Table 10).[4]

According to Simon and Gagnon, effeminacy is especially characteristic of younger homosexuals, representing a transitional stage in their resolution of the identity problems of becoming homosexual.[5] However, controlling for age, the association between effeminacy and psychological problems remains.

Appraisals of One's Homosexuality

In this section, we turn to three processes whereby a person accepts the label of "homosexual" for himself. These processes are acculturation, normalization, and commitment. We would expect each of them to be positively related to psychological well-being.

Acculturation

Acculturation, it will be recalled, refers to the extent to which one is socialized to common homosexual practices, namely, dancing "slow" dances and necking with other males. Acculturation would seem to reflect an increased acceptance by the respondent of the homosexual situation. Neither of these practices is necessarily associated with being an active homosexual, of course. However, a male who has not accepted his homosexuality or who is not involved with other acculturated homosexuals enough to engage in these practices may experience considerable conflict regarding his homosexuality. In this state it may be very difficult for him to get routinized to his homosexuality and to feel comfortable with it.

The more highly acculturated homosexual, on the other hand, by "going all the way" may dissipate some of the uncertainty surrounding the homosexual role and, as a result, become more routinized to his homosexuality. When this type of "settling down" occurs, the homosexual may increase in personal integration. While these homosexual practices might initially seem degrading to the homosexual, over time they may contribute to his sense of well-being by helping him confront and acknowledge his sexual orientation and deal with it in more open and, among homosexuals, acceptable ways.[6] As this suggests, we find that homosexuals who score higher in acculturation report less depression, interpersonal awkwardness, loneliness, and guilt, shame, or anxiety over their homosexuality than do those lower in acculturation (Table 11).

Normalization

One psychological technique used to adapt to one's homosexuality is "normalization." Normalization involves seeing homosexuality as "normal," and not as an illness or mental illness.

We would expect that the more the homosexual normalizes, the less he is influenced by opinions which regard homosexuality less favorably; consequently, we would expect fewer psychological problems. Our data support this notion. Homosexuals who normalize more report greater psychological well-being on seven of the eight measures as well as more homosexual commitment [7] (Table 12).

Commitment

Finally, we test the notion that a commitment to homosexuality is positively related to psychological well-being. We measure commitment as the respondent's unwillingness to give up his homosexuality (if he could). We find a strong negative relationship between commitment and psychological problems, even when age is held constant.[8] Compared with those less committed to homosexuality, those more committed report greater psychological well-being on seven of the eight measures as well as more normalization [9] (Table 13). These findings demonstrate that "deviant identities" may not reflect personal disintegration, as is often supposed, but rather the individual's success in establishing a meaningful sense of identity.[10]

Summary

Focusing on the social psychological aspects of societal reaction theory, this chapter examined the relationships between various aspects of the homosexual's looking glass self and his psychological well-being. First, we considered how the homosexual perceives others as appraising him. We found that the more negative the perceived appraisal of others, the greater the homosexual's psychological problems. These relationships hold regardless of the significance of the appraiser to the homosexual, perhaps because rejection from anyone symbolizes society's more global rejection of the homosexual. Also, feeling accepted by either heterosexuals or homosexuals, regardless of their significance, is correlated with psychological well-being.

Second, we looked at various situations and experiences less directly reflecting the perceived appraisals of others, and which also can augment or diminish a homosexual's sense of social competence. Thus, infrequent sex, never having had an exclusive relationship, and loneliness are related to psychological problems. Furthermore, interpersonal awkwardness and effeminacy are also related to psychological problems.

Finally, we evaluated more direct forms of self-labeling, especially those that signify the respondent's acceptance of the homosexual label. Acculturation (the routinization of secondary homosexual behaviors), normalization (viewing homosexuality from an acceptable interpretative framework), and commitment (a reluctance to give up homosexuality) are all negatively related to psychological problems.

TABLE 1

Psychological Correlates of Perceptions of the Public's Feelings about Homosexuals

	Perception of Disgust or Dislike									
	High		Medium		Low		x^2	df	p	γ
Low self-acceptance										
United States	49.5%	(275)	47.5%	(423)	36.3%	(350)	13.848	2	.001	.18
Netherlands	47.7	(151)	48.1	(501)	33.3	(387)	21.398	2	.001	.23
Denmark	57.1	(21)	70.6	(102)	56.4	(117)	4.955	2	.10	.18
							Pooled $x^2 = 40.201$, $df = 6$, $p < .001$			
Low faith in others										
United States	56.4	(273)	50.6	(417)	43.7	(341)	9.960	2	.01	.16
Netherlands	59.3	(150)	45.5	(503)	36.9	(385)	22.626	2	.001	.26
Denmark	71.4	(21)	64.1	(103)	52.9	(121)	4.307	2	.20	.24
							Pooled $x^2 = 36.893$, $df = 6$, $p < .001$			
High depression										
United States	35.6	(270)	26.3	(414)	16.0	(343)	30.823	2	.001	.32
Netherlands	40.8	(152)	30.8	(510)	18.3	(387)	32.371	2	.001	.33
Denmark	35.0	(20)	40.4	(99)	23.2	(125)	7.775	2	.05	.31
							Pooled $x^2 = 70.969$, $df = 6$, $p < .001$			

TABLE 1—Continued

	Perception of Disgust or Dislike									
	High		Medium		Low		x^2	df	p	γ
High interpersonal awkwardness										
United States	36.4	(272)	33.2	(419)	17.6	(347)	32.868	2	.001	.29
Netherlands	38.0	(150)	30.7	(502)	18.4	(386)	27.038	2	.001	.31
Denmark	38.9	(18)	24.8	(101)	14.2	(120)	7.808	2	.05	.37
							Pooled $x^2 = 67.714$, $df = 6$, $p < .001$			
High loneliness										
United States	65.7	(271)	59.4	(419)	51.0	(349)	13.930	2	.001	.19
Netherlands	62.7	(153)	56.2	(511)	41.4	(391)	28.059	2	.001	.28
Denmark	61.9	(21)	62.5	(104)	46.5	(127)	6.457	2	.05	.28
							Pooled $x^2 = 48.446$, $df = 6$, $p < .001$			
High guilt, shame, or anxiety regarding homosexuality										
United States	29.1	(268)	20.2	(420)	10.1	(347)	35.912	2	.001	.38
Netherlands	15.0	(153)	11.8	(509)	3.6	(390)	25.955	2	.001	.45
Denmark	19.0	(21)	13.3	(105)	4.7	(128)	7.505	2	.05	.49
							Pooled $x^2 = 68.372$, $df = 6$, $p < .001$			

Low commitment										
United States	25.6	(273)	28.9	(422)	17.5	(348)	13.832	2	.001	.16
Netherlands	26.5	(155)	30.1	(511)	17.7	(389)	18.296	2	.001	.21
Denmark	23.8	(21)	30.1	(103)	12.0	(125)	11.511	2	.01	.41
							Pooled $x^2 = 43.639$, $df = 6$, $p < .001$			

TABLE 2

Psychological Correlates of Anticipating Discrimination

	Anticipated Discrimination									
	High		Medium		Low		x^2	df	p	γ
Low self-acceptance										
United States	51.3%	(357)	44.4%	(275)	34.9%	(364)	19.817	2	.001	.23
Netherlands	55.8	(113)	46.2	(279)	38.1	(536)	14.013	2	.001	.22
Denmark	80.0	(30)	64.4	(45)	57.6	(139)	5.413	2	.10	.29
							Pooled $x^2 = 39.243$, df = 6, $p < .001$			
Low faith in others										
United States	59.7	(355)	46.1	(271)	40.6	(357)	27.256	2	.001	.26
Netherlands	65.2	(112)	44.0	(277)	39.2	(536)	25.453	2	.001	.24
Denmark	89.7	(29)	59.2	(49)	52.9	(140)	13.465	2	.01	.40
							Pooled $x^2 = 66.174$, df = 6, $p < .001$			
High psychosomatic symptoms										
United States	59.1	(337)	53.6	(265)	43.0	(351)	18.255	2	.001	.22
Netherlands	64.3	(112)	54.2	(273)	51.7	(524)	5.874	2	.10	.12
Denmark	86.2	(29)	71.7	(46)	59.4	(133)	8.517	2	.02	.40
							Pooled $x^2 = 32.646$, df = 6, $p < .001$			

High depression										
United States	35.8	(349)	24.5	(273)	14.7	(353)	41.633	2	.001	.38
Netherlands	48.7	(115)	31.2	(279)	21.2	(542)	38.483	2	.001	.36
Denmark	64.3	(28)	36.2	(47)	23.9	(142)	18.081	2	.001	.48
							Pooled $x^2 = 98.197$, $df = 6$, $p < .001$			
High interpersonal awkwardness										
United States	38.1	(352)	33.6	(274)	17.5	(360)	39.673	2	.001	.34
Netherlands	43.4	(113)	29.2	(274)	23.0	(539)	20.185	2	.001	.26
Denmark	51.9	(27)	26.7	(45)	15.0	(140)	18.484	2	.001	.52
							Pooled $x^2 = 78.342$, $df = 6$, $p < .001$			
High loneliness										
United States	68.6	(350)	59.9	(274)	46.6	(363)	35.969	2	.001	.31
Netherlands	74.1	(116)	56.4	(280)	43.9	(544)	38.981	2	.001	.35
Denmark	76.7	(30)	53.1	(49)	48.3	(145)	8.046	2	.02	.30
							Pooled $x^2 = 82.996$, $df = 6$, $p < .001$			
High guilt, shame, or anxiety regarding homosexuality										
United States	30.8	(347)	21.5	(274)	6.6	(363)	68.023	2	.001	.52
Netherlands	26.5	(113)	15.6	(282)	3.5	(543)	70.244	2	.001	.65
Denmark	32.3	(31)	14.3	(49)	4.8	(146)	21.205	2	.001	.65
							Pooled $x^2 = 159.472$, $df = 6$, $p < .001$			

TABLE 3

Psychological Correlates of Anticipating/Experiencing Intolerance or Rejection Because of His Homosexuality

	Intolerance or Rejection									
	High		Medium		Low		x^2	df	p	γ
Low self-acceptance										
United States	52.2%	(360)	47.2%	(320)	32.3%	(341)	30.281	2	.001	.27
Netherlands	55.8	(43)	53.2	(188)	39.3	(743)	14.989	2	.001	.27
Denmark	72.7	(11)	68.8	(48)	62.3	(162)	1.023	2	.70	.16
							Pooled $x^2 = 46.293$, $df = 6$, $p < .001$			
High depression										
United States	34.3	(356)	27.2	(313)	13.9	(331)	38.498	2	.001	.36
Netherlands	50.0	(44)	41.7	(187)	23.5	(752)	35.278	2	.001	.41
Denmark	72.7	(11)	31.3	(48)	29.3	(164)	8.981	2	.02	.25
							Pooled $x^2 = 82.757$, $df = 6$, $p < .001$			
High interpersonal awkwardness										
United States	38.9	(357)	32.0	(319)	14.9	(335)	50.920	2	.001	.38
Netherlands	40.0	(45)	39.5	(190)	23.8	(739)	22.154	2	.001	.34
Denmark	66.7	(9)	29.8	(47)	15.9	(164)	16.170	2	.001	.50
							Pooled $x^2 = 89.244$, $df = 6$, $p < .001$			

High loneliness										
United States	67.9	(355)	61.9	(318)	44.5	(339)	41.524	2	.001	.32
Netherlands	68.9	(45)	66.3	(190)	48.1	(755)	25.307	2	.001	.36
Denmark	72.7	(11)	77.6	(49)	48.8	(170)	14.044	2	.001	.52
							Pooled $x^2 = 80.875$, $df = 6$, $p < .001$			
High guilt, shame, or anxiety regarding homosexuality										
United States	27.1	(354)	25.3	(316)	5.0	(339)	66.085	2	.001	.46
Netherlands	22.2	(45)	18.4	(190)	6.5	(752)	33.772	2	.001	.52
Denmark	27.3	(11)	18.4	(49)	6.4	(171)	9.914	2	.01	.55
							Pooled $x^2 = 109.771$, $df = 6$, $p < .001$			

TABLE 4

Psychological Correlates of Heterosexual Acceptance *

	Acceptance									
	High		Medium		Low		x^2	df	p	γ
Low self-acceptance										
United States	26.0%	(416)	49.5%	(370)	65.5%	(255)	107.208	2	.001	–.50
Netherlands	24.9	(145)	39.3	(611)	58.5	(225)	44.442	2	.001	–.39
Denmark	49.4	(85)	67.3	(107)	80.6	(31)	11.591	2	.01	–.40
							Pooled $x^2 = 163.241$, df = 6, $p < .001$			
Low stability of self-concept										
United States	18.7	(401)	29.9	(365)	39.0	(246)	32.834	2	.001	–.15
Netherlands	16.6	(145)	21.0	(618)	25.7	(226)	4.511	2	.20	–.22
Denmark	25.9	(85)	68.1	(116)	54.8	(31)	3.935	2	.20	–.24
							Pooled $x^2 = 41.280$, df = 6, $p < .001$			
Low faith in others										
United States	44.5	(409)	46.4	(364)	63.7	(251)	25.773	2	.001	–.22
Netherlands	43.5	(147)	40.2	(610)	51.1	(221)	7.965	2	.02	–.11
Denmark	54.7	(86)	55.8	(113)	73.3	(30)	3.506	2	.20	–.16
							Pooled $x^2 = 37.244$, df = 6, $p < .001$			

Netherlands	19.6	(143)	22.1	(620)	44.9	(225)	48.171	2	.001	−.38
Denmark	18.8	(85)	31.6	(114)	50.0	(30)	11.004	2	.01	−.40
							Pooled $x^2 = 137.864$, $df = 6$, $p < .001$			
High interpersonal awkwardness										
United States	12.8	(414)	29.5	(363)	53.8	(253)	128.753	2	.001	−.58
Netherlands	16.4	(140)	20.0	(615)	49.1	(224)	80.029	2	.001	−.49
Denmark	14.6	(82)	16.8	(113)	41.9	(31)	11.710	2	.01	−.34
							Pooled $x^2 = 220.492$, $df = 6$, $p < .001$			
High loneliness										
United States	43.0	(412)	59.4	(367)	81.1	(254)	94.297	2	.001	−.48
Netherlands	39.5	(147)	45.7	(619)	70.5	(227)	49.099	2	.001	−.38
Denmark	44.3	(88)	52.1	(117)	80.6	(31)	12.208	2	.01	−.34
							Pooled $x^2 = 155.604$, $df = 6$, $p < .001$			
High guilt, shame, or anxiety regarding homosexuality										
United States	12.9	(410)	19.4	(366)	28.6	(252)	24.796	2	.001	−.31
Netherlands	5.4	(148)	6.8	(618)	15.9	(226)	19.774	2	.001	−.38
Denmark	8.0	(88)	6.8	(118)	18.7	(32)	4.615	2	.10	−.21
							Pooled $x^2 = 49.185$, $df = 6$, $p < .001$			

* Alpha coefficient for heterosexual acceptance scale is .41.

TABLE 5

Psychological Correlates of Homosexual Acceptance *

	Acceptance									
	High		Medium		Low		x^2	df	p	γ
Low self-acceptance										
United States	26.9%	(308)	41.1%	(285)	59.1%	(357)	70.625	2	.001	−.43
Netherlands	23.5	(348)	39.6	(384)	50.6	(183)	36.732	2	.001	−.33
Denmark	50.0	(84)	66.7	(60)	67.9	(82)	6.644	2	.05	−.26
							Pooled $x^2 = 114.001$, $df = 6$, $p < .001$			
Low stability of self-concept										
United States	19.5	(296)	24.3	(280)	36.1	(349)	23.780	2	.001	−.28
Netherlands	9.4	(355)	20.4	(388)	27.0	(181)	22.757	2	.001	−.32
Denmark	27.7	(88)	37.7	(61)	35.2	(83)	1.849	2	.50	−.12
							Pooled $x^2 = 48.386$, $df = 6$, $p < .001$			
High depression										
United States	10.0	(349)	20.5	(278)	39.3	(303)	80.162	2	.001	−.54
Netherlands	14.7	(184)	23.0	(387)	33.9	(354)	25.761	2	.001	−.32
Denmark	19.8	(81)	33.3	(60)	38.6	(88)	7.379	2	.05	−.31
							Pooled $x^2 = 113.302$, $df = 6$, $p < .001$			

High interpersonal awkwardness										
United States	12.4	(354)	22.6	(283)	48.2	(303)	109.830	2	.001	−.57
Netherlands	14.4	(181)	24.9	(382)	33.0	(349)	21.815	2	.001	−.29
Denmark	19.2	(78)	15.0	(60)	23.5	(85)	1.635	2	.50	−.10
							Pooled $x^2 = 133.280$, $df = 6$, $p < .001$			
High loneliness										
United States	38.6	(355)	58.3	(283)	75.9	(303)	93.151	2	.001	−.50
Netherlands	30.3	(185)	47.6	(389)	61.0	(354)	46.719	2	.001	−.36
Denmark	40.0	(85)	45.2	(62)	69.7	(89)	17.179	2	.001	−.41
							Pooled $x^2 = 157.049$, $df = 6$, $p < .001$			

* Alpha coefficient for homosexual acceptance scale is .59.

TABLE 6

Psychological Correlates of Frequency of Homosexual Sex

	Frequency									
	High		Medium		Low		x^2	df	p	γ
Low self-acceptance										
United States	40.8%	(726)	47.7%	(107)	56.4%	(149)	12.918	2	.01	−.23
Netherlands	40.0	(750)	47.6	(126)	56.7	(104)	11.843	2	.01	−.23
Denmark	60.7	(191)	73.8	(23)	87.5	(8)	3.658	2	.20	−.38
							Pooled $x^2 = 28.419$, $df = 6$, $p < .001$			
High psychosomatic symptoms										
United States	48.9	(699)	47.6	(103)	61.0	(141)	7.252	2	.05	−.14
Netherlands	51.4	(734)	69.9	(123)	57.3	(103)	15.014	2	.001	−.22
Denmark	65.2	(187)	73.7	(29)	88.9	(9)	2.595	2	.30	−.33
							Pooled $x^2 = 24.861$, $df = 6$, $p < .001$			
High depression										
United States	19.3	(714)	36.2	(105)	45.3	(148)	51.511	2	.001	−.47
Netherlands	22.7	(761)	40.5	(126)	50.5	(103)	46.146	2	.001	−.45
Denmark	29.2	(195)	39.1	(23)	66.7	(9)	6.216	2	.05	−.37
							Pooled $x^2 = 103.873$, $df = 6$, $p < .001$			

High interpersonal awkwardness										
United States	25.4	(720)	40.2	(107)	36.2	(149)	14.837	2	.001	–.25
Netherlands	24.1	(752)	29.3	(123)	42.9	(105)	17.065	2	.001	–.27
Denmark	17.6	(193)	31.8	(22)	62.5	(8)	11.318	2	.01	–.52
							Pooled $x^2 = 43.220$, $df = 6$, $p < .001$			
High loneliness										
United States	53.9	(724)	70.8	(106)	70.3	(148)	21.314	2	.001	–.32
Netherlands	46.3	(761)	63.8	(127)	75.5	(106)	40.436	2	.001	–.43
Denmark	50.7	(203)	78.3	(23)	77.8	(9)	8.360	2	.02	–.54
							Pooled $x^2 = 70.110$, $df = 6$, $p < .001$			
High guilt, shame, or anxiety regarding homosexuality										
United States	14.6	(726)	27.1	(107)	36.2	(141)	40.542	2	.001	–.45
Netherlands	6.3	(764)	17.5	(126)	23.8	(101)	42.439	2	.001	–.55
Denmark	6.4	(204)	26.1	(13)	33.3	(9)	15.885	2	.001	–.68
							Pooled $x^2 = 98.866$, $df = 6$, $p < .001$			
Low commitment										
United States	21.9	(722)	25.2	(107)	34.9	(149)	11.461	2	.01	–.23
Netherlands	22.1	(763)	28.3	(127)	44.8	(105)	25.656	2	.001	–.36
Denmark	20.0	(200)	21.7	(23)	37.5	(8)	1.445	2	.50	–.17
							Pooled $x^2 = 38.562$, $df = 6$, $p < .001$			

TABLE 7

Psychological Correlates of Exclusive Relationships

	Experience with Exclusive Relationships									
	High		Medium		Low		x^2	df	p	γ
Low self-acceptance										
United States	36.5%	(233)	42.2%	(393)	49.5%	(412)	10.923	2	.01	–.17
Netherlands	33.6	(366)	42.6	(331)	51.4	(321)	22.252	2	.001	–.24
Denmark	55.2	(96)	63.4	(71)	72.7	(66)	5.153	2	.10	–.25
							Pooled $x^2 = 38.328$, df = 6, $p < .001$			
Low stability of self-concept										
United States	21.1	(228)	26.9	(379)	31.8	(403)	8.485	2	.02	–.17
Netherlands	16.6	(368)	22.3	(332)	27.5	(324)	12.012	2	.01	–.21
Denmark	23.8	(105)	42.9	(70)	36.4	(66)	7.445	2	.05	–.23
							Pooled $x^2 = 27.942$, df = 6, $p < .001$			
High depression										
United States	13.0	(230)	22.0	(378)	34.6	(408)	39.285	2	.001	–.38
Netherlands	17.3	(369)	27.9	(333)	38.8	(322)	39.779	2	.001	–.35
Denmark	17.6	(102)	33.8	(68)	47.8	(67)	17.614	2	.001	–.46
							Pooled $x^2 = 96.678$, df = 6, $p < .001$			

High interpersonal awkwardness										
United States	21.3	(230)	25.6	(391)	35.9	(407)	18.245	2	.001	−.24
Netherlands	22.2	(365)	25.8	(326)	33.3	(321)	11.089	2	.01	−.19
Denmark	13.0	(100)	24.6	(69)	27.0	(63)	5.844	2	.10	−.30
							Pooled $x^2 = 35.178$, $df = 6$, $p < .001$			
High loneliness										
United States	45.5	(231)	55.0	(389)	68.3	(410)	34.205	2	.001	−.30
Netherlands	37.6	(372)	53.1	(335)	65.4	(324)	54.160	2	.001	−.36
Denmark	39.6	(106)	63.4	(71)	66.2	(68)	15.387	2	.001	−.38
							Pooled $x^2 = 103.752$, $df = 6$, $p < .001$			

TABLE 8

Psychological Correlates of Loneliness

	Loneliness									
	High		Medium		Low		x^2	df	p	γ
Low self-acceptance										
United States	70.5%	(305)	52.3%	(304)	19.8%	(435)	198.962	2	.001	.65
Netherlands	65.2	(247)	51.4	(290)	26.3	(505)	115.335	2	.001	.52
Denmark	88.9	(63)	63.8	(69)	46.7	(107)	30.199	2	.001	.58
							Pooled $x^2 = 344.496$, $df = 6, p < .001$			
Low stability of self-concept										
United States	46.8	(301)	30.8	(295)	12.2	(425)	107.011	2	.001	.55
Netherlands	32.5	(249)	29.5	(292)	12.2	(510)	54.686	2	.001	.42
Denmark	46.3	(67)	27.9	(68)	27.4	(113)	7.734	2	.05	.26
							Pooled $x^2 = 169.431$, $df = 6, p < .001$			
Low faith in others										
United States	61.8	(430)	50.0	(296)	40.7	(301)	31.555	2	.001	.28
Netherlands	59.9	(247)	41.7	(288)	38.3	(506)	32.499	2	.001	.26
Denmark	80.0	(65)	52.9	(70)	51.8	(110)	15.322	2	.001	.35
							Pooled $x^2 = 79.376$, $df = 6, p < .001$			

High psychosomatic symptoms										
United States	69.7	(287)	52.2	(293)	39.0	(421)	64.594	2	.001	.40
Netherlands	68.2	(236)	62.3	(289)	42.9	(497)	52.056	2	.001	.37
Denmark	81.7	(60)	60.9	(64)	59.0	(105)	9.463	2	.01	.31
							Pooled $x^2 = 126.113$, $df = 6$, $p < .001$			
High depression										
United States	59.4	(303)	21.1	(294)	4.2	(431)	291.073	2	.001	.82
Netherlands	67.1	(249)	32.4	(293)	5.9	(509)	316.225	2	.001	.81
Denmark	67.7	(65)	24.3	(70)	14.7	(109)	55.386	2	.001	.68
							Pooled $x^2 = 662.684$, $df = 6$, $p < .001$			
High interpersonal awkwardness										
United States	59.3	(302)	26.4	(299)	8.8	(432)	222.536	2	.001	.72
Netherlands	54.1	(244)	31.6	(291)	11.5	(504)	154.900	2	.001	.63
Denmark	52.3	(65)	11.8	(68)	6.7	(105)	55.685	2	.001	.75
							Pooled $x^2 = 433.121$, $df = 6$, $p < .001$			
High guilt, shame, or anxiety regarding homosexuality										
United States	38.1	(302)	19.5	(298)	5.5	(437)	123.301	2	.001	.65
Netherlands	23.0	(248)	9.9	(294)	2.3	(512)	84.552	2	.001	.68
Denmark	23.9	(67)	5.7	(70)	3.4	(116)	22.253	2	.001	.66
							Pooled $x^2 = 230.106$, $df = 6$, $p < .001$			

TABLE 8—Continued

	Loneliness									
	High		Medium		Low		x^2	df	p	γ
Low normalization										
United States	34.1	(305)	24.3	(300)	16.9	(433)	29.102	2	.001	.31
Netherlands	12.0	(250)	8.9	(293)	5.6	(514)	9.574	2	.01	.28
Denmark	20.9	(67)	22.9	(70)	17.5	(114)	.822	2	.70	.09
							Pooled $x^2 = 39.498$, $df = 6$, $p < .001$			
Low commitment										
United States	37.6	(303)	23.0	(300)	15.4	(436)	48.725	2	.001	.39
Netherlands	40.5	(252)	28.6	(294)	15.7	(511)	57.718	2	.001	.42
Denmark	33.8	(65)	18.8	(69)	14.0	(114)	10.120	2	.01	.37
							Pooled $x^2 = 116.563$, $df = 6$, $p < .001$			

TABLE 9

Psychological Correlates of Interpersonal Awkwardness

	Awkwardness									
	High		Medium		Low		x^2	df	p	γ
Low self-acceptance										
United States	70.9%	(375)	39.2%	(337)	18.5%	(330)	200.733	2	.001	.66
Netherlands	64.2	(400)	34.6	(399)	19.5	(226)	136.396	2	.001	.57
Denmark	87.3	(71)	68.9	(74)	36.1	(83)	44.668	2	.001	.68
							Pooled $x^2 = 381.797$, df = 6, $p < .001$			
Low stability of self-concept										
United States	44.9	(363)	22.5	(329)	13.4	(322)	91.362	2	.001	.52
Netherlands	33.1	(406)	18.7	(400)	10.1	(227)	41.743	2	.001	.41
Denmark	63.9	(72)	24.7	(81)	15.7	(83)	44.539	2	.001	.64
							Pooled $x^2 = 177.644$, df = 6, $p < .001$			
Low faith in others										
United States	57.7	(371)	47.9	(330)	42.0	(326)	17.568	2	.001	.21
Netherlands	51.2	(404)	39.9	(396)	38.4	(224)	14.146	2	.001	.18
Denmark	71.4	(70)	53.2	(79)	54.2	(83)	6.369	2	.05	.22
							Pooled $x^2 = 38.083$, df = 6, $p < .001$			

TABLE 9—Continued

	Awkwardness									
	High		Medium		Low		x^2	df	p	γ
High psychosomatic symptoms										
United States	68.8	(353)	47.7	(327)	36.6	(314)	72.191	2	.001	.42
Netherlands	66.8	(392)	50.4	(389)	38.2	(225)	50.609	2	.001	.36
Denmark	86.8	(68)	62.5	(72)	50.0	(78)	22.215	2	.001	.51
							Pooled $x^2 = 145.015$, $df = 6$, $p < .001$			
High depression										
United States	48.1	(366)	18.1	(332)	6.8	(323)	168.295	2	.001	.69
Netherlands	49.8	(404)	17.1	(403)	8.0	(226)	163.901	2	.001	.68
Denmark	62.0	(71)	24.4	(78)	9.8	(82)	50.983	2	.001	.72
							Pooled $x^2 = 383.179$, $df = 6$, $p < .001$			
High loneliness										
United States	83.1	(372)	57.6	(335)	30.4	(326)	198.360	2	.001	.66
Netherlands	73.5	(407)	45.5	(404)	22.8	(228)	159.498	2	.001	.61
Denmark	75.3	(73)	63.0	(81)	32.1	(84)	32.062	2	.001	.55
							Pooled $x^2 = 389.920$, $df = 6$, $p < .001$			

High guilt, shame, or anxiety regarding homosexuality										
United States	36.4	(368)	9.0	(333)	9.5	(328)	113.760	2	.001	.58
Netherlands	16.6	(404)	5.7	(403)	2.6	(229)	43.835	2	.001	.58
Denmark	20.5	(73)	6.2	(81)	1.2	(85)	19.432	2	.001	.74
							Pooled $x^2 = 177.027$, $df = 6$, $p < .001$			
Low normalization										
United States	33.2	(371)	23.2	(336)	14.6	(328)	32.874	2	.001	.34
Netherlands	11.3	(407)	7.7	(405)	3.5	(229)	12.148	2	.01	.33
Denmark	30.1	(73)	19.8	(81)	11.9	(84)	8.077	2	.02	.36
							Pooled $x^2 = 53.099$, $df = 6$, $p < .001$			
Low commitment										
United States	33.4	(374)	19.5	(334)	18.1	(331)	28.185	2	.001	.29
Netherlands	33.0	(406)	23.5	(405)	15.3	(229)	25.577	2	.001	.30
Denmark	25.0	(72)	20.3	(79)	17.9	(84)	1.224	2	.70	.14
							Pooled $x^2 = 54.986$, $df = 6$, $p < .001$			

TABLE 10

Psychological Correlates of Effeminacy *

	Effeminacy									
	High		Medium		Low		x^2	df	p	γ
Low self-acceptance										
United States	55.8%	(308)	49.4%	(405)	26.3%	(331)	64.470	2	.001	.38
Netherlands	52.3	(214)	49.6	(357)	32.8	(470)	34.006	2	.001	.29
Denmark	64.7	(85)	65.9	(82)	54.9	(71)	2.288	2	.50	.13
							Pooled $x^2 = 100.764$, $df = 6$, $p < .001$			
Low stability of self-concept										
United States	37.5	(296)	27.7	(394)	18.5	(324)	27.883	2	.001	.30
Netherlands	28.2	(216)	25.3	(360)	16.2	(475)	16.521	2	.001	.24
Denmark	46.6	(88)	28.2	(85)	20.5	(73)	13.419	2	.01	.39
							Pooled $x^2 = 57.823$, $df = 6$, $p < .001$			
High psychosomatic symptoms										
United States	63.1	(290)	51.9	(389)	40.2	(316)	31.842	2	.001	.29
Netherlands	70.6	(211)	55.1	(354)	46.0	(457)	35.543	2	.001	.30

Denmark	75.0	(80)	61.8	(76)	60.6	(71)	4.412	2	.20	.22
							Pooled $x^2 = 71.797$, df = 6, $p < .001$			
High depression										
United States	35.4	(302)	22.6	(393)	18.9	(328)	25.016	2	.001	.27
Netherlands	33.2	(214)	26.2	(362)	26.1	(475)	4.197	2	.20	.09
Denmark	35.7	(84)	37.8	(82)	19.7	(76)	7.086	2	.05	.24
							Pooled $x^2 = 36.299$, df = 6, $p < .001$			
High interpersonal awkwardness										
United States	42.0	(305)	28.9	(401)	16.2	(328)	51.432	2	.001	.39
Netherlands	36.0	(214)	30.4	(358)	20.3	(467)	21.394	2	.001	.26
Denmark	25.6	(86)	16.5	(79)	19.4	(72)	2.186	2	.50	.14
							Pooled $x^2 = 75.012$, df = 6, $p < .001$			
High loneliness										
United States	65.6	(305)	59.5	(398)	49.4	(332)	17.665	2	.001	.21
Netherlands	65.3	(216)	50.4	(363)	46.0	(478)	22.322	2	.001	.22
Denmark	46.0	(87)	59.8	(87)	56.6	(76)	3.624	2	.20	–.15
							Pooled $x^2 = 36.363$, df = 6, $p < .001$			

* Alpha coefficient for effeminacy scale is .63.

TABLE 11

Psychological Correlates of Acculturation

	Acculturation									
	High		Medium		Low		x^2	df	p	γ
High depression										
United States	15.7%	(299)	23.3%	(331)	33.4%	(395)	29.215	2	.001	−.32
Netherlands	21.5	(586)	25.5	(220)	44.5	(245)	46.293	2	.001	−.35
Denmark	26.0	(169)	42.3	(52)	45.8	(24)	7.447	2	.05	−.34
							Pooled $x^2 = 82.955$, $df = 6$, $p < .001$			
High interpersonal awkwardness										
United States	20.8	(303)	25.9	(336)	37.1	(396)	24.280	2	.001	−.27
Netherlands	22.4	(575)	29.0	(217)	36.0	(247)	16.740	2	.001	−.24
Denmark	22.2	(167)	18.0	(50)	13.6	(22)	11.085	2	.01	.17
							Pooled $x^2 = 29.935$, $df = 6$, $p < .001$			
High loneliness										
United States	52.8	(303)	52.7	(336)	66.3	(398)	18.598	2	.001	−.20
Netherlands	45.1	(587)	49.5	(220)	68.8	(250)	39.782	2	.001	−.30
Denmark	50.3	(175)	60.4	(53)	68.0	(25)	3.812	2	.20	−.24
							Pooled $x^2 = 62.192$, $df = 6$, $p < .001$			

High guilt, shame, or anxiety regarding homosexuality										
United States	7.8	(306)	16.1	(336)	30.0	(393)	57.807	2	.001	−.49
Netherlands	5.6	(588)	7.2	(221)	19.9	(246)	43.522	2	.001	−.47
Denmark	7.4	(176)	9.3	(54)	24.0	(25)	7.089	2	.05	−.36
							Pooled $x^2 = 108.418$, $df = 6$, $p < .001$			

TABLE 12

Psychological Correlates of Normalization

	Normalization									
	High		Medium		Low		x^2	df	p	γ
Low self-acceptance										
United States	28.7%	(331)	45.1%	(388)	58.6%	(327)	59.641	2	.001	−.38
Netherlands	32.0	(139)	50.8	(360)	62.6	(544)	57.772	2	.001	−.40
Denmark	52.2	(75)	73.2	(71)	66.7	(92)	8.254	2	.02	−.23
							Pooled $x^2 = 125.667$, $df = 6$, $p < .001$			
Low stability of self-concept										
United States	20.6	(320)	25.0	(376)	37.8	(320)	25.730	2	.001	−.26
Netherlands	17.4	(137)	25.1	(363)	29.2	(551)	12.927	2	.01	−.23
Denmark	23.2	(75)	39.7	(73)	37.3	(99)	6.422	2	.05	−.23
							Pooled $x^2 = 45.079$, $df = 6$, $p < .001$			
High psychosomatic symptoms										
United States	40.6	(315)	53.7	(374)	60.0	(310)	24.608	2	.001	−.25
Netherlands	51.0	(533)	56.3	(355)	61.9	(134)	6.040	2	.05	−.13

Denmark	61.9	(97)	73.5	(68)	64.1	(64)	2.564	2	.30	–.06
							Pooled $x^2 = 33.212$, $df = 6$, $p < .001$			
High depression										
United States	15.4	(319)	22.8	(381)	38.5	(325)	47.473	2	.001	–.39
Netherlands	19.2	(548)	33.7	(362)	44.7	(141)	46.872	2	.001	–.39
Denmark	16.2	(99)	46.5	(71)	38.4	(73)	19.700	2	.001	–.37
							Pooled $x^2 = 114.045$, $df = 6$, $p < .001$			
High interpersonal awkwardness										
United States	20.4	(323)	26.6	(384)	39.0	(328)	28.785	2	.001	–.29
Netherlands	22.3	(543)	30.2	(358)	37.1	(140)	15.260	2	.001	–.23
Denmark	12.6	(95)	24.3	(70)	27.4	(73)	6.334	2	.05	–.31
							Pooled $x^2 = 50.379$, $df = 6$, $p < .001$			
High loneliness										
United States	51.5	(324)	55.7	(384)	67.9	(330)	19.581	2	.001	–.22
Netherlands	44.8	(554)	56.5	(363)	64.3	(140)	22.808	2	.001	–.26
Denmark	42.6	(101)	71.6	(74)	53.9	(76)	14.554	2	.001	–.19
							Pooled $x^2 = 56.943$, $df = 6$, $p < .001$			

TABLE 12—Continued

	Normalization									
	High		Medium		Low		x^2	df	p	γ
High guilt, shame, or anxiety regarding homosexuality										
United States	8.9	(325)	15.7	(381)	33.3	(327)	67.242	2	.001	−.50
Netherlands	4.5	(554)	9.4	(361)	28.1	(139)	73.053	2	.001	−.57
Denmark	3.9	(102)	10.8	(74)	15.8	(76)	7.320	2	.05	−.45
							Pooled $x^2 = 147.615$, $df = 6$, $p < .001$			
Low commitment										
United States	9.2	(331)	21.1	(384)	42.9	(326)	104.784	2	.001	−.57
Netherlands	17.1	(141)	32.3	(362)	38.3	(555)	41.868	2	.001	−.38
Denmark	13.9	(75)	21.1	(71)	28.0	(101)	5.377	2	.10	−.29
							Pooled $x^2 = 152.029$, $df = 6$, $p < .001$			

TABLE 13

Psychological Correlates of Commitment to Homosexuality

	Commitment									
	High		Medium		Low		x^2	df	p	γ
Low self-acceptance										
United States	29.6%	(252)	48.4%	(364)	61.9%	(432)	71.823	2	.001	−.42
Netherlands	29.3	(264)	43.7	(410)	59.5	(368)	57.340	2	.001	−.38
Denmark	49.5	(51)	68.1	(91)	74.5	(95)	11.170	2	.01	−.36
							Pooled $x^2 = 140.333$, df = 6, $p < .001$			
Low stability of self-concept										
United States	56.1	(246)	69.8	(348)	84.0	(424)	62.223	2	.001	−.43
Netherlands	73.7	(266)	76.1	(414)	83.8	(371)	11.162	2	.01	−.20
Denmark	64.7	(51)	63.4	(93)	73.0	(100)	2.262	2	.50	−.15
							Pooled $x^2 = 75.647$, df = 6, $p < .001$			

TABLE 13—Continued

	Commitment									
	High		Medium		Low		x^2	df	p	γ
High psychosomatic symptoms										
United States	40.9	(413)	55.7	(350)	63.4	(235)	34.322	2	.001	−.30
Netherlands	47.9	(359)	56.8	(405)	58.9	(258)	9.125	2	.02	−.15
Denmark	61.0	(100)	66.2	(80)	71.1	(45)	1.493	2	.50	−.14
							Pooled $x^2 = 44.940$, $df = 6$, $p < .001$			
High depression										
United States	13.7	(422)	26.7	(356)	42.2	(249)	67.971	2	.001	−.46
Netherlands	16.0	(375)	25.2	(413)	48.1	(264)	81.901	2	.001	−.46
Denmark	19.8	(101)	30.0	(90)	55.1	(49)	19.325	2	.001	−.45
							Pooled $x^2 = 169.197$, $df = 6$, $p < .001$			
High interpersonal awkwardness										
United States	19.6	(429)	30.6	(360)	41.6	(250)	38.386	2	.001	−.34
Netherlands	24.3	(367)	23.5	(409)	36.7	(264)	16.652	2	.001	−.18
Denmark	14.3	(98)	23.9	(88)	26.5	(49)	4.037	2	.20	−.26
							Pooled $x^2 = 59.075$, $df = 6$, $p < .001$			

High loneliness										
United States	46.5	(428)	61.2	(361)	73.2	(250)	48.512	2	.001	−.36
Netherlands	38.9	(378)	51.6	(413)	69.9	(266)	60.224	2	.001	−.38
Denmark	44.7	(103)	56.4	(94)	68.6	(51)	8.226	2	.02	−.30
							Pooled $x^2 = 116.962$, $df = 6$, $p < .001$			
High guilt, shame, or anxiety regarding homosexuality										
United States	6.8	(429)	17.3	(359)	43.1	(248)	135.786	2	.001	−.65
Netherlands	1.9	(377)	5.8	(414)	25.5	(263)	112.384	2	.001	−.74
Denmark	3.8	(104)	12.8	(94)	15.7	(51)	7.204	2	.05	−.45
							Pooled $x^2 = 255.374$, $df = 6$, $p < .001$			
Low normalization										
United States	9.8	(253)	26.4	(360)	45.1	(428)	109.515	2	.001	−.57
Netherlands	4.2	(266)	6.8	(414)	15.8	(378)	29.620	2	.001	−.44
Denmark	16.3	(50)	22.6	(93)	22.0	(104)	1.384	2	.70	−.14
							Pooled $x^2 = 140.519$, $df = 6$, $p < .001$			

CHAPTER 13

PASSING AND BEING KNOWN ABOUT

Passing means here the concealment of one's homosexuality, namely, to "pass" as heterosexual. Being known about means people know or suspect the respondent to be homosexual. Passing and being known about are usually, though not necessarily, inversely related. Thus, a person may behave very secretly, yet word of his homosexuality may spread; another person may not behave secretly and yet remain above suspicion. In this chapter, we suggest that the effects of passing and being known about on psychological well-being are more subtle than many assume, and we present data which illustrate this point. First, we examine the relationship between passing and various psychological problems. Next, we present a typology of homosexuals based on passing and two other variables and examine the social psychological characteristics that are associated with each type of homosexual. Finally, we examine the correlates of being known about.

Passing

One frequently cited illustration of the negative effects of passing is that covert homosexuals sometimes go to extremes to publicly denounce homosexuality in order to divert attention from their own sexual orientation. As one homosexual writes: "I . . . became city editor of the *Daily Iowan*. . . . I chased girls, never with much enthusiasm I'm afraid, and denounced queers with some regularity in the column I wrote for the *Iowan*. What a fink I was—anything to avoid being called a sissy." [1] This reflects the more general feeling that characterizes many secret homosexuals, that of being "on stage," being unable to present themselves authentically, and having to artificially manage their behaviors and talk so as to maintain a pretense of heterosexuality. Another homosexual says: "The strain of deceiving my family and friends often became intolerable. It was necessary for me to watch every word I spoke, and every gesture that I made, in case I gave myself away." [2] These quotations suggest that passing imposes a substantial psychological burden. Our field work, however, suggests that passing is an even more complex phenomenon.

We would suggest that there are two important antecedents which lead a homosexual to engage in passing: worrying about exposure and anticipating sanctions. Worry about exposure may reflect a general, free-floating fear that discovery would destroy familiar patterns of social relations. The anticipation of negative sanctions reflects a more concrete estimation of the discrimination that would result from exposure as a homosexual. These may signify to the homosexual his low evaluation in the eyes of others as well as the risks at hand and thus be related to psychological problems. Finally, the homosexual's psychological well-being may be affected by passing itself, that is, the deliberate "on stage" behavior that masks sexual orientation can be conducive to anxiety. As one would expect, then, both worry about exposure and anticipated discrimination are correlated with passing (Table 1).

Examining the relationship between passing and psychological problems, we find that passing is significantly related to only three of our eight measures: depression, interpersonal awkwardness, and guilt, shame, or anxiety regarding one's homosexuality. Furthermore, the above discussion suggests that these psychological problems may reflect worry about exposure or anticipated discrimination more than passing per se. Indeed, when we control for these two variables, the relationships do substantially decrease in every country (Table 2). (In the United States, in fact, the relationships between passing and depression and between passing and interpersonal awkwardneses completely disappear.)

The problem that does seem more directly related to passing is guilt, shame, or anxiety over one's homosexuality. As noted above, we would guess that in many cases feelings such as these are partially responsible for motivating the homosexual to pass in the first place.

All in all, our findings suggest that it is worry about exposure and anticipated consequences (rather than passing per se) which leads to many of the covert homosexual's psychological problems. In general, our data support a much more conservative view of the effects of passing on psychological well-being than is often assumed.[3]

Considering the importance of worry about exposure and anticipated discrimination, we theorized that different types of homosexuals could be delineated in terms of different combinations of these three variables (worry about exposure, anticipated discrimination, and passing). The diagram on page 251 designates the eight possible combinations.

All types appear in our sample, although some are represented by only a few respondents. Based on our field work impressions and general social psychological considerations,

DIAGRAM 1

Typology of Male Homosexuals, Based on Passing, Worry about Exposure, and Anticipated Discrimination after Exposure

Type	Anticipated Discrimination	Worry about Exposure	Passing	Per cent of Total Sample within Each Country (Number of Cases) United States		Netherlands		Denmark	
1	high	high	high	23.2%	(212)	8.2%	(75)	12.3%	(26)
2	high	high	low	2.7	(25)	2.3	(21)	2.8	(6)
3	high	low	high	15.1	(138)	5.4	(49)	3.3	(7)
4	high	low	low	5.9	(54)	6.4	(58)	4.2	(9)
5	low	high	high	8.7	(79)	7.7	(70)	12.3	(26)
6	low	high	low	1.6	(15)	3.4	(31)	5.2	(11)
7	low	low	high	17.0	(154)	12.0	(109)	8.5	(18)
8	low	low	low	25.7	(234)	55.5	(506)	51.4	(109)

we had some ideas as to what social psychological characteristics would be associated with each category. These ideas and the social psychological correlates of each type are discussed below. First, we examine the polar types, those who are high and low, respectively, in *both* worry about exposure and anticipated discrimination. At each of these extremes, we compare those who are high in passing with those who are low. We do the same for the mixed types, those which combine high and low on worry about exposure and anticipated discrimination. The social psychological correlates of both polar and mixed types are summarized in Table 3. These relationships are not explained by our demographic variables.

Polar Types

Type 1/This group represents the homosexual who is high in anticipated discrimination, worry about exposure, and passing. Of our eight types, this is the second largest group in the United States but a relatively small group in the Netherlands and Denmark, a difference that we attribute to Europe's greater tolerance. Because they perceive a great deal of societal rejection (signified by anticipated discrimination) and because they worry about being exposed lest they experience this rejection, we would expect Type 1 homosexuals to report more psychological problems than do other types.

Type 2/This group differs from Type 1 in that, while high in anticipated discrimination and worry about exposure, they are low in passing. The homosexuals we would expect this cell to include are those who want to remain unknown but do not due to a variety of reasons. They may be too incompetent to know how to effectively pass, or too lazy to do so, or be so angry at the necessity for remaining unknown that their anger gets the better of their discretion (for example, losing one's "cool" in a group where ignorance and prejudice about homosexuality is being expressed). We would expect psychological problems to be caused among Type 2 homosexuals by the sense of societal rejection which worry about exposure and anticipated discrimination signify.

Type 8/At the opposite pole are Type 8 homosexuals, for whom passing does not play an important role. Homosexuals in this group anticipate little discrimination, do not worry about exposure, and are low in passing. This is the largest group in our sample; in the United States it is only slightly larger than the Type 1 group, but in the Netherlands and Denmark this type is by far the largest. We expected Type 8 homosexuals to have the fewest psychological problems, since they are not disturbed by being identified as homosexual and perhaps also perceive less societal rejection of the homosexual.

Type 7/This group differs from Type 8 in that, while not reporting much worry about exposure or anticipating much discrimination, they score high in passing. It was difficult to imagine what empirical type this would represent, but we employed the term "ritualist"—the person who has developed a routine of passing that is maintained without what seem to be the most "obvious" motivations, that is, worry over exposure and anticipated discrimination (one such example would be the homosexual who personally does not fear exposure but does not want his family hurt by the knowledge). We believe that this type, however, mainly involves habitual passing, especially for those on the way to becoming a Type 8 homosexual. Passing, for the Type 7 homosexual, then becomes merely a precautionary habit against possible social abrasions. Because we see this group as similar in many ways to Type 8, we expected Type 7 homosexuals to also be high in psychological well-being.

Comparison of the Polar Types

In general, our expectation that Types 1 and 2 (those highest in worry *and* anticipated discrimination) have more and Types 7 and 8 (those lowest in worry *and* anticipated discrimination) have fewer psychological problems is supported in the data. In all three countries, the eight psychological problems we measure—low self-acceptance, stability of self-concept, and faith in others and high psychosomatic symptoms, depression, interpersonal awkwardness, loneliness, and guilt, shame, or anxiety regarding one's homosexuality—are all reported substantially more frequently by Types 1 and 2 than by Types 7 and 8 (Tables 3 and 4). Also, it can be seen that generally Types 1 and 2 show the highest and Types 7 and 8 the lowest proportion of psychological problems among *all* of the types we consider (Table 5).

Finally, a comparison of Types 1, 2, 7, and 8 further supports our notion that it is worry about exposure and anticipated discrimination, rather than passing per se, which is important for psychological well-being. Type 1 differs from Type 2, and Type 7 from Type 8, only in terms of passing. Thus, if passing is in and of itself consequential for psychological well-being, we would expect to find differences between Types 1 and 2 and between Types 7 and 8. However, we do not find any substantial, replicated differences in psychological problems between Types 1 and 2 or between Types 7 and 8 (Table 3).

With regard to other measures for which there are significant differences between types, in comparison with all the types, Type 1 is especially low in social involvement with homosexuals, acculturation, and being known about and unusually high in viewing homosexuality as an illness (Table 5). Type 2 is also particularly high in viewing homosexuality as an illness. Type 7 is especially high in social involvement with homosexuals, and Type 8 is in addition particularly high in homosexual commitment, social involvement with homosexuals, acculturation, and being known about and low in viewing homosexuality as an illness. Again comparing Type 1 with 2 and Type 7 with 8, we find little consistent differentiation. Type 2 does show more acculturation than Type 1, however. Also, in accord with our description of Type 7 homosexuals, they report less commitment to homosexuality and being much less known about than do Type 8's.

Mixed Types (Types 3, 4, 5, 6)

These types are produced by other combinations of the three variables. For example, homosexuals in Types 3 and 4 anticipate discrimination against the known homosexual but do not worry about exposure, whereas Types 5 and 6 do not anticipate discrimination, yet worry about exposure. We expected in general that their psychological problems would fall between Types 1 and 2 on the one hand and Types 7 and 8 on the other.

This is what we find—that these mixed types do not consistently stand out as either particularly high or particularly low in psychological problems. There are, however, a few replicated exceptions (Table 5). Type 3 homosexuals are high in passing and anticipated discrimination but low in worry about exposure (apparently confident that they can handle the negative consequences of exposure). High stability of self-concept is reported especially frequently among Type 3 homosexuals—as frequently as among Types 7 and 8. Unlike Types 7 and 8, however, Type 3 is low in being known about.

Type 4 homosexuals, who are low in passing and worry about exposure but high in anticipated discrimination, are particularly low in guilt, shame, or anxiety regarding their homosexuality (scoring about the same as Type 7 on this measure). Type 4's also stand out as low in commitment to homosexuality but high in acculturation and being known about.

Type 5 homosexuals, who are high in passing and worry about exposure but low in anticipated discrimination, are characterized by unusually high faith in others and by high commitment to homosexuality. This type also stands out, however, as low in social involvement with homosexuals and being known about.

We expected Type 6 (low in passing and anticipated discrimination yet high in worry about exposure) to be relatively scarce, and to be characterized by a high degree of free-floating anxiety. Both of these expectations are supported. Regarding the size of the group, Type 6 is the smallest of the eight types in the United States and the next to the smallest in Europe. Because of the small number of Type 6 males in the United States and Denmark, however, generalizations about Type 6 are based only on the Dutch data, without the benefit of replication. Judging from the Dutch homosexuals, Type 6 is high in psychosomatic symptoms, as we expected. They also are low in self-acceptance and stability of self-concept and high in social involvement with homosexuals.

Being Known About

Among people doing research in homosexuality and among homosexuals themselves, a great deal of importance is attributed to the extent to which people know about a person's homosexuality. To homosexuals, being known about is a practical concern reflected in their frequent use of such terms as "coming out" and "closet queen." For researchers, being known about is both a theoretical interest (as indicated by the widespread use of the covert-overt distinction) and a methodological consideration (how representative a sample of homosexuals can a researcher obtain when so many homosexuals are reluctant to disclose the fact?). In this section we compare homosexuals who are more known about with those who are less known about to examine the differences between them and whether or not being known about is as catastrophic as many fear.

Three points regarding our data must be made at the onset. First, our measure of being known about asks whether various groups or individuals suspect or know that the respondent is homosexual (combining Scales I and II, pages 135–136). This variable is obviously not an objective measure of the respondent's being known about; in some cases, it may be that the respondent thinks the person or group in question knows about his homosexuality when in fact they do not, or vice versa. Thus, our measure taps only the homosexual's subjective judgment of whether or not others know about him. For obvious reasons, not many homosexuals are willing to test the truth of this; thus we do not know how accurate these judgments are.

Second, our sample of homosexuals may not be representative. Most of our respondents were obtained from mail organizations, and mail source respondents tend to be somewhat more open about their homosexuality than other respondents. While we were successful in obtaining more covert homosexuals (especially in the bar sample), they are probably underrepresented. For our purposes, however, this may not be a major problem, since we are concerned with the correlates of feeling known about and have achieved sufficient variation in this phenomenon to make a meaningful analysis possible.

Finally, there is the question of causal direction. We can look at correlates of being known about as "causes" or as "consequences." In this section, we consider the correlates of being known about as consequences.

Some homosexuals, for whatever reasons, are known as homosexual by many heterosexuals. Compared with homosexuals who are relatively less known about, what characterizes the former group? We find no differences between these two groups in psychological problems or on measures relating to the homosexual world. We do find, however, that the more known-about homosexuals have less stressful relationships with the heterosexual world. For example, they report anticipating or having experienced *less* rejection or negative reactions toward them from heterosexuals (Table 6). Also, fewer of those more known about say that most people feel negative toward homosexuals, and fewer of them anticipate discrimination from heterosexuals (Table 6).

We would expect those who anticipate less negative reactions and less discrimination to be more known about. In addition, it appears that once a person who is homosexual becomes known as such, tremendous apprehension about managing that social identity often gives way to the realization that the world does not come to an end with the disclosure of this fact. The fatalistic anticipation of disclosure is based upon a reified perception of social reactions. This perception has at least two origins. First, depictions of the homosexual in current literature, the mass media, and scientific publications imply that disclosure is accompanied by ridicule, censure, violence, and imputations of mental illness. Second, among homosexuals themselves, there is a repertoire of "sad tales" that often overdramatize the situation surrounding disclosure. In both cases, of course, the emphasis is on the negative, more sensational aspects of being known about. The truth is that in concrete situations the reaction toward homosexuals is quite varied.[4] The homosexual who becomes publicly known as "homosexual" learns that although there are negative consequences, these may be subtle and/or may be adapted to or avoided. Thus, the more known-about homosexual is more likely to realize that being known as homosexual can have less devastating consequences than those expected by the less known-about homosexual. (This realization that actual consequences are not as bad as those anticipated was also observed in our study of homosexuals given less than honorable discharges from the military.[5])

Compared with less known-about homosexuals, those who are more known about are also less worried about being exposed as homosexual (partially, of course, because they are already more known about). Not only are they more likely to have been officially labeled homosexual, but among those officially labeled, it bothers them less; among those not so labeled, those more known about worry less about such an eventuality. As one might expect, then, they pass less (Table 6). These findings, we suggest, reflect the adaptations, and thus the more realistic evaluations, of the more known-about homosexual.

Arrest

With regard to official labeling, we were interested in the consequences of being arrested in connection with one's homosexuality. Twenty-five per cent of the United States sample, and 16 per cent of both the Dutch and Danish samples, report having experienced this. Unfortunately, we do not know the degree of the official labeling involved, that is, whether those arrested were also "booked," appeared in court, were convicted, and so forth.[6]

What distinguishes members of our sample that have been so arrested from those who have not? Comparing the two groups, no differences are found with regard to psychological problems or the ways in which they relate to either the homosexual or heterosexual world.

The only difference we find is in clinical treatment. Those who have been arrested are more likely to have had it suggested that they receive psychiatric treatment, to have visited a psychiatrist regarding their homosexuality, and to have received psychiatric treatment (Table 7). These findings seem to reflect the common practice wherein the court often makes seeing a psychiatrist a condition of release or probation for persons arrested for homosexual offenses.

The general lack of differences between homosexuals who have been arrested and those who have not could indicate that, like being known about, arrest regarding homosexual offenses may in the long run be relatively inconsequential for psychological well-being or for social adaptations. We believe the reason for this is that with arrest the homosexual is officially labeled, but that this does not necessarily involve his being *publicly* labeled, that is, the arrest may not become public knowledge.

Summary

In this chapter we explored the problematic relationships between passing, being known about, and psychological well-being. Passing seems to be a more complex phenomenon than is generally assumed. Although homosexuals who behave in a secretive manner do show greater psychological problems than those who do not, it does not seem that passing per se leads to great psychological strain. Instead, those psychological problems which appear seem to be, by and large, more directly associated with the factors which lead to passing. Thus, worry about exposure and anticipated discrimination against the known homosexual are associated with psychological problems and with certain aspects of relating to the homosexual world. A typology, based on worry about exposure, anticipated discrimination, and passing, and the social psychological correlates of the types was discussed.

Compared with less known-about homosexuals, the more known about are not found to have greater psychological problems, as many would expect. Thus, being known about is not the "end of the world," as many homosexuals fear. In fact, the more known-about homosexuals seem to experience less stress with regard to the heterosexual world, indicating that the covert homosexual's fears of exposure may be exaggerated. Finally, with regard to official labeling, arrest did not correlate with psychological problems or with relations to the homosexual and heterosexual worlds.

TABLE 1

Relationships Between Passing and Worry About Exposure and Between Passing and Anticipated Discrimination

	Passing and Worry About Exposure		Passing and Anticipated Discrimination	
	γ	Probability	γ	Probability
United States	.75	.001	.64	.001
Netherlands	.83	.001	.65	.001
Denmark	.85	.001	.71	.001

TABLE 2

Relationship Between Passing and Psychological Problems, Holding Constant Worry About Exposure and Anticipated Discrimination

	Original γ *	Partial γ Controlling for Worry About Exposure and Anticipated Discrimination	Partial γ Controlling for Worry About Exposure	Partial γ Controlling for Anticipated Discrimination
Depression				
United States	.23 (.01)	.02	.01	.04
Netherlands	.36 (.001)	.18	.26	.24
Denmark	.49 (.001)	.28	.50	.32
Interpersonal awkwardness				
United States	.30 (.001)	.02	.14	.24
Netherlands	.32 (.001)	.20	.29	.26
Denmark	.54 (.001)	.25	.50	.31

* Chi-square probabilities for the original tables are noted in parentheses.

TABLE 2—Continued

	Original γ *	Partial γ Controlling for Worry About Exposure and Anticipated Discrimination	Partial γ Controlling for Worry About Exposure	Partial γ Controlling for Anticipated Discrimination
Guilt, shame, or anxiety regarding homosexuality				
United States	.68 (.001)	.45	.46	.54
Netherlands	.68 (.001)	.36	.56	.60
Denmark	.69 (.001)	.38	.51	.66

TABLE 3

Social Psychological Correlates of Polar Homosexual Types (Types 1, 2, 7, and 8)*,†

	Type 1	Type 2	Type 7	Type 8	Probability
Number of cases					
United States	212	25	154	234	
Netherlands	75	21	109	506	
Denmark	26	6	18	109	
Low self-acceptance					
United States	56.3%[l]	64.0%[hh]	34.6%[l]	32.5%[ll]	<.001
Netherlands	68.0[hh]	57.1	45.4	34.9[ll]	<.001
Denmark	80.8	—	82.4	53.5	<.20
Low stability of self-concept					
United States	34.1	44.0[hh]	20.5[l]	20.1[l]	<.001
Netherlands	29.7	30.0[h]	15.5[ll]	19.4[l]	<.001
Denmark	42.3	—	22.2	30.2	<.50
Low faith in others					
United States	55.1	68.0[hh]	34.2[ll]	44.5	<.001
Netherlands	51.4	71.4[hh]	44.4	39.6[l]	<.001
Denmark	76.9	—	50.0	54.3	<.10
High psychosomatic symptoms					
United States	63.3	76.2[hh]	44.4[l]	41.3[ll]	<.001
Netherlands	66.7[h]	75.0[hh]	48.6[l]	51.9	<.05
Denmark	87.5	—	66.7	59.6	<.20
High depression					
United States	38.4[h]	44.0[hh]	11.5[ll]	11.7[l]	<.001
Netherlands	50.7[hh]	47.4[h]	25.5[l]	20.1[ll]	<.001
Denmark	57.7[hh]	—	41.2	21.9[ll]	<.02

* *hh* marks the homosexual type with the highest percentage showing this characteristic of all eight types in that country; *h*, other types with unusually high percentages; *ll*, the type with the lowest percentage; and *l*, other types with unusually low percentages. These symbols are not used for Denmark when the differences between homosexual types are not statistically significant at the .05 level. Since for Denmark each row contains only four percentages, only the highest and lowest are so designated.

† Percentages are deleted for cells with fifteen or fewer cases.

TABLE 3—Continued

	Type 1	2	7	8	Probability
High interpersonal awkwardness					
United States	44.1[h]	48.0[hh]	20.9[l]	15.9[ll]	<.001
Netherlands	47.3[hh]	28.6	32.4	21.4[ll]	<.001
Denmark	52.0[hh]	—	33.3	10.4[ll]	<.001
High loneliness					
United States	71.6[h]	80.0[hh]	46.8[l]	45.7[ll]	<.001
Netherlands	73.0[h]	76.2[hh]	45.5[l]	44.4[ll]	<.001
Denmark	88.5[hh]	—	55.6	44.4[ll]	<.01
High guilt, shame, or anxiety regarding homosexuality					
United States	39.6[hh]	36.0[h]	9.7[l]	1.7[ll]	<.001
Netherlands	35.1[hh]	33.3[h]	9.2[l]	2.6[ll]	<.001
Denmark	30.8[hh]	—	22.2	1.8[ll]	<.001
Low normalization					
United States	29.8[h]	29.2[h]	22.9	14.7[ll]	<.01
Netherlands	20.0[hh]	14.3	11.0	5.3[ll]	<.001
Denmark	46.2[hh]	—	22.2	16.7	<.02
Low commitment					
United States	28.5	36.0[hh]	27.0	9.9[ll]	<.001
Netherlands	48.0[h]	28.6	33.0	15.1[ll]	<.001
Denmark	36.0	—	29.4	14.8	<.30
High social involvement with homosexuals					
United States	55.2[ll]	60.9	71.7[h]	76.7[hh]	<.001
Netherlands	53.4[ll]	77.8[hh]	73.1[h]	74.5[h]	<.01
Denmark	69.2	—	58.8	77.2	<.30
High acculturation					
United States	29.0[ll]	48.0	48.7	50.4[h]	<.001
Netherlands	33.3[ll]	38.1[l]	51.4	66.0[hh]	<.001
Denmark	69.2	—	77.8	81.7	<.50
High in being known about (Scale I)					
United States	9.0[ll]	13.6[l]	17.4	60.8[hh]	<.001
Netherlands	5.7[ll]	35.3	27.8	75.5[hh]	<.001
Denmark	16.0	—	33.3	61.4[hh]	<.001

TABLE 3—Continued

	Type 1	Type 2	Type 7	Type 8	Probability
High in being known about (Scale II)					
United States	23.5[l]	42.1	26.8	53.0[h]	<.001
Netherlands	65.1	83.3	83.8[h]	89.9[hh]	<.001
Denmark	52.2[l]	—	83.3	85.1[hh]	<.01

TABLE 4

Comparisons Between Types 1 and 2 and Types 7 and 8

	Types 1 and 2 (Average %)*	Types 7 and 8 (Average %)	Difference
Low self-acceptance			
United States	60.1%	33.5%	26.6%
Netherlands	62.5	42.1	20.4
Denmark	80.8	67.9	12.9
Low stability of self-concept			
United States	39.0	20.3	18.7
Netherlands	29.8	17.4	12.4
Denmark	42.3	26.2	16.1
Low faith in others			
United States	61.5	39.3	22.2
Netherlands	61.4	42.0	19.4
Denmark	76.9	52.1	24.8
High psychosomatic symptoms			
United States	69.5	42.8	26.7
Netherlands	70.8	50.2	20.6
Denmark	87.5	63.1	24.4

* The per cent for Denmark in this column is not an average, but the per cent for Type 1. This is because the N for Type 2 was so small that an average percentage including this type would be misleading.

TABLE 4—Continued

	Types 1 and 2 (Average %)*	Types 7 and 8 (Average %)	Difference
High depression			
United States	41.2	11.6	29.8
Netherlands	49.0	22.8	26.2
Denmark	57.7	31.5	26.2
High interpersonal awkwardness			
United States	46.0	18.4	27.6
Netherlands	37.9	26.9	11.0
Denmark	52.0	19.4	32.6
High loneliness			
United States	75.8	46.2	29.6
Netherlands	74.6	44.9	39.7
Denmark	88.5	50.0	38.5
High guilt, shame, or anxiety regarding homosexuality			
United States	37.8	5.7	32.1
Netherlands	34.2	5.9	28.3
Denmark	30.8	12.0	18.8
Low normalization			
United States	29.5	18.8	10.7
Netherlands	17.1	8.1	9.0
Denmark	46.2	19.5	26.7
Low commitment			
United States	32.2	18.4	13.8
Netherlands	38.3	24.0	14.3
Denmark	36.0	22.1	13.9
High social involvement with homosexuals			
United States	58.0	74.2	16.2
Netherlands	65.6	73.8	8.2
Denmark	69.2	65.5	—3.7
High acculturation			
United States	38.5	49.5	11.0
Netherlands	35.7	58.7	23.0
Denmark	69.2	79.7	10.5

TABLE 4—Continued

	Types 1 and 2 (Average %)*	Types 7 and 8 (Average %)	Difference
High in being known about. (Scale I)			
United States	11.3	39.1	27.8
Netherlands	20.5	51.6	31.1
Denmark	16.0	47.3	31.3
High in being known about (Scale II)			
United States	32.8	39.9	7.1
Netherlands	74.2	86.8	12.6
Denmark	52.2	84.2	32.0

TABLE 5

Social Psychological Correlates of the Eight Types *,†

	1	2	3	4	5	6	7	8	Probability
Number of cases									
United States	212	25	138	54	79	15	154	234	
Netherlands	75	21	49	58	70	31	109	506	
Denmark	26	6	7	9	26	11	18	109	
Low self-acceptance									
United States	56.3%[h]	64.0%[hh]	37.2%[l]	59.3%[h]	45.6%	—	34.6%[l]	32.5%[ll]	<.001
Netherlands	68.0[hh]	57.1	48.0	46.6	47.1	64.5[h]	45.4	34.9[ll]	<.001
Denmark	80.8	—	—	—	61.5	—	82.4	53.5	<.20
Low stability of self-concept									
United States	34.1	44.0[hh]	19.5[ll]	35.3	38.5[h]	—	20.5[l]	20.1[l]	<.001
Netherlands	29.7	30.0[h]	18.0[l]	25.9	20.0	46.7[hh]	15.5[ll]	19.4[l]	<.001
Denmark	42.3	—	—	—	36.0	—	22.2	30.2	<.50
Low faith in others									
United States	55.1	68.0[hh]	53.3	60.4[h]	41.8[l]	—	34.2[ll]	44.5	<.001
Netherlands	51.4	71.4[hh]	68.0[h]	56.4	30.4[ll]	54.8	44.4	39.6[l]	<.001
Denmark	76.9	—	—	—	48.0	—	50.0	54.3	<.10

High psychosomatic symptoms									
United States	63.3	76.2[hh]	45.3	73.5[h]	52.6	—	44.4[l]	41.3[ll]	$<.001$
Netherlands	66.7[h]	75.0[hh]	46.8[ll]	56.1	54.5	64.3	48.6[l]	51.9	$<.05$
Denmark	87.5	—	—	—	56.5	—	66.7	59.6	$<.20$
High depression									
United States	38.4[h]	44.0[hh]	25.0	36.5	30.8	—	11.5[ll]	11.7[l]	$<.001$
Netherlands	50.7[hh]	47.4[h]	42.0	28.1	37.1	32.3	25.5[l]	20.1[ll]	$<.001$
Denmark	57.7[hh]	—	—	—	34.6	—	41.2	21.9[ll]	$<.02$
High interpersonal awkwardness									
United States	44.1[h]	48.0[hh]	24.8	29.4	34.2	—	20.9[l]	15.9[ll]	$<.001$
Netherlands	47.3[hh]	28.6	34.7	27.3	30.0	33.3	32.4	21.4[ll]	$<.001$
Denmark	52.0[hh]	—	—	—	13.0	—	33.3	10.4[ll]	$<.001$
High loneliness									
United States	71.6[h]	80.0[hh]	54.7	67.9	59.5	—	46.7[l]	45.7[ll]	$<.001$
Netherlands	73.0[h]	76.2[hh]	58.0	62.7	56.5	58.1	45.5[l]	44.4[ll]	$<.001$
Denmark	88.5[hh]	—	—	—	53.8	—	55.6	44.4[ll]	$<.01$

* *hh* marks the homosexual type with the highest percentage showing this characteristic of all eight types in that country; *h*, other types with unusually high percentages; *ll*, the type with the lowest percentage; and *l*, other types with unusually low percentages. These symbols are not used for Denmark when the differences between homosexual types are not statistically significant at the .05 level. Since for Denmark each row contains only four percentages, only the highest and lowest are so designated.

† Percentages are deleted for cells with fifteen or fewer cases.

TABLE 5—Continued

	1	2	3	4	5	6	7	8	Probability
High guilt, shame, or anxiety regarding homosexuality									
United States	39.6[hh]	36.0[h]	13.1	9.6[l]	29.1	—	9.7[l]	1.7[ll]	<.001
Netherlands	35.1[hh]	33.3[h]	18.4	10.3[l]	21.7	16.7	9.2[l]	2.6[ll]	<.001
Denmark	30.8[hh]	—	—	—	11.5	—	22.2	1.8[ll]	<.001
Low normalization									
United States	29.8[h]	29.2[h]	22.5	20.8	34.2[hh]	—	22.9	14.7[ll]	<.01
Netherlands	20.0[hh]	14.3	9.2	6.8[l]	12.9	9.7	11.0	5.3[ll]	<.001
Denmark	46.2[hh]	—	—	—	12.5[ll]	—	22.2	16.7	<.02
Low commitment									
United States	28.5	36.0[hh]	24.8	18.5[l]	32.9[h]	—	27.0	9.9[ll]	<.001
Netherlands	48.0[h]	28.6	42.0	16.9[l]	54.3[hh]	32.3	33.0	15.1[ll]	<.001
Denmark	36.0	—	—	—	32.0	—	29.4	14.8	<.30
High social involvement with homosexuals									
United States	55.2[ll]	60.9	65.6	64.6	57.5[l]	—	71.7[h]	76.7[hh]	<.001
Netherlands	53.4[ll]	77.8[hh]	64.6	70.0	60.3[l]	77.4[h]	73.1[h]	74.5[h]	<.01
Denmark	69.2	—	—	—	56.0	—	58.8	77.2	<.30

High acculturation									
United States	29.0[ll]	48.0	31.2[l]	53.7[hh]	41.8	—	48.7	50.4[h]	< .001
Netherlands	33.3[ll]	38.1[l]	44.9	63.8[h]	35.7[l]	54.8	51.4	66.0[hh]	< .001
Denmark	69.2	—	—	—	50.0	—	77.8	81.7	< .50
High in being known about (Scale I)									
United States	9.0[ll]	13.6[l]	12.3[l]	48.0[h]	9.0[ll]	—	17.4	60.8[hh]	< .001
Netherlands	5.7[ll]	35.3	10.4[l]	50.0[h]	8.6[l]	45.8	27.8	75.5[hh]	< .001
Denmark	16.0	—	—	—	13.0[ll]	—	33.3	61.4[hh]	< .001
High in being known about (Scale II)									
United States	23.5[l]	42.1	22.2[ll]	53.5[hh]	30.6	—	26.8	53.0[h]	< .001
Netherlands	65.1	83.3	53.8[l]	83.3	53.2[ll]	78.6	83.8[h]	89.9[hh]	< .001
Denmark	52.2[ll]	—	—	—	66.7	—	83.3	85.1[hh]	< .01

TABLE 6

Correlates of Being Known About

	Extent of Being Known About									
	High		Medium		Low		x^2	df	p	γ
Anticipates or has experienced intolerance or rejection because of his homosexuality										
United States	26.9%	(334)	52.1%	(334)	72.7%	(355)	144.239	2	.001	−.57
Netherlands	4.0	(404)	8.6	(279)	26.5	(310)	87.222	2	.001	−.65
Denmark	1.2	(82)	8.8	(80)	27.5	(69)	26.164	2	.001	−.76
							Pooled $x^2 = 257.625$, $df = 6$, $p < .001$			
Thinks most people feel disgusted or repelled by homosexuals										
United States	58.7	(349)	66.1	(342)	74.9	(359)	20.954	2	.001	−.24
Netherlands	53.5	(445)	65.4	(295)	74.0	(319)	34.530	2	.001	−.31
Denmark	40.0	(95)	52.3	(88)	59.7	(72)	6.700	2	.05	−.26
							Pooled $x^2 = 62.184$, $df = 6$, $p < .001$			

Anticipates a great deal of discrimination										
United States	32.0	(319)	47.4	(329)	68.6	(350)	90.618	2	.001	—.47
Netherlands	9.1	(363)	21.3	(268)	40.3	(313)	93.061	2	.001	—.57
Denmark	5.5	(73)	25.0	(84)	37.7	(69)	21.503	2	.001	—.57
							Pooled $x^2 = 205.182$, $df = 6$, $p < .001$			
Worries about exposure of his homosexuality										
United States	19.5	(343)	37.8	(341)	55.8	(351)	97.186	2	.001	—.49
Netherlands	3.1	(447)	21.6	(296)	44.1	(320)	191.262	2	.001	—.75
Denmark	9.7	(93)	31.4	(86)	54.9	(71)	39.382	2	.001	—.64
							Pooled $x^2 = 327.830$, $df = 6$, $p < .001$			
Is officially labeled as homosexual										
United States	57.0	(349)	41.3	(341)	26.9	(360)	65.985	2	.001	.40
Netherlands	45.2	(442)	35.1	(288)	18.2	(318)	60.025	2	.001	.40
Denmark	41.3	(92)	22.7	(88)	11.3	(71)	19.545	2	.001	.50
							Pooled $x^2 = 145.555$, $df = 6$, $p < .001$			

TABLE 6—Continued

	Extent of Being Known About									
	High		Medium		Low		x^2	df	p	γ
Is bothered over being officially labeled as homosexual *										
United States	52.2	(207)	67.9	(156)	72.9	(107)	16.237	2	.001	−.31
Netherlands	34.7	(222)	61.7	(120)	62.1	(87)	31.651	2	.001	−.42
Denmark	42.5	(40)	61.9	(21)	44.4	(9)	2.146	2	.50	−.19
							Pooled $x^2 = 50.034$, $df = 6$, $p < .001$			
Would be bothered if officially labeled as homosexual †										
United States	63.4	(183)	80.4	(219)	93.3	(268)	62.946	2	.001	−.58
Netherlands	46.8	(301)	69.6	(214)	81.7	(268)	78.552	2	.001	−.52
Denmark	64.5	(62)	80.0	(70)	89.1	(64)	11.318	2	.001	−.45
							Pooled $x^2 = 152.816$, $df = 6$, $p < .001$			

Is high in passing										
United States	34.5	(342)	68.0	(319)	86.8	(317)	197.799	2	.001	−.68
Netherlands	8.6	(442)	32.1	(290)	63.5	(310)	255.148	2	.001	−.75
Denmark	10.3	(87)	38.8	(85)	61.2	(67)	44.151	2	.001	−.67
							Pooled $x^2 = 497.098$, df = 6, $p < .001$			

* Among those who have been officially labeled.
† Among those who have not been officially labeled.

TABLE 7

Correlates of Arrest in Connection with Homosexuality

	Ever Arrested							
	Yes		No		x^2	df	p	γ
Psychiatric treatment has been suggested								
United States	58.7%	(252)	42.7%	(778)	38.801	1	.001	.31
Netherlands	65.0	(163)	49.6	(889)	25.648	1	.001	.31
Denmark	46.3	(41)	40.4	(213)	.793	1	.70	.12
					Pooled $x^2 = 65.242$, $df = 3$, $p < .001$			
Visited a psychiatrist regarding homosexuality								
United States	54.3	(254)	38.9	(781)	36.561	1	.001	.30
Netherlands	59.0	(166)	40.1	(885)	40.056	1	.001	.37
Denmark	36.6	(41)	21.8	(211)	7.414	1	.01	.35
					Pooled $x^2 = 84.031$, $df = 3$, $p < .001$			

Received psychiatric treatment regarding homosexuality								
United States	45.8	(253)	28.0	(776)	54.958	1	.001	.37
Netherlands	29.3	(164)	20.0	(877)	13.698	1	.001	.25
Denmark	29.3	(41)	12.4	(209)	13.812	1	.001	.49
					Pooled $x^2 = 82.468$, $df = 3$, $p < .001$			

CHAPTER 14

SOCIAL INVOLVEMENT WITH OTHER HOMOSEXUALS

Sociologists studying deviant behavior have long recognized that involvement with others in a similar situation has important ramifications for personal adaptation and well-being. Becker, for example, notes that deviant groups help to solidify a deviant identity, neutralize the effect of conventional judgments, and help continue the deviant behavior.[1] We would expect, therefore, that, compared with homosexuals who have low social involvement with other homosexuals, those homosexuals who have high involvement would have achieved a better adaptation to their homosexuality.

Our index of social involvement with other homosexuals is composed of items dealing with the proportion of leisure time spent socializing with other homosexuals and with the proportion of friends and close friends who are homosexual.[2]

Relating to the Heterosexual World (Table 1)

It is reasonable to expect that homosexuals who score high on social involvement with other homosexuals might have a particular conception of the heterosexual world. For example, they may have opted out of relationships with heterosexuals because they fear or have actually experienced exposure or ridicule. In this case, we might expect homosexuals more highly involved with other homosexuals to see reactions of heterosexuals to homosexuals in more consistently negative terms.

Contrary to this expectation, however, homosexuals who are most socially involved with other homosexuals are found to be *least* likely to anticipate or to have experienced rejection from heterosexuals, to impute very negative feelings about homosexuals to them, or to expect discrimination from them. Our data, therefore, suggest another logic than the above.

It was noted before that fellow homosexuals can act as negative role models and be the source of "sad tales" as to what homosexuals can expect from the heterosexual world. This seems especially likely to be the case for those homosexuals who have little association with other homosexuals. During our field work, we observed that homosexuals who are low in social involvement with homosexuals tend to have more superficial, relatively anonymous social encounters with other homosexuals. We have observed that in such encounters, discussions usually focus on sex or on the problems of being homosexual (the hassles, and so on). With a high degree of social involvement, however, the scope of the interaction is likely to broaden so that people rely less on "sad tales" to make conversation. Also, the homosexual high in social involvement with homosexuals is more likely to meet many more homosexuals who get along quite successfully. And, as we noted in the last chapter, he is more likely to meet homosexuals who can more accurately describe the variety of heterosexual responses. As a consequence, those with high social involvement with other homosexuals are more likely to replace a stereotype of the rejecting heterosexual world with an outlook that is more subtle and complex, involving all sorts of qualifications as to heterosexual reactions to homosexuality.[3]

Nonetheless, concern over being known as homosexual is a fear that most homosexuals continue to face. This concern may center around a fear of sanctions, embarrassment over being homosexual, or simply a wish to be regarded on the basis of other personal characteristics besides sexual orientation. Like most minorities, homosexuals generally prefer other sources of social identity to be central, for example, their occupation. They point out that they are doctors, lawyers, bookkeepers, clerks, and so forth and that their sexual preference is no one's business but their own and should be irrelevant to their social identity. Few, therefore, want the status of "homosexual" to override other identities (although some, for example, young militant homosexuals, are less reluctant to be so labeled than are others).

Through social involvement with other homosexuals, one can meet persons who are known about, yet handle the homosexual social identity in such a way that it fails to disrupt their lives. One learns that being known about does not necessarily mean the end of the world, that all heterosexuals do not reject homosexuals, and that a supportive social environment exists which can dull the anticipation of sanctions. This knowledge may do much to reduce the fear of becoming known about.

Thus, we would also expect the homosexual who associates least with other homosexuals to be more concerned and apprehensive about being publicly labeled homosexual, which is exactly what we find. Homosexuals who score low are more worried about being exposed as homosexual, more concerned with passing, and more bothered by the thought of being officially labeled homosexual. Furthermore, they report themselves to be less known about.[4]

Relating to the Homosexual World (Table 2)

The majority of our respondents have had, at one time or another, an exclusive sexual relationship with another homosexual. Such a relationship was expected to be related to social involvement with other homosexuals in the following way. It would certainly contribute to a higher score on social involvement. In addition, we also expected such social involvement to facilitate the opportunity to find such a relationship. High social involvement with homosexuals provides a person with more opportunities to develop such a relationship than do, for example, "one-night stands," as well as providing social support for maintaining an exclusive homosexual relationship. We expected, therefore, that those who have the most social contact with other homosexuals would more often report having had an exclusive homosexual relationship, and the data support this.

On commonsense grounds, we might also theorize that greater social involvement with other homosexuals presents greater opportunities for sex, and, therefore, we expected to find a positive relationship between such involvement and frequency of sex. We do find such a relationship.[5] Its explanation, however, we feel, is more subtle than many might assume.

The relationship is not necessarily explained by homosexuals having sex with those with whom they are "socially" involved. For example, homosexuals do not usually have sex with their homosexual friends.[6] Because of an "incest taboo" among homosexual friends (and because homosexuals are not "oversexed," as many assume[7]), the correlation between social involvement and frequency of sex is best explained by the increased opportunities that social involvements can indirectly furnish. Close associates provide introductions to homosexuals outside of the friendship clique, invitations to parties, and so forth. For the homosexual high in social involvement with homosexuals, all this increases the probability of finding a sexual partner.

We also expected social involvement to be related to acculturation. Our field work suggested that the practices to which the items of our acculturation scale refer—dancing slow dances with another male and necking with another male—are acquired through socialization by other homosexuals. The respondent's sexual techniques are also considered an indicator of acculturation. In conversations, many homosexuals recounted the difficulty they had in learning many of the common homosexual sex practices. For example, a few subjects, who were approaching the point of admitting their homosexuality, spoke of the socialization they required before reciprocating *any* sexual act with another male. A crucial stage in learning these common practices is sometimes reached when the other homosexual refuses to continue the relationship unless there is some such reciprocation. Thus, social involvement with other homosexuals is important for acculturation in that the practices mentioned above are accepted behaviors by a large number of homosexuals, and the novice, through such association, learns to interpret sexual practices from this point of view. These practices, then, lose their "perverted" character and become just another part of his life, often enhancing his sexual gratifications and helping to alleviate his identity problems. The more the respondent is involved with other homosexuals, therefore, the more we would expect him to acquire the social and sexual practices that are distinctive of the homosexual subculture. The data support this notion. Extent of social involvement is positively related to acculturation and to having experienced all the sexual practices common among homosexuals.

If social, sexual, and psychological rewards accrue from social involvement with other homosexuals, then involvement should also be positively related to commitment to homosexuality. The data support this reasoning. Those who are higher in social involvement do report less desire to renounce their homosexuality.

Psychological Problems (Table 3)

If there are social and psychological rewards in social involvement with other homosexuals, one would also expect those more involved to have fewer psychological problems. If those more involved with fellow homosexuals live with less fear of exposure, due to a supportive environment that has altered the way in which they conceive of homosexuality and the homosexual's place in the world, then one would expect them to be less likely to reject themselves because of their homosexuality. If the putative attitudes and responses of companions provide the basis for one's looking glass self, then those more involved with fellow homosexuals should report greater psychological well-being.

We are aware of the opposite hypothesis that those homosexuals who are better adjusted could more easily live in the heterosexual world and be less dependent on other homosexuals, or that social contact with other homosexuals only serves to exaggerate the importance and "degenerateness" of one's predilection. While this hypothesis may hold for some other types of so-called deviants (for example, physician drug addicts), it does not seem to be the case among homosexuals. There seem to be two reasons for this. First, if someone like a physician who was a drug addict associated with other drug addicts, they would probably be below him in social class, due to the low likelihood of his knowing other upper-class addicts. Second, because a physician drug addict has access to drugs, he is not dependent on such association. The homosexual, on the other hand, can more easily become involved with other homosexuals of his same class and social type (homosexual bars, for example, are often differentiated in this way), and he is sexually dependent on other homosexuals. The homosexual who does not associate much with other homosexuals is more concerned with passing. Thus, he is more likely to frequent anonymous settings which may be demeaning (for example, cruising streets, bus stations) and to end up with sexual partners who are below him in social class.

Our results show that respondents who are low in social involvement with other homosexuals have more psychological problems. They report less self-acceptance and more depression, loneliness, and guilt, shame, or anxiety regarding their homosexuality. Also, they are more likely to desire psychiatric treatment.

It seems clear, therefore, that the social support derived from social involvement with other homosexuals enhances the homosexual's self-image and psychological well-being.

Summary

This chapter examined the effect of social involvement with other homosexuals on the way the homosexual manages his homosexuality. Compared with those low in involvement, those who are higher are less threatened by the heterosexual world. They anticipate less rejection and discrimination from heterosexuals and are less likely to impute negative feelings to them. This was explained in terms of the learning experiences from other homosexuals whereby stereotypes of a universally hostile heterosexual world are replaced by a more subtle, less generalized, and more realistic appreciation of the situation. Such social involvement also provides models of homosexuals who successfully manage a deviant public identity as well as provide a cushion or retreat to fall back on if heterosexual relationships prove problematic. Thus, homosexuals who are more socially involved with other homosexuals are less concerned with passing, less fearful of exposure, and less bothered by labeling. In addition, they are more known about.

With regard to the homosexual world, homosexuals with greater social involvement are more likely to have had an exclusive homosexual relationship and to have higher frequencies of sex. This was explained by seeing social involvement as providing opportunities for meeting potential partners.

Those higher in such involvement are also more acculturated. Again, association was viewed as providing a socializing situation whereby, for example, certain practices could be learned and their meaning reinterpreted. The greater homosexual commitment of those higher in social involvement with other homosexuals was further seen as a product of the rewards that such association can bring.

Finally, those higher in social involvement report fewer psychological problems. This was seen as a function of the social psychological support coming from other homosexuals and the effect of this support on self-image.

TABLE 1

Relating to the Heterosexual World, by Social Involvement with Other Homosexuals

	Extent of Involvement									
	High		Medium		Low		x^2	df	p	γ
Anticipates or has experienced intolerance or rejection because of his homosexuality										
United States	45.3%	(459)	46.7%	(285)	68.9%	(212)	35.157	2	.001	–.26
Netherlands	10.8	(427)	10.5	(353)	19.2	(167)	9.375	2	.01	–.17
Denmark	8.2	(97)	12.0	(92)	23.8	(21)	4.175	2	.20	–.31
							Pooled $x^2 = 48.707$, $df = 6$, $p < .001$			
Thinks most people feel disgusted or repelled by homosexuals										
United States	66.3	(472)	57.9	(292)	78.1	(219)	22.915	2	.001	–.10
Netherlands	62.8	(465)	59.7	(372)	73.7	(171)	10.096	2	.01	–.08
Denmark	55.0	(109)	39.8	(98)	73.9	(23)	10.436	2	.01	–.05
							Pooled $x^2 = 43.447$, $df = 6$, $p < .001$			

Anticipates a great deal of discrimination										
United States	45.5	(444)	43.1	(281)	66.5	(209)	31.693	2	.001	—.22
Netherlands	20.4	(416)	19.2	(323)	33.1	(160)	13.476	2	.01	—.16
Denmark	26.5	(98)	16.3	(86)	26.1	(23)	3.009	2	.30	.15
							Pooled $x^2 = 42.160$, $df = 6$, $p < .001$			
Worries about exposure of his homosexuality										
United States	71.6	(464)	72.9	(288)	84.1	(214)	12.962	2	.01	—.19
Netherlands	52.4	(464)	49.9	(373)	66.1	(174)	13.281	2	.01	—.11
Denmark	56.1	(107)	60.4	(96)	78.3	(23)	3.892	2	.20	—.19
							Pooled $x^2 = 30.135$, $df = 6$, $p < .001$			
Would be bothered if officially labeled as homosexual *										
United States	78.9	(279)	75.3	(198)	91.9	(149)	16.562	2	.001	—.22
Netherlands	64.5	(344)	62.4	(271)	76.5	(132)	8.409	2	.02	—.11
Denmark	74.4	(86)	87.1	(70)	89.5	(19)	5.050	2	.10	—.39
							Pooled $x^2 = 30.021$, $df = 6$, $p < .001$			

* Among those who have not been officially labeled.

TABLE 1—Continued

	Extent of Involvement									
	High		Medium		Low		x^2	df	p	γ
Is high in passing										
United States	61.0	(444)	53.8	(279)	77.3	(194)	27.582	2	.001	−.14
Netherlands	30.9	(453)	25.7	(370)	49.7	(169)	31.301	2	.001	−.15
Denmark	35.6	(104)	29.5	(88)	56.5	(23)	5.811	2	.10	−.08
							Pooled $x^2 = 64.694$, df $= 6$, $p < .001$			
Is high in being known about (Scale I)										
United States	32.8	(436)	28.9	(270)	13.2	(204)	27.346	2	.001	.30
Netherlands	56.3	(375)	59.0	(305)	32.2	(149)	31.876	2	.001	.21
Denmark	51.6	(91)	45.8	(72)	10.0	(20)	11.551	2	.01	.34
							Pooled $x^2 = 70.773$, df $= 6$, $p < .001$			

TABLE 2

Relating to the Homosexual World, by Social Involvement with other Homosexuals

	Extent of Involvement									
	High		Medium		Low		x^2	df	p	γ
Has had an exclusive homosexual relationship										
United States	65.7%	(467)	51.9%	(289)	32.7%	(217)	66.012	2	.001	.41
Netherlands	68.7	(454)	56.5	(363)	41.7	(168)	39.601	2	.001	.33
Denmark	62.9	(105)	67.4	(95)	30.4	(23)	10.831	2	.01	.16
							Pooled $x^2 = 116.444$, $df = 6$, $p < .001$			
Has high frequency of homosexual sex										
United States	67.3	(446)	49.6	(278)	20.8	(207)	123.022	2	.001	.56
Netherlands	60.6	(439)	53.9	(347)	36.0	(164)	29.117	2	.001	.27
Denmark	67.6	(105)	58.9	(90)	25.0	(20)	12.794	2	.01	.35
							Pooled $x^2 = 164.933$, $df = 6$, $p < .001$			
Is high in acculturation										
United States	59.2	(471)	34.5	(293)	12.1	(214)	142.910	2	.001	.62
Netherlands	69.1	(463)	58.5	(372)	28.3	(173)	86.191	2	.001	.43
Denmark	86.2	(109)	76.5	(98)	22.7	(23)	42.394	2	.001	.60
							Pooled $x^2 = 271.495$, $df = 6$, $p < .001$			

TABLE 2—Continued

	Extent of Involvement									
	High		Medium		Low		x^2	df	p	γ
Has experienced the most common homosexual sex practices										
United States	69.3	(449)	59.0	(271)	32.1	(193)	76.699	2	.001	.44
Netherlands	40.4	(421)	35.4	(347)	27.1	(155)	8.818	2	.02	.17
Denmark	59.8	(82)	60.9	(69)	21.4	(14)	7.902	2	.02	.19
							Pooled $x^2 = 93.419$, $df = 6$, $p < .001$			
Is high in commitment										
United States	80.4	(470)	78.2	(293)	63.4	(216)	24.514	2	.001	.26
Netherlands	78.4	(464)	76.5	(370)	59.4	(175)	25.451	2	.001	.24
Denmark	79.0	(105)	81.4	(97)	60.9	(23)	4.698	2	.05	.12
							Pooled $x^2 = 54.663$, $df = 6$, $p < .001$			

TABLE 3

Psychological Problems, by Social Involvement with Other Homosexuals

	Extent of Involvement									
	High		Medium		Low		x^2	df	p	γ
Has low self-acceptance										
United States	43.6%	(472)	38.1%	(294)	50.9%	(218)	8.370	2	.02	−.05
Netherlands	40.9	(465)	39.4	(373)	48.6	(175)	4.339	2	.20	−.06
Denmark	55.0	(109)	57.1	(98)	78.3	(23)	4.297	2	.20	−.17
							Pooled $x^2 = 17.006$, $df = 6$, $p < .001$			
Is high in depression										
United States	21.1	(465)	19.9	(286)	41.2	(216)	37.727	2	.001	−.27
Netherlands	27.0	(463)	21.4	(370)	40.9	(171)	22.643	2	.001	−.11
Denmark	27.9	(104)	28.1	(96)	54.5	(22)	6.574	2	.05	−.19
							Pooled $x^2 = 66.944$, $df = 6$, $p < .001$			
Is high in loneliness										
United States	54.9	(470)	52.2	(291)	68.8	(218)	15.950	2	.001	−.14
Netherlands	48.6	(465)	48.4	(370)	64.6	(175)	14.956	2	.001	−.14
Denmark	51.9	(108)	49.0	(98)	69.6	(23)	3.190	2	.30	−.08
							Pooled $x^2 = 34.096$, $df = 6$, $p < .001$			

TABLE 3—Continued

	Extent of Involvement									
	High		Medium		Low		x^2	df	p	γ
Is high in guilt, shame, or anxiety regarding homosexuality										
United States	12.1	(471)	15.4	(293)	39.4	(213)	74.777	2	.001	−.46
Netherlands	7.5	(464)	8.0	(373)	17.8	(169)	16.456	2	.001	−.26
Denmark	7.3	(109)	8.2	(98)	26.1	(23)	8.105	2	.02	−.33
							Pooled $x^2 = 99.338$, $df = 6, p < .001$			
Desires psychiatric treatment regarding homosexuality *										
United States	9.6	(376)	14.4	(236)	22.7	(181)	17.405	2	.001	−.33
Netherlands	3.0	(432)	5.6	(324)	7.4	(148)	5.811	2	.10	−.31
Denmark	8.6	(105)	6.2	(97)	13.6	(22)	1.424	2	.50	−.01
							Pooled $x^2 = 24.640$, $df = 6, p < .001$			

* Among those who have not seen a psychiatrist regarding their homosexuality.

CHAPTER 15

BISEXUALITY[1]

Kinsey . . . puts it this way. . . .

Eighteen percent of the males have at least as much of the homosexual as the heterosexual in their histories for at least three years between the ages of 16 and 55. This is more than one in six of the white male population. . . .

[And] four percent of the white males are exclusively homosexual throughout their lives, after the onset of adolescence.

You see what I mean? If you plan to be an exclusive homosexual, you're in a very small minority. Sooner or later you're going to have to deal with women, if you haven't already. Worse things could happen to you and they probably will.[2]

The term "homosexual," which we have employed so far, should not be understood to mean that we see sexual orientation as a simple dichotomy. As Kinsey and his co-workers have pointed out, ". . . males do not represent two discrete populations, heterosexual and homosexual. The world is not to be divided into sheep and goats." [3] Thus, some persons are more exclusively homosexual than others. Homosexuality is not an all-or-nothing phenomenon, and many people have learned to respond in varying degrees to both males and females.

Based on these considerations, Kinsey and his associates developed their famous scale, which indicates degrees of homosexual experience or response.[4] This scale, however, has been criticized for not distinguishing between sexual feelings and behaviors, so that two persons getting the same score could actually be quite different in the nature of their "sexual orientations." Furthermore, the problem exists of whom to classify as a "homosexual" on the basis of this scale. If homosexuality is seen as a *condition*, the decision has to be made as to how much of the condition is necessary before a person is defined as homosexual.[5]

Sociologists have argued that homosexuality can more profitably be viewed as a status rather than a condition. The status of homosexual refers not to behaviors themselves but to the expectations and typifications surrounding those defined as homosexual. And it is these typifications rather than the sexual behaviors which affect the self-conception of anyone who views himself as homosexual.[6]

The important thing to understand is that "homosexual" can refer to a number of things—inclination, activity, status, role, or self-concept—and that a person need not be equally "homosexual" in all respects. Thus, we find a variety of combinations of being homosexual which include some of these factors and exclude others, for example, hustlers who engage in homosexual activity but deny the self-concept, the married man who has the inclination but does not act on it, and so forth.

Which aspect the investigator should concentrate on depends upon his objective, what it is he is trying to understand. In this chapter, we are most interested in the repondents' self-conception. We thus asked respondents to rate themselves on the Kinsey Scale. Our questionnaire item and the distribution of our samples are as follows:

Item Do you think of yourself as:	Distribution of Respondents (in %) U.S.	 Netherlands	 Denmark
0. Exclusively heterosexual	—	—	—
1. Predominantly heterosexual, only insignificantly homosexual	—	—	—
2. Predominantly heterosexual, but significantly homosexual	2.1	—	.4
3. Equally homosexual and heterosexual	4.4	1.1	3.2
4. Predominantly homosexual, but significantly heterosexual	13.1	7.5	6.3
5. Predominantly homosexual, only insignificantly heterosexual	29.8	33.5	26.6
6. Exclusively homosexual	50.6	55.3	63.5

We were interested in the social and psychological correlates of typing one's self as more, or as less, exclusively homosexual. Research in other contexts suggests that those persons who are not 0's (exclusively heterosexual) or 6's (exclusively homosexual) are akin to "marginal men"—not integrated into either heterosexual or homosexual life, being unsure of what they are, and having psychological problems. As Cory and LeRoy have written:

Without a group to belong to, the case of the . . . [bisexual] seems to be peculiarly pathetic. While appearing to encompass a wider choice of love objects, he actually becomes a product of abject confusion; his self-image is that of an overgrown young adolescent whose ability to differentiate one form of sexuality from another has never developed. He lacks above all a sense of identity, a feeling of group identification. As James Baldwin has so poignantly demonstrated in *Giovanni's Room,* he cannot answer the question: What am I? [7]

According to this model, therefore, heterosexuals who have "the traditions of our culture and the institutions of our society with which they can identify themselves and as a result feel a sense of solidarity and personal worth," [8] have fewer problems than homosexuals. And among homosexuals, those who are more exclusively homosexual can identify more with the homosexual subculture and, as a result, have fewer problems. The bisexual is seen as not being able to identify with either the homosexual subculture or the larger society and thus as having the most problems. Comparing respondents who rate themselves as bisexual (2–4 on the Kinsey Scale) with those who rate themselves as more exclusively homosexual (5 or 6 on the Kinsey Scale), we now examine this model in light of our data.[9]

Relating to the Heterosexual World (Table 1)

Compared with more exclusive homosexuals, bisexuals anticipate more discrimination, score higher in passing, and are less known about. Also as one might expect, bisexuals have greater social involvement with heterosexuals. Finally, bisexuals have more frequent and more enjoyable heterosexual sex and are more likely to have been married. (As no demographic differences were found, they do not explain any of the findings in this chapter.)

Relating to the Homosexual World (Table 2)

We expected that the more exclusive homosexual, in contrast, would be more involved in the homosexual world. Indeed, this is what we find. Compared with bisexuals, the more exclusive homosexuals are more socially involved with other homosexuals. They also are more likely to have restricted their friends to other homosexuals for a substantial period of time and are more likely to have had an exclusive homosexual relationship. Finally, more exclusive homosexuals have homosexual sex more frequently than do bisexuals. Thus, the more exclusive homosexuals are more likely to lead lives circumscribed by other homosexuals. (Holding the degree of social involvement with other homosexuals constant, however, does not affect any of the findings reported in this chapter.)

We also find that compared with our bisexuals, more exclusive homosexuals are more acculturated (although this is not replicated in Denmark) and more likely to have experienced all the sexual practices common among homosexuals. In addition, more exclusive homosexuals are more likely to want to change their occupation to one which could be considered stereotypically homosexual (for example, beautician). We are uncertain what this means; while it might signify acculturation, it might signify something else—identification with a certain type of homosexual role, less fear of being known about, and so forth. Perhaps as a result of their greater homosexual socializing and acculturation, those who see themselves as more exclusively homosexual are also more likely to subscribe to a belief which is frequently expounded by homosexuals and in homosexual literature—that becoming homosexual was beyond their control.

Psychological Problems (Table 3)

It has been suggested that bisexuals are "marginal men," confused about their sexual identities and suffering negative psychological consequences. Our data present only limited support for this. With only one exception, we do not find bisexuals reporting greater psychological difficulties; the exception is that they are more likely to report feeling guilt, shame, or anxiety over being homosexual. However, these feelings do not seem to generalize to other psychological problems. They may well be neatly compartmentalized, experienced only occasionally, and associated with a behavior that is only peripheral in their lives.

On the other hand, it may be that our failure to find more global differences in psychological problems is due in part to our sampling procedures. Bisexuals who are not at all involved in the homosexual subculture (for example, the one whose only contact with homosexuals occurs when he goes into a public rest room for impersonal sex) would not have received our questionnaire. It could be that, among bisexuals, *these* are the marginal men. Thus, while the folk model cannot, strictly speaking, be regarded as disproved, it certainly must be called into question with regard to its generality.

What seems to emerge from the data on both bisexuality and passing (Chapter 13) is evidence of man's ability to compartmentalize self-image, role, and behavior. Thus, it seems that bisexuals, and people in general, may be flexible enough to adjust to any number of life-styles without more general and debilitating psychological problems ensuing.[10]

Summary

In this chapter, respondents who view themselves as bisexual were compared with those who consider themselves as more homosexual. Bisexuals were found to be more likely to associate with heterosexuals and less likely to associate with homosexuals and to score lower in acculturation. Furthermore, they report themselves to be more concerned with passing and to be less known about as homosexual. However, the preponderance of psychological problems which many commentators attribute to bisexuals is not supported by our data. On only one psychological measure did we find a difference—bisexuals report more guilt, shame, or anxiety over being homosexual. Thus, they do not appear to be a "product of abject confusion," as Cory and LeRoy suggest. Homosexuality may be somewhat peripheral to their general existence, and the various social features of homosexual life may simply hold little interest for them. Thus, their sexual orientation may be of little concern or cause few problems in their everyday life.

TABLE 1

Relating to the Heterosexual World, by Sexual Orientation Score

	Sexual Orientation							
	2–4		5–6		x^2	df	p	γ
Anticipates a great deal of discrimination								
United States	59.0%	(195)	47.4%	(782)	7.848	1	.01	−.23
Netherlands	29.9	(107)	21.9	(825)	2.973	1	.10	−.21
Denmark	36.0	(25)	20.7	(198)	2.170	1	.20	−.37
					Pooled $x^2 = 12.991$, $df = 3$, $p < .001$			
Is high in passing								
United States	74.9	(179)	59.5	(776)	13.913	1	.001	−.34
Netherlands	45.1	(113)	29.5	(918)	10.703	1	.01	−.33
Denmark	39.1	(23)	34.0	(215)	.071	1	.80	−.11
					Pooled $x^2 = 24.687$, $df = 3$, $p < .001$			
Is high in being known about (Scale I)								
United States	13.8	(188)	29.8	(758)	18.888	1	.001	.45
Netherlands	36.6	(101)	55.7	(759)	12.311	1	.001	.37
Denmark	27.3	(22)	46.9	(129)	2.318	1	.20	.40
					Pooled $x^2 = 33.517$, $df = 3$, $p < .001$			

Is high in social involvement with heterosexuals								
United States	71.0	(200)	44.7	(824)	43.616	1	.001	−.50
Netherlands	52.1	(117)	44.3	(931)	2.300	1	.20	−.16
Denmark	56.0	(35)	43.9	(223)	.877	1	.50	−.24
					Pooled $x^2 = 46.793$, $df = 3$, $p < .001$			
Has had heterosexual intercourse								
United States	80.1	(196)	51.0	(820)	53.451	1	.001	−.59
Netherlands	59.3	(118)	35.6	(931)	24.059	1	.001	−.45
Denmark	88.0	(25)	58.6	(227)	7.031	1	.01	−.68
					Pooled $x^2 = 84.541$, $df = 3$, $p < .001$			
Enjoyed heterosexual intercourse the first time								
United States	81.6	(158)	58.5	(412)	25.866	1	.001	−.52
Netherlands	60.9	(69)	37.9	(322)	11.398	1	.001	−.44
Denmark	52.4	(21)	43.8	(130)	0.243	1	.70	−.17
					Pooled $x^2 = 37.507$, $df = 3$, $p < .001$			

TABLE 1—Continued

	Sexual Orientation							
	2–4		5–6		x^2	df	p	γ
Would enjoy having heterosexual intercourse *								
United States	68.0	(75)	19.2	(563)	81.705	1	.001	−.80
Netherlands	24.6	(61)	9.0	(700)	13.178	1	.001	−.53
Denmark	66.7	(9)	11.8	(161)	16.315	1	.001	−.87
					Pooled $x^2 = 111.198$, $df = 3, p < .001$			
Has heterosexual sex more than once a month								
United States	26.3	(194)	1.5	(817)	161.061	1	.001	−.92
Netherlands	13.8	(116)	0.8	(931)	75.694	1	.001	−.91
Denmark	28.0	(25)	0.9	(225)	40.161	1	.001	−.95
					Pooled $x^2 = 276.916$, $df = 3, p < .001$			
Has been married								
United States	41.1	(197)	11.1	(817)	99.158	1	.001	−.70
Netherlands	16.0	(106)	7.5	(816)	7.809	1	.05	−.40
Denmark	32.0	(25)	5.8	(223)	16.631	1	.001	−.77
					Pooled $x^2 = 123.598$, $df = 3, p < .001$			

* Among those who have never had heterosexual intercourse.

TABLE 2

Relating to the Homosexual World, by Sexual Orientation Score

	Sexual Orientation 2–4		5–6		x^2	df	p	γ
Is high in social involvement with homosexuals								
United States	37.6%	(186)	72.6%	(777)	79.967	1	.001	.63
Netherlands	57.7	(111)	72.3	(891)	9.484	1	.01	.31
Denmark	52.2	(23)	77.5	(204)	5.743	1	.02	.52
					Pooled $x^2 = 95.194$, $df = 3$, $p < .001$			
Has had mostly homosexual friends for more than two years								
United States	28.6	(196)	59.5	(817)	59.492	1	.001	.57
Netherlands	28.0	(118)	41.0	(932)	6.895	1	.01	.28
Denmark	20.0	(25)	58.3	(223)	11.793	1	.001	.70
					Pooled $x^2 = 78.180$, $df = 3$, $p < .001$			

TABLE 2—Continued

	Sexual Orientation							
	2–4		5–6		x^2	df	p	γ
Has had an exclusive homosexual relationship								
United States	40.2	(199)	56.4	(817)	16.276	1	.001	.32
Netherlands	45.0	(111)	61.4	(911)	10.271	1	.01	.32
Denmark	52.0	(25)	62.1	(219)	.585	1	.50	.20
					Pooled $x^2 = 27.132$, $df = 3$, $p < .001$			
Has high frequency of homosexual sex								
United States	30.5	(187)	56.6	(774)	40.062	1	.001	.50
Netherlands	44.6	(112)	54.5	(874)	3.461	1	.10	.19
Denmark	54.5	(22)	60.7	(211)	0.108	1	.80	.12
					Pooled $x^2 = 43.631$, $df = 3$, $p < .001$			
Is high in acculturation								
United States	21.6	(199)	46.2	(822)	39.015	1	.001	.51
Netherlands	47.9	(117)	59.5	(931)	5.323	1	.05	.23
Denmark	72.0	(25)	75.3	(227)	.015	1	.95	.09
					Pooled $x^2 = 44.353$, $df = 3$, $p < .001$			

Has experienced the most common homosexual sex practices								
United States	39.9	(183)	61.9	(784)	28.453	1	.001	.42
Netherlands	26.2	(103)	37.6	(859)	4.673	1	.05	.26
Denmark	40.0	(20)	55.2	(165)	1.093	1	.30	.30
					Pooled $x^2 = 34.219$, $df = 3$, $p < .001$			
Seeks an occupation stereotyped as homosexual								
United States	13.3	(60)	33.6	(229)	8.477	1	.01	.53
Netherlands	10.0	(30)	18.0	(211)	0.694	1	.50	.33
Denmark	11.1	(9)	20.0	(45)	0.251	1	.90	.33
					Pooled $x^2 = 9.422$, $df = 3$, $p < .05$			
Believes homosexuality is beyond one's control								
United States	40.8	(201)	58.3	(827)	19.268	1	.001	.34
Netherlands	74.4	(117)	85.3	(933)	8.531	1	.01	.33
Denmark	76.0	(25)	89.9	(227)	3.000	1	.10	.47
					Pooled $x^2 = 30.799$, $df = 3$, $p < .001$			

TABLE 3

Psychological Problems, by Sexual Orientation Score

	Sexual Orientation							
	2–4		5–6		x^2	df	p	γ
Is high in guilt, shame, or anxiety regarding homosexuality								
United States	33.2%	(199)	15.5%	(819)	31.355	1	.001	−.46
Netherlands	24.8	(117)	7.4	(929)	34.860	1	.001	−.61
Denmark	16.0	(25)	8.8	(227)	.645	1	.50	−.33
					Pooled $x^2 = 66.860$, $df = 3$, $p < .001$			

CHAPTER 16

AGE

It is generally recognized that the process of aging can be stressful and problematic. For the male homosexual, aging is depicted as exceptionally stressful. Since homosexual relationships often involve no special commitment between partners and none of the legal supports and sanctions that help keep heterosexual marriages intact, the older homosexual is often described as isolated and lonely. In addition, it has been said that as the homosexual grows older, he often finds it difficult to maintain his involvement with many aspects of the homosexual world, where youthfulness appears to be a sine qua non for sociosexual success.

The older homosexual is often described, therefore, as unhappy, depressed, and lonely, isolated from the more exciting aspects of homosexual life, and lacking in self-esteem because of the rejection which he experiences from other homosexuals. The following is a typical description:

> In Greenwich Village gay boys laughingly pass around cards which read: "Nobody loves you when you're old and gay."
>
> To many, including the homosexual colony, the aging homosexual is an object of scorn and derision. Though his loneliness

is often abject, he seldom arouses sympathy or interest, unless he has money or influence. . . .

Ordinarily, . . . the aging process begins as they approach thirty. Recently addressing a scientific group, Dr. Alfred A. Gross, executive secretary of the George Henry Foundation, noted: "The homosexual's world is a young person's one. Among men without special gifts, a man is middle-aged at thirty, elderly at forty, and unless he has unusual endowments of talent or wealth, by the time a homosexual reaches fifty, he is obliged to buy companionship. . . ." For the most part, though, the aging homosexual is usually his own worst problem, so desperately lonely and frightened at times that he frantically beats the walls in his anguish.[1]

In this chapter we examine the social and psychological characteristics which, among homosexuals, seem to be associated with the aging process. We begin with an examination of how the social life of the homosexual varies by age, followed by a consideration of his psychological problems.

With regard to the social situation of the homosexual, the data support some aspects of the folk view (Table 1). As this view suggests, older respondents attend homosexual bars and clubs much less frequently. In addition, the older homosexual is more likely to be living alone. The folk view is also corroborated in that older homosexuals report less frequent homosexual sex. (These findings are not explained by sample source.)

To this extent, then, the commonly espoused description of the older homosexual is supported by the data. (Also, in the United States, older homosexuals are lower in overall social involvement with other homosexuals, but this difference does not replicate.[2])

The folk view also portrays the "old" homosexual as lacking in self-acceptance, anxious, depressed, lonely, and generally unhappy. The present data contradict this image. We find no age-related differences in self-acceptance, anxiety, depression, or loneliness. In fact, our data suggest that in some respects our older homosexuals have greater well-being than our younger homosexuals. Older respondents worry less about exposure of their homosexuality, have more stable self-concepts, and are less effeminate (Table 2). (In Chapter 12, we suggested that effeminacy is associated with the younger homosexual's identity problems.) Finally, the older homosexual is less apt to desire psychiatric treatment. (Generation differences in one's perspective toward psychiatric treatment are probably also involved here.[3])

Why these discrepancies between the folk view and the data? The following explanation, based on our field work and questionnaire data, is proposed. The homosexual world places a premium on youth. This means that as far as certain forms of social interaction and sexual gains are concerned, the older homosexual is less valued. Thus, as one gets older there is a decreased participation in certain public institutions of the subculture, such as homosexual bars. There is also a greater problem in obtaining sexual partners.[4]

The younger homosexual correctly observes this sociosexual situation, that is, that the older homosexual is isolated from certain public facets of the homosexual scene and that his sexual frequency is lower. On the basis of these facts, the younger person views the older homosexual's situation as unenviable. The same limited perspective appears among journalists and social scientists. From their position (for example, as a married person with a family), the social situation of the older homosexual seems miserable. What heterosexuals and younger homosexuals do not know, our data suggest, is that the older homosexual can often adapt to his social situation.

The present study provides no data concerning the ways in which the older homosexual's increased psychological well-being may be achieved. A study by Gurin, Veroff, and Feld, however, does bear on this question. These researchers found that in a sample of the general population, older respondents report more positive self-images, fewer perceived shortcomings, fewer problems and feelings of self-doubt, and more satisfaction in their jobs and interpersonal relationships. The authors of the study suggested *that what appear to be problems or inadequacies at the time of youthful involvement may seem less serious with the passage of time.*

> Age differences seem most of all to reflect differences in the current level of aspiration in older and younger people. Older people are on the whole not dissatisfied or troubled about most aspects of their lives—either because of a lowering of aspirations and expectations as a result of a positive adaptation to the realistic possibilities in their life situation or as a more passive resignation to their life situation. But neither are they particularly happy or optimistic about their lives. Their satisfactions seem to be based on limited expectations and a passive acceptance of their status.[5]

Thus, the folk beliefs about the older homosexual erroneously attribute (or overgeneralize) to the older homosexual the perspectives and expectations of younger homosexuals and heterosexuals who hold these beliefs. Moreover, the psychological well-being of older people is not peculiar to homosexuals but is probably associated with the aging process in general.[6]

Summary

As a whole, our older homosexuals are less involved in the homosexual world, have homosexual sex less frequently, and are more likely to be living alone. These findings were interpreted as reflecting the social, psychological, and sexual changes that accompany aging among homosexuals.

Contrary to popular beliefs, however, our older homosexuals are no worse off than our younger homosexuals on various psychological dimensions, and are, on some dimensions, better off. This finding is in accord with trends found in the general population.

The stereotype which portrays the homosexual as decreasing in psychological well-being as he gets older results, we believe, from incorrectly attributing or overgeneralizing meanings to the sociosexual situation of the older homosexual which he himself does not experience.[7]

TABLE 1

Social Characteristics, by Age

	Age											
	Under 26		26–35		36–45		Over 45		x^2	df	p	γ
Attends homosexual bars and clubs more than once a month												
United States	55.7%	(183)	56.5%	(315)	49.5%	(289)	24.9%	(249)	66.594	3	.001	−.33
Netherlands	84.2	(240)	72.0	(414)	61.4	(249)	46.3	(160)	71.937	3	.001	−.41
Denmark	82.3	(79)	77.4	(106)	54.1	(37)	53.6	(28)	16.491	3	.001	−.39
									Pooled $x^2 = 155.022$, $df = 9$, $p < .001$			
Lives alone												
United States	30.4	(168)	45.9	(296)	54.8	(261)	57.4	(209)	39.478	3	.001	.27
Netherlands	42.0	(231)	45.6	(390)	56.3	(224)	60.6	(142)	19.539	3	.001	.20
Denmark	52.5	(80)	64.6	(99)	57.6	(33)	70.4	(27)	4.058	3	.30	.16
									Pooled $x^2 = 59.075$, $df = 9$, $p < .001$			

Has high frequency of homosexual sex												
United States	46.4	(168)	59.4	(298)	55.0	(271)	40.9	(230)	20.889	3	.001	−.10
Netherlands	57.1	(226)	58.5	(383)	46.4	(237)	44.0	(150)	15.141	3	.01	−.16
Denmark	64.4	(73)	62.2	(98)	54.3	(35)	50.0	(26)	2.345	3	.70	−.15
									Pooled $x^2 = 38.375$, $df = 9$, $p < .001$			

TABLE 2

Psychological Characteristics, by Age

	Age											
	Under 26		26–35		36–45		Over 45		x^2	df	p	γ
Worries about exposure of his homosexuality												
United States	83.0%	(182)	78.5%	(316)	74.9%	(287)	65.9%	(249)	19.383	3	.001	–.23
Netherlands	51.7	(240)	56.5	(414)	53.4	(249)	48.4	(159)	3.488	3	.50	–.03
Denmark	67.1	(79)	60.0	(105)	43.2	(37)	53.6	(28)	6.320	3	.10	–.22
									Pooled $x^2 = 29.191$, $df = 9$, $p < .001$			
Has low stability of self-concept												
United States	37.2	(180)	32.0	(303)	25.3	(285)	18.5	(243)	21.987	3	.001	–.25
Netherlands	24.9	(237)	26.4	(409)	18.6	(247)	10.0	(160)	20.986	3	.001	–.22
Denmark	40.5	(79)	33.3	(102)	24.3	(37)	14.3	(28)	7.733	3	.10	–.29
									Pooled $x^2 = 50.706$, $df = 9$, $p < .001$			

Is high in effeminacy												
United States	21.3	(183)	9.0	(312)	8.1	(285)	7.2	(250)	28.256	3	.001	–.31
Netherlands	15.1	(239)	7.5	(413)	5.2	(249)	7.0	(158)	17.497	3	.001	–.29
Denmark	22.8	(79)	10.5	(105)	13.9	(36)	10.7	(28)	5.903	3	.02	–.28
									Pooled $x^2 = 51.656$, df = 9, $p < .001$			
Desires psychiatric treatment regarding homosexuality *												
United States	24.1	(158)	13.6	(264)	13.9	(252)	7.9	(229)	20.376	3	.001	–.28
Netherlands	5.6	(214)	5.2	(366)	5.8	(226)	0.7	(147)	6.422	3	.10	–.19
Denmark	10.4	(77)	8.7	(103)	5.4	(37)	3.6	(28)	1.717	3	.70	–.24
									Pooled $x^2 = 28.515$, df = 9, $p < .001$			

* Among those who have not seen a psychiatrist regarding their homosexuality.

CHAPTER 17

OCCUPATION

Status of Occupation

High-status occupations, more so than lower-status ones, have an image of "respectability." In many higher-status occupations disreputability is often believed to reflect poorly upon the occupation or one's associates or to make a person somehow less qualified for such a position. Breaching a respectable image may thus jeopardize the person's prestige, material rewards, and other gratifications which higher-status occupations provide, as well as advancement in the occupation.

Obviously these considerations affect homosexuals in higher-status occupations. One might thus expect homosexuals in such occupations to be more secret about their homosexuality than those in lower-status occupations. Based on field research, Leznoff and Westley conclude:

> In our society, homosexuality is defined . . . as a . . . depraved practice and the homosexual is threatened by powerful legal and social sanctions. . . . Therefore, all homosexuals face the problem of evading social controls. They do this in two predominant ways.

Some pass for heterosexuals on the job and in most of their social relationships. . . .

Others openly admit and practice homosexuality. . . .

The mode of adaptation is largely dependent upon the extent to which identification as a homosexual is a status threat. . . . Thus we find a rough relationship between form of evasion and occupation. The overt homosexual tends to fit into an occupation of low status rank; the secret homosexual into an occupation with a relatively high status rank.[1]

According to Leznoff and Westley, the homosexual in a lower-status occupation, being less threatened by status loss, is less likely either to conceal his homosexual activities or to be socially involved with heterosexuals. On the other hand, the homosexual in a higher-status occupation is more likely to be discreet in his homosexual practices and to attempt to conceal his homosexuality (to pass), and he is less likely to be involved in the more public homosexual world.

This section examines the relationship between the status of the homosexual's occupation and the way in which he manages his life. It thus provides a further test of Leznoff and Westley's fieldwork conclusions.[2]

Relating to the Heterosexual World (Table 1)

Homosexuals in higher-status occupations report greater investments in and commitments to their jobs. They are more likely to have had fewer job changes over the last five years, and they are less likely to state that they would like to change their occupations. (These and other findings in this chapter are not explained by age.)

Our data on passing strongly support Leznoff and Westley's assertion that the status of a homosexual's occupation is positively related to his covertness. Respondents in occupations with higher status are more worried over exposure and would be more bothered about being officially labeled homosexual. In light of these data, we would also expect homosexuals in higher-status occupations to pass more and to be less known about, which is what we find. (Results related to status of occupation are not due to differences in type of employment, which we discuss later in this chapter.)

Homosexuals in higher-status occupations often cannot dissociate themselves from heterosexuals as completely as can those in lower-status occupations. In addition to inevitable job-related social occasions, the homosexual in a higher-status occupation may also, because of wider interests more characteristic of higher-status people, be more reluctant to confine his social life to other homosexuals. In addition, social involvement with heterosexuals can be a method of preventing one's sexual orientation from being called into question. Thus, we find that homosexuals in high-status occupations have greater social involvement with heterosexuals and feel more accepted by them (except in the Danish sample).

In addition, homosexuals from higher-status occupations identify more with heterosexuals, being more likely to report that they feel closer to a heterosexual of their own social class than to a homosexual of a much lower class. That is, among homosexuals in higher-status occupations, class identification appears to take precedence over "minority" identification more often than among homosexuals in lower-status occupations.[3]

Relating to the Homosexual World (Table 2)

According to Leznoff and Westley, homosexuals in higher-status occupations, being more discreet in their homosexuality, are less willing than homosexuals in lower-status occupations to associate with known homosexuals. Our data support this view (although no differences are found for the Netherlands).[4]

Throughout the book we describe the homosexual world in somewhat abstract terms. Here we present a group of pictures to bring this world to life for the reader. It should be noted, however, that these pictures do not represent the entire homosexual world. They capture only the most visible, public aspects of that world.

1. Scene of the Stonewall riot (Courtesy of Fred W. McDarrah)

2. Gay Liberation (Courtesy of Fred W. McDarrah)

3. Gay Pride march (Courtesy of Fred W. McDarrah)

4. Parents "come out" too (Courtesy of Fred W. McDarrah)

5. Entrance to a gay bar (Courtesy of Fred W. McDarrah)

6. Inside a gay club (Courtesy of Fred W. McDarrah)

7. Advertisement for a gay bath

8. Window display in a gay bookstore (Courtesy of *Gay*)

9. Dancing at a gay bath (Courtesy of *Gay*)

10. Out of the closets and into the streets (Courtesy of Fred W. McDarrah)

This supports the idea that homosexuals in higher-status occupations are more covert in their homosexuality.[5] As for degree of social involvement with other homosexuals, number of homosexual friends, frequency of sex, and acculturation, however, we find no differences. The reason for this is, as Leznoff and Westley recognize, that there is no such thing as *the* homosexual world, but rather a variety of homosexual worlds or communities. Thus, social involvement with other homosexuals may be as great for a homosexual in a higher-status occupation as for one in a lower-status occupation, yet, for the former, it may be primarily confined to a circle of friends who are equally covert. These overlapping homosexual worlds produce *a* homosexual community as both types of homosexuals may come into contact in their sexual pursuits. Leznoff and Westley conclude: ". . . it is the casual and promiscuous sexual contacts between the members of different categories of evasion (i.e., the secret and the overt) which weld . . . homosexuals into a community." [6]

Psychological Problems (Table 3)

As a result of being more concerned with passing, homosexuals in higher-status occupations are often assumed to have greater psychological problems. One commentator suggests the following relationships between psychological processes and occupational milieus:

> One encounters with great frequency homosexuals who themselves hold a low opinion of homosexuality. . . . The Closet Queen is . . . subject to low self-esteem which is related to his homosexuality. . . . Among Closet Queens, physicians continue to have the highest rate of suicide and drug addiction. Much of this can be attributed to their inability in reconciling personal and professional roles. Inheritor of a superior social status within our society, the doctor finds it most anxiety creating to acknowledge his own personal sexual variations from the Amer-

ican Medical Association norms. He cannot admit to his own colleagues his sexual object preference.[7]

This view—that difficulty in reconciling personal and professional roles leads to low self-esteem and high anxiety —could be applied to high-status occupations in general. Our data, however, show no differences between homosexuals in high- and low-status occupations on any of our psychological dimensions but self-acceptance and faith in others. And these differences are the opposite of those suggested above; that is, self-acceptance and faith in others are higher for respondents with high occupational status.

The following interpretations are offered. With regard to self-acceptance, homosexuals in high-status occupations undoubtedly experience many social psychological rewards from occupying an enviable status, as well as the intrinsic gratifications which such occupations offer. Thus, in Rosenberg's words: "If a person's self-esteem is influenced by what others think of him, then there is reason to expect those with the highest prestige in society . . . to be more likely than others to accept themselves." [8] Research, which finds high-status people to be happier and more self-accepting, supports Rosenberg's expectation.[9] Thus, even if the homosexual in a high-status occupation faces greater strain associated with the way in which he manages his homosexuality, this would appear to be outweighed by the greater social psychological rewards associated with his social position.

With regard to his greater faith in others, we generally expect higher status to increase positive sentiments toward others and to decrease cynicism.[10]

Thus, as we suggested in an earlier chapter, there is a tendency for popular notions to overestimate the importance of sexual orientation in the homosexual's larger life situation, and the psychological maladjustment attributed to the higher-status homosexual seems to be a case in point.

Type of Employment

In addition to expecting differences by the status of occupations, we also expected to find differences associated with type of employment. For example, it is generally assumed that the personal lives of those in educational or governmental positions are subject to greater surveillance than the lives of those who are self-employed or in private firms. Also, regulations prohibiting the employment of homosexuals are more common in educational and governmental institutions than in private firms.[11] Consequently, we expected that homosexuals in educational and governmental positions would be more covert in their homosexuality and anticipate more discrimination, whereas those who are self-employed would be the most overt and anticipate the least discrimination.

Our findings regarding type of employment are shown in Table 4; these differences remain when the status of occupations is held constant. First, respondents in government positions and those in private firms are similar to each other (thus, we combine them in our table). The range in types of jobs the above respondents hold is probably too great to allow for any overall differences between these categories of employment. For example, a government job that requires a security clearance and a job as clerk in a county agency are both "government" jobs, yet they differ widely in how they would affect the homosexual's adaptations. Thus, respondents in governmental and private employment do not stand out on any of our measures. Second, with regard to those employed in educational institutions, they are the least likely to have been arrested in connection with their homosexuality. (To some extent they also are less likely to have been officially labeled as homosexual, they anticipate more discrimination, and they pass more—although the differences between respondents in education and those in government or private employment do not reach our substantive criterion.) Third, it is the self-employed who stand out the most. As a group, they anticipate the least discrimination, are the most likely to have been officially labeled homosexual, and are the least concerned with passing. For some homosexuals, then, self-employment does appear to lessen the fear of occupational sanctions. (Note, however, that we do not have a large enough number of respondents in the professions, or the highest-status category, to examine this type of self-employed homosexual.) Finally (in general, and only in terms of our gross differentiation of occupations) our data suggest that the status of the homosexual's occupation is more highly related to his adaptations than is his type of employment.

Summary

This chapter considered the way in which the homosexual's occupation affects the management of his homosexuality. Being homosexual is a potential threat to the investments and rewards associated with a higher-status occupation. Thus, it was expected that homosexuals in higher-status occupations would be more discreet in their homosexuality, pass more, and be less involved in the overt homosexual world than would homosexuals in lower-status occupations. Our results were as expected. Homosexuals in higher-status occupations are less known about, more worried about exposure, and more concerned with passing. These findings replicate those of Leznoff and Westley. Homosexuals in high-status occupations also report more social involvement with heterosexuals and feel more accepted by them. Finally, homosexuals in higher-status occupations more often report that they feel closer to a heterosexual of the same class than to a homosexual from a lower class, indicating that for them class identification may override identification based on sexual orientation.

With respect to relating to the homosexual world, homosexuals from higher-status occupations are less willing to associate with known homosexuals, which we interpreted as indicative of their greater discretion.

Finally, with regard to most psychological problems, we found no difference between homosexuals in higher-status occupations and those in lower-status occupations. However, homosexuals in high-status occupations report more self-acceptance and faith in others. These results contradict notions that homosexuals in high-status occupations experience greater psychological maladjustment. They seemingly reflect the self-esteem and other social psychological advantages that accrue from a high-status occupation, regardless of one's sexual orientation. None of the above results was explained by type of employment.

With regard to type of employment, homosexuals who are self-employed stand out the most, anticipating the least discrimination, being the least concerned with passing, and being the most likely to have been officially labeled. Those employed in educational institutions are the least likely to have been arrested in connection with their homosexuality. None of these findings was explained by the status of the homosexual's occupation. Caution was suggested in interpreting these findings due to our gross differentiation of occupations, but it was suggested that type of employment may be less highly related to a homosexual's adaptations than is the status of the occupation in which he is employed.

TABLE 1

Relating to the Heterosexual World, by Status of Occupation

	Status									
	High		Medium		Low		x^2	df	p	γ
Had two or more job changes in last five years										
United States	25.1%	(347)	36.2%	(401)	47.5%	(99)	21.074	2	.001	−.29
Netherlands	14.2	(254)	23.0	(543)	37.9	(116)	26.061	2	.001	−.35
Denmark	12.8	(39)	30.1	(103)	40.5	(37)	7.468	2	.05	−.39
							Pooled $x^2 = 54.603$, $df = 6$, $p < .001$			
Desires change of occupation										
United States	27.6	(359)	44.8	(422)	52.5	(101)	33.404	2	.001	−.34
Netherlands	22.6	(257)	37.8	(550)	50.9	(112)	31.744	2	.001	−.35
Denmark	25.0	(40)	45.2	(104)	41.0	(39)	4.939	2	.10	−.20
							Pooled $x^2 = 70.087$, $df = 6$, $p < .001$			

Worries about exposure of his homosexuality										
United States	78.4	(366)	76.0	(437)	64.8	(108)	8.422	2	.02	.16
Netherlands	61.8	(259)	51.3	(567)	44.6	(121)	12.022	2	.01	.21
Denmark	67.5	(40)	61.7	(107)	37.5	(40)	8.959	2	.02	.35
							Pooled $x^2 = 29.403$, $df = 6$, $p < .001$			
Would be bothered if officially labeled as homosexual *										
United States	86.9	(237)	81.1	(259)	62.7	(75)	21.850	2	.001	.36
Netherlands	72.6	(190)	64.1	(415)	52.9	(87)	10.640	2	.01	.23
Denmark	81.8	(33)	85.0	(80)	53.6	(28)	12.308	2	.01	.39
							Pooled $x^2 = 44.798$, $df = 6$, $p < .001$			
Is high in passing										
United States	67.9	(336)	62.7	(408)	49.5	(101)	11.313	2	.01	.19
Netherlands	39.1	(256)	30.8	(556)	25.0	(116)	8.783	2	.01	.19
Denmark	51.4	(37)	32.7	(101)	15.4	(39)	11.150	2	.01	.46
							Pooled $x^2 = 31.246$, $df = 6$, $p < .001$			

* Among those who have not been officially labeled.

TABLE 1—Continued

	Status									
	High		Medium		Low		x^2	df	p	γ
Is high in being known about (Scale II)										
United States	30.7	(205)	39.0	(272)	51.9	(77)	11.077	2	.01	–.24
Netherlands	76.5	(234)	83.3	(496)	87.2	(94)	7.001	2	.05	–.21
Denmark	63.9	(36)	82.5	(97)	79.4	(34)	5.319	2	.10	–.25
							Pooled $x^2 = 23.397$, $df = 6$, $p < .001$			
Is high in social involvement with heterosexuals										
United States	54.6	(368)	46.7	(437)	43.0	(107)	7.059	2	.05	.15
Netherlands	58.7	(259)	39.5	(565)	40.8	(120)	27.437	2	.001	.26
Denmark	50.0	(40)	44.2	(104)	42.5	(40)	.529	2	.80	.09
							Pooled $x^2 = 35.024$, $df = 6$, $p < .001$			
Feels accepted by heterosexuals										
United States	82.7	(365)	71.7	(428)	70.6	(102)	15.042	2	.001	.25
Netherlands	80.9	(251)	78.5	(530)	68.5	(108)	6.931	2	.05	.16
Denmark	84.2	(38)	90.2	(102)	86.8	(38)	1.039	2	.70	–.07
							Pooled $x^2 = 20.934$, $df = 6$, $p < .01$			

Identifies more with social class than with homosexuals										
United States	46.5	(370)	47.4	(437)	26.2	(107)	16.604	2	.001	.12
Netherlands	41.2	(260)	31.5	(565)	19.0	(121)	19.152	2	.001	.27
Denmark	35.0	(40)	31.4	(105)	15.4	(39)	4.526	2	.20	.28
							Pooled $x^2 = 40.282$, $df = 6$, $p < .001$			

TABLE 2

Relating to the Homosexual World, by Status of Occupation

	Status									
	High		Medium		Low		x^2	df	p	γ
Is willing to associate with known homosexuals										
United States	58.0%	(369)	53.4%	(436)	72.0%	(107)	12.132	2	.01	−.35
Netherlands	75.0	(260)	70.4	(565)	70.6	(119)	1.909	2	.50	.05
Denmark	66.7	(39)	73.3	(105)	85.0	(40)	3.652	2	.20	−.38
							Pooled $x^2 = 13.875$, $df = 6$, $p < .05$			

TABLE 3

Psychological Problems, by Status of Occupation

	Status									
	High		Medium		Low		x^2	df	p	γ
Has low self-acceptance										
United States	38.1%	(370)	45.4%	(438)	50.0%	(108)	6.829	2	.05	–.15
Netherlands	34.6	(260)	42.9	(567)	45.5	(121)	6.184	2	.05	–.15
Denmark	47.5	(40)	62.6	(107)	62.5	(40)	2.966	2	.30	–.23
							Pooled $x^2 = 15.979$, $df = 6$, $p < .02$			
Has low faith in others										
United States	41.0	(366)	52.2	(429)	62.3	(106)	18.641	2	.001	–.25
Netherlands	33.1	(257)	45.7	(558)	63.2	(114)	29.991	2	.001	–.32
Denmark	41.0	(39)	63.1	(103)	69.2	(39)	7.620	2	.05	–.33
							Pooled $x^2 = 56.252$, $df = 6$, $p < .001$			

TABLE 4

Correlates of Employment *

	Employer								
	Self-employed		Private Firm or Government Agency		Educational Institution		x^2	df	p
Anticipates a great deal of discrimination									
United States	30.0%	(130)	50.7%	(605)	58.7%	(184)	26.371	2	.001
Netherlands	16.1	(93)	22.2	(671)	30.9	(81)	5.462	2	.02
							Pooled $x^2 = 31.833$, df = 4, $p < .001$		
Has been arrested									
United States	33.1	(136)	25.2	(635)	15.1	(185)	14.403	2	.001
Netherlands	21.7	(106)	16.4	(762)	5.9	(85)	9.100	2	.02
							Pooled $x^2 = 23.503$, df = 4, $p < .001$		

Is officially labeled as homosexual									
United States	52.6	(137)	41.1	(643)	36.2	(188)	9.110	2	.02
Netherlands	44.8	(105)	33.1	(753)	24.1	(83)	9.322	2	.01
							Pooled $x^2 = 18.442$, $df = 4$, $p < .01$		
Is high in passing									
United States	48.4	(128)	62.7	(600)	66.5	(176)	11.394	2	.01
Netherlands	25.2	(107)	31.1	(748)	41.0	(83)	5.439	2	.10
							Pooled $x^2 = 16.833$, $df = 4$, $p < .01$		

* Data for Denmark are omitted because of the small N's in the Self-employed and Educational Institution categories.

CHAPTER 18

LIVING ARRANGEMENTS

The homosexual's mode of residence—that is, whom he lives with—is important in considering the way he manages his day-to-day existence. Various living arrangements can promote or impede particular life-styles and can reflect greater or lesser commitment to homosexuality. In this chapter, respondents with four different living arrangements—living with a homosexual roommate, living alone, living with one's parents, and living with one's wife—are compared in terms of the type of life they lead and the problems they confront.[1] (None of the findings is explained by age or the degree of social involvement with other homosexuals, two variables associated with living arrangements.)

Living with a Homosexual Roommate

Among many homosexuals the ideal arrangement is to live with a homosexual partner, especially one who is loved and with whom one's life is shared. Although not without their difficulties, these relationships are often recognized as solving a number of the homosexual's problems and as increasing his overall happiness.[2]

> Whatever the pattern, the ages, the races, the nature of the adjustment to the outside world, the degree of sexual fidelity involved, it can be said without equivocation that those who have . . . [such a] relationship . . . have gone a long way toward solving the problem of the adjustment of the homosexual in a hostile society. . . . That such a . . . [relationship] brings with it new problems does not at all mean that it is a poor solution to the old ones.[3]

Living with a homosexual roommate can provide a continuing sense of support with regard to being homosexual. One might expect this to be associated with less fear of a homosexual *social* identity. Compared with those with other living arrangements, respondents living with homosexual roommates anticipate or have experienced the least intolerance or rejection on account of their homosexuality, anticipate the least discrimination, are the least worried about exposure of their homosexuality, the least concerned with passing, and the most known about (Table 1).

Of the four groups, homosexuals living with homosexual roommates are the least socially involved with heterosexuals (except in Denmark) and the most socially involved with other homosexuals (Tables 1 and 2). As we suggested earlier, social involvement with other homosexuals may indirectly increase the probability of finding a partner with whom to live[4]; at the same time, it seems reasonable to expect that a homosexual with such a living arrangement would spend more time with other homosexuals.

Homosexuals living with a homosexual roommate are the most integrated into the homosexual world in other ways as well. They are the most likely to have had mostly homosexual friends for over two years and to have experienced an exclusive homosexual relationship. (The latter finding perhaps reflects that this group includes respondents involved in homosexual "marriages.") Respondents with homosexual roommates seem to utilize the "social" aspects of the homosexual subculture more than do those in other living arrangements. Not surprisingly, they also show the greatest frequency of homosexual sex.[5] Respondents with homosexual roommates are also the most likely to be high in acculturation and to have experienced the most common homosexual sex practices (Table 2).

Earlier we presented the notion that living together—despite the problems such a relationship might present—is psychologically beneficial for the homosexuals involved. Living with a homosexual roommate is found to be associated with greater psychological well-being (although in addition to being a consequence of this living arrangement, this probably also reflects the greater difficulty a homosexual with many psychological problems might have in obtaining such a relationship). In any case, compared with homosexuals with other modes of residence, those living with a homosexual roommate show high self-acceptance (not replicated in Denmark), high stability of self-concept, low depression, loneliness, and guilt, shame, or anxiety over being homosexual, and they are somewhat less likely to desire psychiatric treatment (Table 3).[6] Note that the magnitude of the differences between this group and the others in depression, loneliness, and guilt, shame, or anxiety regarding their homosexuality is especially large.

Living Alone

Living by oneself is probably the chief residential pattern for male homosexuals. It provides the freedom to pursue whatever style of homosexual life one chooses, whether it be furtive encounters in parks or immersion in the homosexual subculture. In addition, homosexual relationships are fragile enough to make this residential pattern common, whether deliberately chosen or not.

As a group, homosexuals living alone do not stand out on any of our measures, generally falling between those with homosexual roommates, on the one hand, and those living with their parents or wives, on the other. Compared with those living with their parents or wives, homosexuals who live alone are low in worry about exposure and high in having had mostly homosexual friends for more than two years (except in the Netherlands), and in having experienced the most common homosexual sex practices (Tables 1 and 2).

The data also indicate that, despite some switching back and forth between living alone and living with a homosexual roommate, as a whole these two residential groups are clearly distinguishable on a number of measures. Compared with homosexuals with homosexual roommates, those who live alone anticipate more discrimination, are less known about, and are more socially involved with heterosexuals (Table 1). In addition, for every measure of relating to the homosexual world reported in this chapter, homosexuals who live alone are less integrated into that world (Table 2). Homosexuals living alone also report more depression, loneliness, and guilt, shame, or anxiety regarding their homosexuality than do those with homosexual roommates, indicating the specific ways in which having a roommate may benefit the homosexual psychologically (Table 3).

Finally, homosexuals living alone are older than are those with homosexual roommates, although this does not replicate in Denmark (Table 4). This may reflect the social handicap which characterizes the older homosexual in the youth-oriented homosexual subculture.

Living with Parents

Beyond a certain age, living with parents has obvious disadvantages for both heterosexuals and homosexuals. Parents can often limit independence by setting curfews and by placing restrictions on geographical mobility, finances, selection of friends, and the like. Simply by being near, parents can monitor much of what goes on—for example, phone calls may be overheard, visitors observed, and questions asked.

Although this can be frustrating for the heterosexual male, the situation is probably exacerbated for the homosexual male. The homosexual living with his parents is usually more concerned about his sexual activities being found out. He may feel forced to feign an interest in girls, or to date, or to invent heterosexual friends with whom he says he spends his leisure time in order to allay parental suspicions. Because of these disadvantages, we would expect homosexuals to move away from home and thus diminish parental surveillance as soon as they are able.

As this description suggests, homosexuals who live with their parents are the youngest in our sample, but as noted above, this does not explain the other differences found for them. Homosexuals living with their parents are also the least likely of our respondents to have close friends (Table 4). On measures of relating to the heterosexual world, they stand out only in being high in worry over exposure of their homosexuality (Table 1).

Homosexuals living with parents are less integrated into, and less acculturated to, the homosexual world than are homosexuals living with homosexual roommates, but more so than those living with wives. The same pattern also holds for the following variables: social involvement with homosexuals, having mostly homosexual friends for more than two years, acculturation, frequency of homosexual sex, and having experienced the most common homosexual sex practices (Table 2). (In the United States they also score lower on these measures than do respondents living alone; however, such a difference is often small or not replicated in the European samples.)

Given that homosexuals who live with their parents are generally young, concerned about exposure of their sexual orientation, and somewhat isolated in terms of close friends, one might expect them to have greater psychological problems. We find that homosexuals living with their parents do have less self-acceptance, less stable self-concepts, and more depression than do those with other modes of residence; they also more frequently desire psychiatric treatment (Table 3). (Only the finding for stability of self-concept replicates in Denmark.)

Thus, among our respondents, living with parents appears to exacerbate some of the homosexual's problems. Of course, it is also possible that the homosexual with more personal problems is more likely to deliberately choose this particular residential pattern.

Living with His Wife

As discussed in Chapter 15, not all "homosexuals" are exclusively so in orientation or behavior. Many persons who engage in homosexual sex also have as much or more heterosexual sex, do not consider themselves homosexual, and do not participate in the social activities of the homosexual world. Such males often are married and living with their wives. On the other hand, some males who are married and live with their wives are more homosexual than heterosexual in their orientation. The reasons for their entering into such a heterosexual union are complex and can involve such things as a desire for children or bowing to social pressure.[7]

Our sample includes a number of males who are heterosexually married and living with their wives, yet engaging in homosexual activities. One might expect the homosexual who is living with his wife to feel even more threatened by the possibility of his homosexuality being discovered than the one living with his parents. For the homosexual living with his parents, exposure could breach a residential arrangement that probably would eventually have been dissolved anyway. For the homosexual living with his wife, however, it might destroy an arrangement that otherwise could have endured.

Thus, of all the residential groups, homosexuals living with wives are the most likely to worry about being exposed as homosexual, the highest in passing, and the least known about (Table 1).[8] The greater concern with passing by respondents living with wives also seems to be reflected in the fact that they are the most likely to anticipate intolerance or rejection on account of their homosexuality and to expect a great deal of discrimination. At the same time, as we might expect, this group is the most socially involved with heterosexuals (Table 1).

Compared with those with other living arrangements, homosexuals living with their wives are more likely to be bisexual and less likely to be integrated into the homosexual world, especially with regard to its "social" aspects. They are much less socially involved with other homosexuals, much less likely to have had mostly homosexual friends for more than two years, and much less acculturated. They also less often report having experienced the most common homosexual sex practices and have homosexual sex less frequently, although compared with respondents living with parents the differences are small on this last item (Table 2).

It may well be that homosexuals living with their wives limit their forays into the homosexual world in order to decrease the probability of being discovered. However, married homosexuals could obtain from their families and from other heterosexuals the gratifications which homosexuals with other living arrangements obtain from the homosexual world. Thus, their lesser integration into the homosexual world may reflect alternative sources of gratifications.

Given their greater worry about the exposure of their homosexuality, one might expect homosexuals living with wives to experience greater psychological strain than would those with other living arrangements. In general, however, this particular arrangement does not seem to produce this. The only psychological problem on which homosexuals living with wives stand out is guilt, shame, or anxiety regarding their homosexuality, which might reflect the conflicting involvements and commitments peculiar to their situation (Table 3).

Finally, homosexuals living with wives are older than those in other living arrangements, but as previously noted, none of the findings reported in this chapter is explained by age.

Summary

In this chapter, the relationships of homosexuals' living arrangements to their life-styles and problems were examined.

Homosexuals with homosexual roommates were found to be the most open about their homosexuality and the least socially involved with heterosexuals. They are the most integrated into the homosexual world and show the greatest psychological well-being. Homosexuals with homosexual roommates seem to be the most effectively insulated from negative responses by heterosexuals and from psychological stress.

Homosexuals who live alone are not outstanding on any

of our measures, generally scoring between those with homosexual roommates and those with other living arrangements.

Homosexuals who live with their parents are the youngest, high in worry about their homosexuality being exposed, and the least likely to have close friends. They also show the most psychological problems.

Homosexuals living with wives are the most integrated into the heterosexual world and the least integrated into the homosexual world, especially the social aspects of the homosexual world. They report the most guilt, shame, or anxiety regarding their homosexuality but do not stand out in terms of other psychological problems.

None of the findings in this chapter is due to the age differences or degree of social involvement with other homosexuals.

TABLE 1

Relating to the Heterosexual World,* by Living Arrangements

	Living Arrangements					
	Homosexual Roommate	Alone	Parents †	Wife ‡	x^2	df	p
Anticipates or has experienced intolerance or rejection because of his homosexuality							
United States	44.1% (313)[l]	51.5% (435)	58.3% (139)	75.8% (62)[h]	24.097	3	.001
Netherlands	7.3 (328)[l]	12.2 (460)	17.5 (126)	40.0 (30)[h]	32.471	3	.001
Denmark	3.5 (57)	15.2 (132)	16.7 (24)	—	5.746	3	.20
					Pooled $x^2 = 62.314$, $df = 9, p < .001$		

* *h* indicates an unusually high percentage, and *l* indicates an unusually low one. Unusually high and low percentages are not designated in rows for which the probability is equal to or greater than .05.

† Respondents living with either one or both parents are combined because of a lack of significant differences between these groups.

‡ Percentages are not presented for the category "wife" in the Danish sample because of the small number of respondents (five).

TABLE 1—Continued

	Living Arrangements										
	Homosexual Roommate		Alone		Parents †		Wife ‡		x^2	df	p
Anticipates a great deal of discrimination											
United States	39.8	(304)[l]	50.8	(425)	59.1	(137)	72.1	(64)[h]	29.263	3	.001
Netherlands	15.3	(321)[l]	25.5	(428)	30.6	(121)	44.8	(29)[h]	23.932	3	.001
Denmark	18.4	(49)	22.2	(135)	34.8	(23)	—		2.454	3	.50
									Pooled $x^2 = 55.649$, $df = 9$, $p < .001$		
Worries about exposure of his homosexuality											
United States	72.0	(318)[l]	73.3	(449)[l]	84.0	(144)[h]	88.9	(63)[h]	15.043	3	.01
Netherlands	43.1	(357)[l]	56.1	(487)	65.7	(134)	75.0	(32)[h]	30.597	3	.001
Denmark	45.3	(64)[l]	62.2	(143)	76.9	(26)[h]	—		9.041	3	.05
									Pooled $x^2 = 54.681$, $df = 9$, $p < .001$		
Is high in passing											
United States	54.8	(292)[l]	64.5	(423)	64.2	(134)	83.9	(53)[h]	19.288	3	.001
Netherlands	22.8	(351)[l]	34.7	(476)	38.6	(132)	54.8	(31)[h]	25.427	3	.001
Denmark	16.1	(62)[l]	39.1	(133)	57.7	(26)[h]	—		16.636	3	.001
									Pooled $x^2 = 61.351$, $df = 9$, $p < .001$		

Is high in being known about (Scale I)											
United States	61.9	(299)[h]	52.0	(408)	46.2	(130)	16.4	(61)[i]	44.441	3	.001
Netherlands	89.4	(301)[h]	71.0	(396)	62.5	(104)	40.7	(27)[i]	63.025	3	.001
Denmark	87.2	(47)[h]	65.5	(116)	47.6	(21)[i]	—		12.588	3	.01
									Pooled $x^2 = 120.054$, $df = 9$, $p < .001$		
Is high in being known about (Scale II)											
United States	63.1	(314)[h]	43.5	(437)	43.4	(143)	44.4	(63)	32.150	3	.001
Netherlands	61.6	(354)[h]	35.8	(483)	27.1	(133)	19.4	(31)[i]	80.737	3	.001
Denmark	55.7	(61)[h]	29.8	(141)[i]	48.0	(25)	—		16.319	3	.001
									Pooled $x^2 = 129.206$, $df = 9$, $p < .001$		
Is high in social involvement with heterosexuals											
United States	39.5	(319)[i]	50.2	(446)	58.0	(143)	76.2	(63)[h]	34.985	3	.001
Netherlands	36.2	(356)[i]	49.6	(484)	45.1	(133)	68.8	(32)[h]	22.460	3	.001
Denmark	43.8	(64)	45.4	(141)	38.5	(26)	—		.467	3	.95
									Pooled $x^2 = 57.912$, $df = 9$, $p < .001$		

TABLE 2

Relating to the Homosexual World,* by Living Arrangements

	Living Arrangements								x^2	df	p
	Homosexual Roommate		Alone		Parents †		Wife ‡				
Is 5 or 6 on sexual orientation scale											
United States	91.1%	(316)	81.0%	(447)	78.3%	(31)	22.2%	(63)[i]	156.956	3	.001
Netherlands	92.2	(357)	88.8	(482)	86.2	(130)	67.7	(31)[i]	19.040	3	.001
Denmark	93.8	(64)	91.7	(145)	92.3	(26)	—		30.989	3	.001
									Pooled $x^2 = 206.985$, $df = 9$, $p < .001$		
Is high in social involvement with homosexuals											
United States	85.0	(301)[h]	66.4	(417)	49.6	(131)	15.9	(63)[i]	136.061	3	.001
Netherlands	81.0	(343)[h]	66.1	(466)	67.7	(124)	39.3	(28)[i]	36.477	3	.001
Denmark	84.7	(59)	69.2	(130)	78.3	(23)	—		5.336	3	.20
									Pooled $x^2 = 177.874$, $df = 9$, $p < .001$		

Has had mostly homosexual friends for more than two years											
United States	67.5	(317)[h]	53.7	(441)	41.1	(141)	16.4	(61)[l]	67.434	3	.001
Netherlands	50.6	(356)[h]	35.6	(486)	35.1	(134)	16.1	(31)[l]	29.115	3	.001
Denmark	54.0	(63)	56.3	(142)	46.2	(26)	—		1.347	3	.80
									Pooled $x^2 = 97.896$, $df = 9$, $p < .001$		
Has had an exclusive homosexual relationship											
United States	77.8	(316)[h]	47.2	(441)	33.8	(142)	33.3	(63)	114.885	3	.001
Netherlands	89.1	(349)[h]	44.1	(476)	42.0	(131)	40.0	(30)	195.345	3	.001
Denmark	91.9	(62)[h]	52.1	(140)	44.0	(25)	—		33.686	3	.001
									Pooled $x^2 = 343.916$, $df = 9$, $p < .001$		

* *h* indicates an unusually high percentage, and *l* indicates an unusually low one. Unusually high and low percentages are not designated in rows for which the probability is equal to or greater than .05.

† Respondents living with either one or both parents are combined because of a lack of significant differences between these groups.

‡ Percentages are not presented for the category "wife" in the Danish sample because of the small number of respondents (five).

TABLE 2—Continued

	Living Arrangements										
	Homosexual Roommate		Alone		Parents †		Wife ‡		x^2	df	p
Has high frequency of homosexual sex											
United States	72.6	(296)[h]	51.3	(417)	27.2	(136)[i]	26.2	(16)[i]	100.152	3	.001
Netherlands	77.1	(328)[h]	44.8	(466)	31.5	(127)[i]	29.0	(31)[i]	119.888	3	.001
Denmark	85.5	(62)[h]	50.0	(138)	56.0	(25)	—		22.457	3	.001
									Pooled $x^2 = 242.497$, df = 9, $p < .001$		
Is high in acculturation											
United States	52.4	(317)[h]	41.1	(445)	29.9	(144)	14.5	(62)[i]	42.092	3	.001
Netherlands	69.0	(355)[h]	54.2	(487)	55.6	(133)	21.9	(32)[i]	38.007	3	.001
Denmark	84.4	(64)[h]	71.0	(145)[i]	73.1	(26)	—		4.334	3	.001
									Pooled $x^2 = 84.433$, df = 9, $p < .001$		

Has experienced the most common homosexual sex practices											
United States	68.2	(305)[h]	58.3	(429)	43.8	(128)	36.8	(57)[i]	34.207	3	.001
Netherlands	44.9	(336)[h]	34.5	(449)	26.8	(112)	11.5	(26)[i]	22.555	3	.001
Denmark	63.3	(49)	51.4	(105)	43.8	(16)	—		3.035	3	.50
									Pooled $x^2 = 59.797$, $df = 9$, $p < .001$		

TABLE 3

Psychological Problems,* by Living Arrangements

	Living Arrangements								x^2	df	p
	Homosexual Roommate		Alone		Parents †		Wife ‡				
Has low self-acceptance											
United States	38.6%	(319)[g]	46.8%	(449)	52.1%	(144)[h]	38.1%	(63)[g]	9.891	3	.02
Netherlands	31.0	(352)[i]	46.2	(480)	52.3	(128)[h]	53.1	(32)[h]	28.419	3	.001
Denmark	59.6	(57)	67.1	(140)	54.2	(24)	—		2.633	3	.50
									Pooled $x^2 = 40.943$, $df = 9$, $p < .001$		
Has low stability of self-concept											
United States	20.5	(312)[g]	29.6	(432)	36.9	(141)[h]	25.8	(62)	14.947	3	.01
Netherlands	16.7	(354)[i]	24.2	(484)	27.8	(133)[h]	19.4	(31)	9.986	3	.01
Denmark	28.6	(63)	33.1	(142)	38.5	(26)	—		1.432	3	.70
									Pooled $x^2 = 26.365$, $df = 9$, $p < .01$		

Is high in depression											
United States	15.9	(314)[l]	28.4	(437)	35.0	(143)[h]	28.6	(63)	24.226	3	.001
Netherlands	13.3	(354)[l]	33.3	(483)	41.4	(133)[h]	41.9	(31)[h]	60.104	3	.001
Denmark	14.8	(61)[l]	39.0	(141)[h]	32.0	(25)	—		13.238	3	.01
									Pooled $x^2 = 97.568$, $df = 9$, $p < .001$		
Is high in loneliness											
United States	47.5	(318)[l]	62.4	(447)	64.8	(142)	66.7	(63)	22.656	3	.001
Netherlands	28.9	(356)[l]	63.4	(487)	68.2	(132)	62.5	(32)	116.930	3	.001
Denmark	37.5	(64)[l]	60.4	(144)	61.5	(26)	—		14.174	3	.01
									Pooled $x^2 = 153.760$, $df = 9$, $p < .001$		

* *h* indicates an unusually high percentage, and *l* indicates an unusually low one. Unusually high and low percentages are not designated in rows for which the probability is equal to or greater than .05.

† Respondents living with either one or both parents are combined because of a lack of significant differences between these groups.

‡ Percentages are not presented for the category "wife" in the Danish sample because of the small number of respondents (five).

TABLE 3—Continued

	Living Arrangements										
	Homosexual Roommate		Alone		Parents †		Wife ‡		x^2	df	p
Is high in guilt, shame, or anxiety regarding homosexuality											
United States	7.5	(318)[l]	21.8	(444)	27.9	(140)	30.2	(63)[h]	42.321	3	.001
Netherlands	2.5	(357)[l]	12.9	(482)	14.3	(133)	21.9	(32)[h]	35.243	3	.001
Denmark	3.1	(64)	12.4	(145)	7.7	(26)	—		4.755	3	.20
									Pooled $x^2 = 82.319$, $df = 9$, $p < .001$		
Desires psychiatric treatment regarding homosexuality [1]											
United States	9.4	(288)[l]	14.3	(385)	21.5	(121)[h]	14.3	(56)	10.924	3	.02
Netherlands	2.4	(331)	5.3	(436)	9.6	(114)[h]	0.0	(23)[g]	11.663	3	.01
Denmark	3.2	(63)	11.3	(141)	8.0	(25)	—		3.790	3	.30
									Pooled $x^2 = 26.377$, $df = 9$, $p < .01$		

[1] Among those who have not seen a psychiatrist regarding their homosexuality.

TABLE 4

Other Characteristics,* by Living Arrangements

	Living Arrangements										
	Homosexual Roommate		Alone		Parents †		Wife ‡		x^2	df	p
Is under 35 years of age											
United States	53.3%	(319)	41.6%	(450)	63.2%	(144)[h]	22.2%	(63)[l]	41.036	3	.001
Netherlands	65.3	(357)	56.5	(487)	83.6	(134)[h]	25.0	(32)[l]	53.111	3	.001
Denmark	71.9	(64)	73.6	(144)	88.5	(26)	—		6.000	3	.20
									Pooled $x^2 = 100.147$, $df = 9$, $p < .001$		

* *h* indicates an unusually high percentage, and *l* indicates an unusually low one. Unusually high and low percentages are not designated in rows for which the probability is equal to or greater than .05.

† Respondents living with either one or both parents are combined because of a lack of significant differences between these groups.

‡ Percentages are not presented for the category "wife" in the Danish sample because of the small number of respondents (five).

TABLE 4—Continued

	Living Arrangements										
	Homosexual Roommate		Alone		Parents †		Wife ‡		x^2	df	p
Has few close friends											
United States	10.0	(290)	16.0	(419)	26.7	(135)[h]	10.0	(60)	21.238	3	.001
Netherlands	10.5	(351)	12.3	(471)	23.3	(129)[h]	24.1	(29)[h]	16.553	3	.001
Denmark	11.5	(61)	14.9	(134)	24.0	(25)	—		2.369	3	.70
									Pooled $x^2 = 40.160$, $df = 9$, $p < .001$		

CHAPTER 19

RELIGIOUS BACKGROUND

> . . . it is beyond dispute that when Americans are grouped according to their religious affiliation, significant differences in behavior can be observed from one religious category to another.[1]

In this chapter, we examine the relationship between the homosexual's religious background and the way he experiences and manages his homosexuality. Unfortunately, replication in this chapter is limited to Catholics and Protestants in our Dutch sample. This is due to the small number of persons classifying themselves as Jewish in the Dutch sample or as Catholic, Protestant, or Jewish in the Danish sample.[2] Most of the differences we find related to religious background are merely the demographic differences that exist among Catholics, Protestants, and Jews in the general population (and are described in Note 3).[3] Thus, these differences are not really related to the "homosexuality" of our respondents, but rather are more general correlates of these religions. With regard to differences which do relate to their homosexuality, we find only two.

(Neither of these differences is explained by the demographic differences that we found.)

Relating to the Heterosexual World

Our Jewish homosexuals are the most known about to their fathers (Table 1). This probably reflects Jewish family structure, which according to various studies has more equalitarianism, positive sentiments, and family involvement than do Protestant and Catholic families.[4] Thus, perhaps Jewish respondents are more known about because they confide more in their fathers.

Relating to the Homosexual World

We find no differences by religious background in the manner in which respondents relate to the homosexual world.

Psychological Problems

Given the Roman Catholic Church's condemnation of homosexuality, one might expect the Catholic homosexual to react severely to his sexual orientation. Also, the conservative sexual attitudes associated with the Jewish emphasis on "family" and "morality" might be expected to take a toll on the Jewish homosexual. However, we find no significant differences by religion on any of our eight measures of psychological problems. In the United States we do find that Jewish respondents are more likely to have visited a psychiatrist regarding their homosexuality, but this may reflect a difference in group attitudes toward psychiatry more than a difference in the extent of psychological problems (Table 1).

Summary

We found no general relationship between the life-styles or psychological problems of homosexuals and their religious backgrounds. The only differences we found regarding our respondents' homosexuality is that Jewish respondents in the United States are more known about to their fathers and more likely to have visited a psychiatrist regarding their homosexuality. (Because of the small number of Jewish respondents in our European samples, we could not attempt replication.)

Kinsey and his associates found that religious affiliation is not so strongly correlated with sexual behavior as is religiosity. They note that the "differences between religiously devout persons and religiously inactive persons of the same faith are much greater than the differences between two equally devout groups of different faiths." [5]

In the next chapter, we examine religiosity and its relationship to the respondent's management of his homosexuality.

TABLE 1

Correlates of Religious Background

	Religion								
	Catholic		Protestant		Jewish		x^2	df	p
Father knows or suspects respondent's homosexuality									
United States	36.2%	(271)	33.1%	(501)	51.6%	(93)	11.617	2	.01
Netherlands	64.2	(349)	63.6	(407)	—		1.967	2	.50
							Pooled $x^2 = 13.584$, $df = 4, p < .01$		
Visited a psychiatrist regarding homosexuality									
United States	39.0	(295)	39.8	(538)	61.7	(94)	17.177	2	.001
Netherlands	46.6	(382)	41.0	(446)	—		5.999	2	.05
							Pooled $x^2 = 23.176$, $df = 4, p < .001$		

CHAPTER 20

RELIGIOSITY

On the whole, homosexual contacts occur most frequently among the males who are not particularly active in their church connections. They occur less frequently among devout Catholics, Orthodox Jewish groups, and Protestants who are active in the church. The differences are not always great, but lie constantly in the same direction.[1]

Both Christianity and Judaism have traditionally held to the belief that homosexual practices are unnatural and immoral. Such evaluations, as we have previously noted, formed the basis for legal prohibitions of homosexuality and perhaps also for the rejection of homosexuals by the general public. Consequently, we might expect a greater condemnation of homosexuals among persons who hold strong religious beliefs than among those who are less devout.

Moreover, religious homosexuals may be more likely to experience a conflict between their sexual orientation and their religious beliefs. Feeling pressure to work out some accommodation between their homosexuality and their religious beliefs, some religious homosexuals may try to suppress their sexual orientation. Others may renounce their religion. And still others may retain both their homosexuality and their religious convictions but reduce the conflict between them by rationalization or compartmentalization.

This chapter examines the relationship between religiosity—as measured by the importance a person attributes to formal religion—and our respondents' evaluation and management of their homosexuality.[2]

Relating to the Heterosexual World (Table 1)

Respondents who attribute the most importance to religion are more worried about exposure of their homosexuality, more concerned with passing, and less known about than homosexuals for whom religion is not important at all. In addition, respondents who personally evaluate religion as important are more likely to define other people's opinions as important to them, suggesting that religious respondents are more other-directed. (None of the findings reported in this chapter is explained by demographic differences between more religious and less religious respondents.[3])

These findings may reflect a number of things. First, although religious respondents do not expect more discrimination or intolerance if they become known as homosexual, they may be less willing to risk losing the respect of others. Also, religious homosexuals may be more hesitant to disclose a sexual orientation which they believe *should* be sanctioned.

Relating to the Homosexual World (Table 2)

Compared with respondents who regard religion as not very important or not important at all, the more religious homosexuals tend to be less socially involved with other homosexuals and less likely to have experienced the most common homosexual sex practices.

Those higher in religiosity are also more likely to believe they were born homosexual. However, while homosexuals who consider religion very important may somewhat neutralize the conflict between religious dictates and homosexuality in this way, they are still the least committed to their homosexuality.

Psychological Problems (Table 3)

Not only can the reactions of others toward a homosexual cause psychological problems for him, but so can the conflict that one might assume exists *within* the homosexual himself between his sexuality and his religious beliefs. Therefore, one might expect greater psychological problems to characterize those homosexuals who view religion as more important. This is generally not the case, however. The only difference we find is that the least religious homosexuals are less likely than others to have experienced guilt, shame, or anxiety after having homosexual relations for the first time.[4]

The lack of psychological differences between more religious and less religious homosexuals suggests that, among many homosexuals, some kind of accommodation between religious beliefs and sexual orientation is achieved. Some homosexuals may refuse to relate homosexuality to religious doctrine; they may simply not think about religion when involved in homosexual activities or vice versa. Others may reinterpret traditional religion in a way that effectively neutralizes its condemnation of homosexuality. For example, a homosexual minister writes:

> The fact that we are homosexual has not changed or altered God's love for us as human beings and eternity bound souls. Christ did not die just for heterosexuals; He did not rise from

the grave and bring life, hope, and happiness only for heterosexuals; and neither are His promises and blessings only for their world. . . .

At no time in the ministry of Jesus did He touch upon the subject of homosexuality. His moral teachings regarding sexual expression are as adaptable and right for the homosexual person as they are for the heterosexual.[5]

To the extent that the religious homosexual neutralizes the conflict between homosexuality and religion, his religiosity should not produce as much strain. Thus, we expected psychological problems to be related to the perception that homosexuality violates religion. We expected the strength of this relationship to be strongest among those who attribute the most importance to religion. (That is, if a person rejects religion, whether or not he sees homosexuality as breaching it should not affect his psychological well-being.)

Holding religiosity constant, we find some support for our expectations. Among those who regard religion as very important, those who perceive homosexuality as more in violation of religion score lower in stability of self-concept (and, in the United States, self-acceptance [6]) and higher in depression than do those who do not perceive such a violation (Table 4). We find no significant relationships among those who do not regard religion as very important.[7]

These findings suggest that how well the religious homosexual can neutralize the conflict between religion and homosexuality can have consequences for his psychological well-being. As Durkheim pointed out long ago, ". . . each individual's moral consciousness expresses the collective morality in its own way. Each one sees it and understands it from a different angle." [8] When the individual's perspective obscures the conflict between his homosexuality and a value that is important to him—in this case, religion—the effects of that conflict are in some instances decreased.

Summary

Because the Judeo-Christian tradition condemns homosexuality, homosexuals who ascribe importance to religion face a dilemma. In this chapter, we examined the situation of the religious homosexual and the success of accommodations between his religious beliefs and his homosexuality. Measuring religiosity as the personal importance attributed to formal religion, we found that religious homosexuals are less known about, more concerned with passing, more worried about exposure, and more likely to attribute importance to the opinion of others. Homosexuals for whom religion is more important are also less socially involved with other homosexuals and less likely to have experienced all the sexual practices common among homosexuals, are more likely to believe they were born homosexual, and are the least committed to their homosexuality.

It was expected that the conflict between religiosity and sexuality would result in greater psychological problems for religious homosexuals. Other than showing greater guilt, shame, or anxiety after their first homosexual experience, however, this is not the case. We found that many religious homosexuals reinterpret religion as *not* violated by homosexuality. And among the most religious homosexuals, whom we had expected to show the greatest psychological problems, such an interpretation can neutralize the negative psychological effects of their dilemma. Thus, we found that some psychological problems are correlated with the perception that homosexuality violates religion, but that this relationship holds only among the most religious respondents.

TABLE 1

Relating to the Heterosexual World, by Importance Attributed to Formal Religion

	Importance of Religion						
	Very Important	Somewhat Important	Not Very Important	Not Important at All	x^2	df	p	γ
Worries about exposure of his homosexuality								
United States	80.3% (188)	81.7% (278)	78.3% (217)	65.2% (345)	28.431	3	.001	.26
Netherlands	60.3 (78)	65.9 (185)	54.8 (325)	45.9 (468)	23.861	3	.001	.23
Denmark	—	64.3 (42)	64.5 (62)	55.7 (131)	4.140	3	.30	.06
					Pooled $x^2 = 56.432$, $df = 9$, $p < .001$			
Is high in passing								
United States	72.0 (175)	64.5 (265)	63.4 (205)	55.2 (326)	14.661	3	.01	.19
Netherlands	42.1 (76)	41.6 (178)	31.1 (318)	25.6 (464)	19.772	3	.001	.22
Denmark	—	36.6 (41)	38.6 (57)	32.5 (126)	.971	3	.90	.05
					Pooled $x^2 = 35.404$, $df = 9$, $p < .001$			

Is high in being known about (Scale I)												
United States	22.6	(177)	22.0	(273)	26.6	(203)	33.8	(311)	12.494	3	.01	–.18
Netherlands	34.3	(67)	45.8	(153)	49.6	(264)	63.2	(350)	29.438	3	.001	–.28
Denmark	—		36.1	(36)	45.1	(51)	45.6	(103)	1.527	3	.70	–.05
									Pooled $x^2 = 43.459$, $df = 9$, $p < .001$			
Thinks opinions of others important												
United States	67.2	(186)	56.5	(285)	44.2	(215)	43.2	(340)	35.108	3	.001	.26
Netherlands	55.7	(70)	48.0	(173)	49.2	(321)	47.0	(451)	1.946	3	.70	.05
Denmark	—		43.9	(41)	46.8	(62)	34.6	(130)	5.517	3	.20	.22
									Pooled $x^2 = 42.571$, $df = 9$, $p < .001$			

TABLE 2

Relating to the Homosexual World, by Importance Attributed to Formal Religion

	Importance of Religion											
	Very Important		Somewhat Important		Not Very Important		Not Important at All		x^2	df	p	γ
Is high in social involvement with homosexuals												
United States	68.3%	(180)	74.9%	(271)	83.3%	(204)	81.3%	(328)	16.610	3	.001	−.20
Netherlands	74.6	(67)	80.6	(175)	85.4	(316)	83.1	(449)	5.330	3	.20	−.07
Denmark	—		80.0	(40)	96.6	(58)	89.8	(118)	20.560 *	3	.001	−.37
									Pooled $x^2 = 42.500$, df = 9, $p < .001$			
Has experienced the most common homosexual sex practices												
United States	49.1	(169)	51.2	(260)	63.3	(207)	63.9	(330)	17.586	3	.001	−.19
Netherlands	30.0	(70)	34.5	(165)	33.2	(295)	40.3	(434)	5.656	3	.20	−.12
Denmark	—		44.8	(29)	54.5	(44)	57.8	(102)	2.471	3	.50	−.18
									Pooled $x^2 = 25.713$, df= 9, $p < .01$			

Believes homosexuals are born homosexual												
United States	28.4	(190)	20.5	(288)	16.4	(220)	15.6	(347)	14.657	3	.01	.20
Netherlands	57.7	(78)	59.8	(184)	46.0	(324)	45.5	(470)	14.356	3	.01	.15
Denmark	—		39.5	(43)	41.0	(61)	36.6	(131)	.648	3	.90	.03
									Pooled $x^2 = 29.661$, df = 9, $p < .001$			
Is high in commitment												
United States	68.3	(189)	76.0	(288)	78.9	(218)	78.2	(348)	8.095	3	.05	−.13
Netherlands	70.5	(78)	70.1	(184)	70.4	(324)	80.6	(468)	14.526	3	.01	−.19
Denmark	—		76.7	(43)	79.0	(62)	81.7	(131)	1.147	3	.80	−.13
									Pooled $x^2 = 23.768$, df = 9, $p < .01$			

* While Cochran's recommendations (William G. Cochran, "Some Methods for Strengthening the Common X^2 Tests," *Biometrics* 10 [1954], pp. 417–51) for expected frequencies are not met here, the significance level for Denmark would be significant without the associated inflation, as would the pooled x^2.

TABLE 3

Psychological Problems, by Importance Attributed to Formal Religion

	Importance of Religion											
	Very Important		Somewhat Important		Not Very Important		Not Important at All		x^2	df	p	γ
Is high in guilt, shame, or anxiety after first homosexual experience												
United States	61.7%	(188)	63.9%	(285)	65.1%	(218)	50.7%	(341)	16.360	3	.001	.14
Netherlands	59.0	(78)	62.5	(184)	56.8	(322)	49.3	(467)	11.274	3	.02	.16
Denmark	—		61.4	(44)	59.0	(61)	53.0	(132)	1.455	3	.70	.13
									Pooled $x^2 = 29.089$, $df = 9$, $p < .001$			

TABLE 4

Psychological Problems among Respondents Regarding Formal Religion as Very Important, by Extent to Which Homosexuality is Perceived as Violating Formal Religion *

	Extent of Violation									
	High		Medium		Low		x^2	df	p	γ
Has low stability of self-concept										
United States	45.5%	(55)	29.3%	(82)	18.7%	(48)	8.789	2	.02	.38
Netherlands	25.0	(16)	23.1	(26)	5.7	(35)	4.780	2	.10	.50
							Pooled $x^2 = 13.569$, $df = 4$, $p < .01$			
Is high in depression										
United States	47.3	(55)	21.0	(81)	14.3	(49)	16.961	2	.001	.50
Netherlands	43.8	(16)	32.0	(25)	25.7	(35)	1.656	2	.50	.25
							Pooled $x^2 = 18.617$, $df = 4$, $p < .001$			

* Data from Denmark are not included because the number of cases is too small for this type of analysis. For example, there are only eleven Danish respondents who regard formal religion as very important.

CHAPTER 21

RACE

In this chapter, we compare black homosexuals with white homosexuals in our United States sample. Although the number of blacks is small, only thirty-nine, this comparison is made because very little is known about the black homosexual in America. (There are too few blacks in our European samples to make similar comparisons.)

There are a number of demographic differences between our black and white samples which seem unrelated to homosexuality (and these are described in Note 1).[1] The demographic differences do not explain any of the findings reported in this chapter.

Relating to the Heterosexual World (Table 1)

Compared with white homosexuals, black homosexuals expect less negative reaction to their homosexuality and anticipate less discrimination from other people on account of it. They are less concerned with passing as heterosexual and are more known as homosexual.

These findings may be interpreted as follows. Staples, in codifying extant knowledge on black sexuality, notes that in general blacks in America have less puritanical attitudes than do whites. This is accounted for by the history of blacks and their experiences in America, namely, their African past (with its particular sexual patterns), the influence of slavery (the sexual exploitation and "promiscuity" encouraged by slave masters), and the continuation of racial oppression and exploitation (which has led to life conditions which promote and sustain a naturalistic and less puritanical view of sexual relations).[2] Thus, Staples reports that while they may be no less likely than whites to regard homosexuality as an aberration, blacks are "more comfortable around homosexuals and . . . [do] not perceive them as any kind of threat."[3]

Relating to the Homosexual World (Table 2)

Compared with white homosexuals, black homosexuals more often had their first homosexual experience at an early age. We suspect that this finding simply reflects differences between blacks and whites in general, rather than differences between black and white homosexuals. That is, there is evidence of a pattern of earlier initiation to sex among black heterosexuals as well.[4] Blacks in our sample are also more likely to be having an exclusive relationship and less likely to be living with a homosexual who is not their lover.[5]

Psychological Problems (Table 3)

The only difference we find in psychological well-being is that black homosexuals are more self-accepting (although it must be noted that this difference is not large).[6] Thus, while blacks in general are usually thought to have less self-acceptance than whites, this is not the case for our respondents. (Moreover, recent research has shown that this is not always the case among the general population either.[7])

Summary

Comparisons between black and white homosexuals in the United States showed that blacks expect less negative reaction to their homosexuality and anticipate less discrimination from other people on account of it. In addition, blacks are more known as homosexual and less concerned with passing as heterosexual. It was suggested that this is related to the less puritanical attitudes of blacks and the greater tolerance of homosexuals by the black community.

Blacks in our sample more often had their first homosexual experience at an early age, are more likely to be having an exclusive homosexual relationship, and, when living with another homosexual, are more likely to be lovers with their roommate.

Finally, with regard to psychological measures, we found only one difference—that black homosexuals are somewhat more self-accepting. It seems to be the case, however, that among our homosexuals, race is generally uncorrelated with our psychological measures.

TABLE 1

Relating to the Heterosexual World, by Race

	Race							
	Black		White		x^2	df	p	γ
Anticipates or has experienced intolerance or rejection because of his homosexuality	28.9%	(38)	52.3%	(969)	15.087	1	.001	.46
Anticipates a great deal of discrimination	29.7	(37)	51.7	(948)	6.286	1	.01	.42
Is high in passing	36.8	(38)	63.6	(925)	11.124	1	.001	.50
Is high in being known about (Scale I)	53.8	(39)	25.3	(917)	29.896	1	.001	.55

TABLE 2

Relating to the Homosexual World, by Race

	Race							
	Black		White		x^2	df	p	γ
Was under thirteen years of age at first homosexual experience	52.6%	(38)	34.3%	(972)	5.429	1	.01	.36
Had exclusive homosexual relationship at time of questionnaire completion	51.3	(39)	32.5	(991)	5.156	1	.05	.37
Roommate is lover	92.3	(13)	60.9	(327)	5.253	1	.05	.77

TABLE 3

Psychological Problems, by Race

	Race					
	Black	White	x^2	df	p	γ
Has low self-acceptance	30.8% (39)	44.8% (1006)	3.008	1	.05	.29

PART V

CONCLUSIONS

CHAPTER 22

THEORETICAL IMPLICATIONS

The orientation of this study was derived from the sociological viewpoint known as the societal reaction perspective.[1] While our aim has been primarily to examine sociological and social psychological aspects of homosexual adaptations, our data do have theoretical implications for this particular perspective per se, and it is to these that we now turn.[2]

Societal Reaction and Its Effects

In our cross-cultural comparisons, we find European homosexuals to be less threatened by the heterosexual world than are American homosexuals, though we generally find no corresponding differences in psychological well-being. This suggests a number of points concerning societal reaction and its possible effects on homosexuals.

First, what is the nature of the *societal reaction?* The answer to this question is complex.[3] On the most formal level, it takes the form of particular legislation. But in practice, the effect of such legislation depends less on what the law says than on how it is enforced. And, as we have seen, law enforcement practices can vary among various city administrations, police chiefs, individual officers, and so on.

In addition, we believe that for the majority of homosexuals in the societies we studied, the impact of the legal situation is not *direct*. Instead, we believe, the most universal (though not necessarily the most serious) effect of legal repression is to symbolize society's rejection of the homosexual. This rejection seems to be a major source of the homosexual's problems.

On a less formal level, societal reaction refers to the responses of heterosexuals in everyday interaction. And on this level the complexity of societal reaction becomes even more apparent. Although public opinion polls show most Americans to be antihomosexual, they do not tell us how heterosexuals actually react to homosexuals in concrete situations. As many commentators point out, morality is "situated," and it is never clear how abstract rules and moral judgments will be utilized in a particular situation.[4] Douglas writes: "There is no necessary 'logical' or 'rational' relationship between our abstract moral statements and our situational uses of moral statements that would allow us to deduce the situational from the abstract or infer the abstract from the situational." [5]

How a heterosexual responds to a person he knows or suspects is homosexual depends on many factors: the social context, the relationship between the parties, their aims and interests, the things they see as relevant to the situation, and their perception of "what is going on." Even though our European countries are more tolerant in terms of attitudes and legislation, the daily life of the European homosexual as a homosexual may not differ from that of the American homosexual as much as we might expect. In other words, in middle-class society (from which most of our respondents come) American homosexuals may not confront personal "rejection" much more frequently or to the degree that the "attitudinal" differences might suggest.

Second, what and how far-reaching are the *effects* of societal reaction? We would suggest that societal rejection should not be conceived of in terms of a "linear" model. Rather, given a certain level of "rejection," which we found in all three societies, additional increments of rejection seem to have little effect. We also question the *invariable* importance of the effect of general societal reactions for psychological well-being. Among the homosexual's problems, perhaps societal rejection is *not directly* the most important, and the effect of societal reaction on psychological problems may be small compared with the effects of other factors, namely, what we have called the "social nature of homosexuality" (Chapter 7). A complete picture of the effects of societal reaction, however, might be masked in our study by a sampling problem. Homosexuals who are the most covert and inactive in the subculture are probably not adequately represented in our sample. If the societal reaction model is correct, it would be among these homosexuals that we might expect to find the greatest psychological effects because they do not have subcultural supports. A complete test of the model, therefore, may be precluded because of sampling difficulties.

What we *can* say for now is that the model is not specific and detailed enough to avoid reifications and overgeneralizations. For example, the key variable may not be the societal reaction so much as how the person adapts to it. Thus, the negative effects of societal reaction may be neutralized by living with another homosexual and being involved in the homosexual subculture. The societal reaction approach seems to suggest, on the one hand, that such adaptations do have positive consequences but, on the other hand, it is unclear as to whether societal reaction should still produce negative effects, regardless of such adaptations.[6] Thus, some theoretical clarification is needed regarding the extent to which the impact of societal reaction is limited by the person's adaptations.

Finally, we would suggest that, when looking at the effects of societal reaction, one look at the distinctively *sociological* as well as *social psychological* effects. For homosexuals, we have suggested, the sociological consequences of societal reaction include the development of the homosexual subculture, militant homophile movements, and distinctive homosexual life styles.

Adaptations to Societal Reaction

We have been discussing societal reaction and its effects on homosexuals. Now we examine the adaptations homosexuals make to their "deviant" status. These adaptations mediate the effects of societal reaction, and they must be appreciated if one is to understand how societal reaction affects homosexuals.

The Subculture

In explaining our findings, we suggested that homosexuals in our three societies have different ways of adapting to their most salient problems. Homosexuals in the United States, due to the particular response toward them and their particular sociohistorical context, rely more on the homosexual subculture and/or militant action. Homosexuals in Europe, on the other hand, rely more on other solutions. Each type of solution may be effective in the country where it is used most, resulting in few cross-cultural differences in psychological well-being.

Each mode of adaptation, however, seems to have its costs. For the homosexual in the United States, legal repression and low social acceptance make for a thriving homosexual subculture in which some of the homosexual's problems can be handled. The cost of this adaptation, however, is segregation from the wider society. For the European homosexual, there is greater tolerance and a lack of legal repression. This seems to make for a relatively undeveloped homosexual subculture, however, and the European homosexual lacks many of the supportive homosexual institutions found, for example, in San Francisco.

Such considerations show how the conventional world strongly influences the character of the "deviant world." At the same time, we do not wish to suggest that the development of deviant subcultures is provoked solely by particular societal reactions. Other important preconditions involve, for example, the difficulty of carrying out the "deviant" behaviors without the support and/or cooperation of other like individuals. We are suggesting, however, that the homosexual subculture (and perhaps *any* subculture) cannot be understood in isolation from the wider society in which it is found.

It is our impression that greater involvement in the subculture is generally related to greater social involvement with other homosexuals, and our findings show the importance of such social involvement for the homosexual's well-being. What is needed is more investigation into *the manner* in which social involvement with other homosexuals produces its positive effects. Learning from other homosexuals who function as role models seems to be one major process. In addition, from other homosexuals one learns more subtle stereotypes of heterosexuals, how to handle a homosexual social identity, and so on. At the same time, other homosexuals give one support in the trial and error process of becoming homosexual. Acculturation to a homosexual way of life routinizes behaviors that perhaps initially seemed shameful; this makes acceptance of the self-label "homosexual" easier. Such acculturation may also facilitate normalization, that is, placing homosexual behaviors in an acceptable interpretive framework provided by the subculture. In general, our findings appear to support the notion, suggested by the societal reaction approach, that associating with similarly situated others enhances a sense of well-being.

Finally, we must note that in the past, deviant groups have been conceptualized in more or less passive terms. They have been viewed as inward looking, concerning themselves primarily with bandaging the wounds their members receive from a hostile conventional world. Recently, however, many social deviants have begun to demand social change to alleviate their problems (as they themselves define those problems rather than as "experts" do). This "politicization of deviance," as Horowitz and Liebowitz call it, suggests that we will see a merger between political marginality and social deviance which not only will create a new style of politics, but also a new style of "being different." [7] In any case, sociology must revise its theoretical formulations in the light of these changes. We must recognize the homosexual subculture as having active political interests, and we must pay as much attention to the demands and conceptualizations of the homophile movement concerning homosexuality as to those of psychiatrists, sociologists, and legal authorities.[8]

Passing

Rather than engulfing themselves in the homosexual subculture, the majority of homosexuals make only occasional and transitory use of its institutions. Moreover, since most homosexuals prefer not to be known as such, they pass in the everyday world as heterosexual. Thus, many commentators conceptualize passing as dividing the homosexual's life into two worlds. One is the homosexual world where he can be "himself" without fear; the other is the heterosexual world in which he spends most of his time, worried about being exposed, and "on stage" playing a role he would rather not. All this is believed to produce great psychological stress.

On the basis of our research, however, we would conceptualize passing and its effects in a different manner.

First, we found that any psychological problems associated with passing are associated more with worrying about exposure and anticipating sanctions than with passing per se. Second, while the "two-worlds" model may be analytically useful in attempting to understand the homosexual, the findings of the present study suggest that there is a danger in reifying it. Passing seems to be a more subtle phenomenon. Due to the predominance of heterosexual socialization, the homosexual knows how to present himself as heterosexual without much learning or practice. In addition, passing becomes routinized. The homosexual is not confronted by two highly distinct lives, and only on certain occasions does he ever phenomenologically differentiate his life world into two.[9]

If the homosexual does not necessarily feel "on stage" in his relationship to the heterosexual world, it must also be understood that his relationship to the homosexual world is not without stress. In fact, it could be argued that the covert homosexual runs more risk of "discovery" when he is in the homosexual world, where he is behaving "homosexually," than in the heterosexual world where there are fewer public occasions which might call his sexuality into question. Our data support Leznoff and Westley's findings, for example, that fear may exist among higher-status homosexuals when they make forays into the homosexual world in search of partners. Their main concern is that they may be recognized as homosexual at a later date while attempting to pass in heterosexual company. The homosexual world, therefore, for many homosexuals, is not a fully comfortable refuge.

By the same token, it is also interesting to note that bisexuals in our sample, who are generally imagined to be torn between opposite worlds and impulses, do not turn out to have any more psychological problems than do exclusive homosexuals. We view the lack of psychological differences for bisexuals and others who pass as heterosexuals as evidence of the human capacity for adaptation and compartmentalization, which social scientists often ignore.[10]

Moreover, other factors which diminish the supposed effects of passing must be recognized. Homosexuals with high occupational status are found to be very secretive but to have fewer psychological problems than do those with lower occupational status, who are generally more overt. Thus, the psychological advantages accompanying higher-status positions outweigh any psychological disadvantages which may accrue from the fear of discovery.

It would appear, therefore, that theoretical descriptions of passing, and "secret deviance" in general, should be modified to show two things. (1) Phenomenologically, a person's "deviance" is not as invariably salient, nor as much in conflict with other parts of his life, as is often supposed. (2) The stressful effects of passing are modified by a number of other factors, some of which we have outlined.

Finally, theoretical models of the consequences of being known about need to be modified, especially for certain types of social deviance. Our findings show that being known about, rather than producing more stress for the homosexual in relation to the heterosexual world, can, in certain ways, make for a generally less stressful situation.[11] Our interpretation is that the known homosexual finds that he can still function adequately and continues to do so with a more realistic conception of societal reactions.

Demographic Factors

Previously we quoted Simon and Gagnon's injunction that researchers studying homosexuality should overcome their "excessive concern with the sexuality of the individual." In other words, simply knowing a person is homosexual does not tell us much about him. His other social characteristics will help us understand the type of homosexual he is and how he handles his sexuality.

Occupational status, for example, seems to operate this way. Homosexuals in high-status occupations identify more with members of their social class than with other homosexuals, associate more with heterosexuals, and are more covert. In this case, then, social status apparently affects the ways in which the person manages his homosexuality.

Race also has an important effect. The fact that black homosexuals pass less and are more known about is associated with the greater tolerance of homosexuals shown by the black community.

Age is another demographic variable that affects the social and psychological character of the homosexual's life. Contrary to the expectations of many homosexuals and professionals, older homosexuals are found to be as well off psychologically as younger homosexuals. Like the older heterosexual, the older homosexual adapts to aging (probably earlier than his heterosexual counterpart) and does not exhibit the psychological problems that younger homosexuals envision.

Although we have discussed social factors that seem to affect the homosexual's adaptations, one must not extrapolate an overly deterministic model of the way the homosexual manages his life. The homosexual is a very active participant in working out a congenial life style, and there is a large amount of variance that is unexplained by all of these factors.[12]

Conceptualizing Homosexuals and Homosexuality

Our final suggestion is that homosexuality be conceptualized in terms of social statuses and roles rather than as a condition. "Homosexual" is a social status, and the role expectations surrounding it account for the types of homosexuals that any society produces. Thus, McIntosh suggests, some societies have a great deal of homosexual activity but no "homosexuals." [13] In other words, the notion of "the homosexual," for some purposes, can usefully be seen as a cultural product, a status. This status is not inherent in the individuals associated with it, but it influences them by organizing other persons' reactions to them and giving those persons who occupy the status a stereotyped set of traits to orient their own behaviors and attitudes toward themselves.[14]

Thus, it is important to look at the types of homosexual roles which a given society delineates and how homosexuals themselves attempt to modify the society's concept of "homosexual." Gay Liberation illustrates one such attempt to change a homosexual stereotype. Also, in terms of "coming out" and self-acceptance, Dank has suggested that persons who eventually identify themselves as homosexual must perceive a change in the "meaning of the cognitive category *homosexual* before placing themselves in the category." [15] In short, the politics of identity vis-à-vis the cultural conception of the homosexual has important effects on heterosexuals and homosexuals alike, and deserves further study, especially in understanding the homosexuals of tomorrow. It is our wish, moreover, that societies come to conceptualize homosexuality in less negative terms, and as not being "deviant," thereby reducing the differentiation of human beings on the basis of sexual orientation.[16]

CHAPTER 23

PRACTICAL CONSIDERATIONS

In this chapter we suggest ways in which the homosexual's immediate mode of adaptation might be improved. We then discuss strategies for bringing about changes in those societal conditions which make such adaptations necessary.

Individual Adaptations

We feel that the results of our research have implications for the individual homosexual seeking a satisfactory way of life. As our findings are based on survey research and limited field work, however, our suggestions are broad. Moreover, they reflect probability statements rather than certainties and, as they deal with categories of persons, may not fit the contingencies of a particular individual's situation. In addition, we did not study the various longitudinal routes to successful adaptations. With these reservations in mind, we present grids which may be employed as a broad set of guidelines.

Probably our most salient finding pertains to the beneficial effects of a supportive environment. Thus, the homosexual may want to cultivate social relations with other homosexuals and/or utilize the institutions and publications of the homosexual subculture. Through such involvement he most likely will learn that a homosexual identity may not have all the negative consequences that are feared, and perhaps may have more rewards than he has considered. He may, through such association, also learn how to best handle the practical problems of being homosexual, for example, how to handle parents, deal with job discrimination, make the best use of the institutions in the homosexual subculture.[1]

New York and San Francisco do have very well-developed homosexual subcultures, but it is generally not necessary to move to one of these cities in order to get involved in the homosexual world. Many other American cities have an established (though less open) homosexual scene, and it will be recalled that respondents who do not live in New York or San Francisco have no more psychological problems than those who do.

The homosexual should also remember that his sexual needs are only one aspect of his life and should think about the nonsexual features of the city he is considering before he decides to move.

If the homosexual *is* interested in a very well-developed homosexual subculture, Amsterdam and Copenhagen are overrated. Homosexual folklore notwithstanding, New York and San Francisco are better developed in terms of the proliferation of homosexual institutions.

The homosexual should consider rooming with another homosexual. In general, it seems best for him not to live with parents.

Also, there are some exaggerated notions about the consequences of passing. First is the belief that passing is inevitably debilitating psychologically. Our data show that passing does not produce as much psychological strain as many assume and that much of the strain associated with passing is due to fears of exposure. The homosexual should keep this in mind if passing is the style of adaptation he chooses to adopt. Moreover, being more known about is generally not associated with greater psychological stress. Thus, while passing is not so psychologically harmful as many assume, neither is being known about likely to be as bad as is feared. We would add a caveat, however. Whereas we are referring to the long-term effects of being known about, it is often the case that the experience of "coming out"—of initially telling parents, friends, and so on, about one's homosexuality—can be a distressing period.

A second exaggerated notion in connection with passing is that homosexuals in higher-status occupations typically suffer more psychological problems than do those in lower-status occupations due to a greater need for discretion. Our data indicate that, to the contrary, homosexuals in higher-status occupations have fewer psychological problems. Thus, the homosexual should not let such fears limit his occupational aspirations.

The homosexual should realize that others may behave less negatively to homosexuals than he expects. Compared with those less known about, homosexuals who are more known about, and therefore presumably in a position to more realistically evaluate others' reactions, less often rate others as actually acting very negatively. Since expecting more negative reactions is associated with greater psychological problems, one should try not to exaggerate how negative people's actions might be. This is not to say, however, that there are not many persons to whom homosexuality is abhorrent, and some of these persons might react in this way. In any case, the homosexual should try not to internalize the moral evaluations of such people.

The homosexual should in general re-evaluate moral interpretations which make him uncomfortable with his sexuality. If he values traditional religion, he should realistically consider the historical character of its pronouncements. He might also examine the moral frameworks provided by religious groups that are more accepting of homosexuality (especially note the emergence of "homosexual" churches, for example, the Reverend Troy Perry's church in Los Angeles).

The homosexual should try to rid himself of notions that homosexuality is "sick" and that he would necessarily be better off if he were heterosexual. If he seeks counseling, he should try to avoid practitioners who subscribe to these views.

The homosexual should recognize that the usual picture of the aging homosexual is a caricature. The facts we have presented suggest that as homosexuals get older, their life styles may change somewhat, but that psychological problems do not necessarily increase with age.

Bisexuals do not seem to exhibit the problems that many writers invariably attribute to them. So those who enjoy both homosexual and heterosexual sex may want to continue their bisexuality without worrying about the inevitability of some of the stereotyped consequences.

Homosexuals need not shun all heterosexuals. There are many heterosexuals who do not reject homosexuals. Relationships with such heterosexuals can be socially and psychologically rewarding.

The homosexual shares far more in common with many heterosexuals than he may realize. While he should enjoy the homosexual aspect of his life and while identification with other homosexuals is functional, he need not make his sexual orientation *the* central part of his identity.

Suggestions such as these are not always easy to adopt, but we have presented data which support their efficacy. We also appreciate that while generally it may not be easy to be homosexual (especially in the United States), the adaptations and satisfactions of homosexuals are often ignored. (Thus, we find no major differences in psychological well-being between homosexuals and the general population, nor do many other studies find such differences.) In conclusion, as one homosexual writer suggests, a more balanced and realistic view of the homosexual's situation is required.

> There is prejudice, and now and then oppression. But on the average, comparatively few people are actually ever arrested, fired from a job, or abused for being gay. . . . Our younger, less liberated brothers and sisters seize upon every isolated example of gay tragedy as another proof of how sad it is to be gay. It behooves those of us who really like being gay and who want to help our self oppressed sisters and brothers to accentuate the positive side of gay life.[2]

Societal Change

It is evident that among homosexuals, psychological and social functioning is affected by the perception and internalization of societal rejection. Prejudice and discrimination do exist. It seems obvious, therefore, that a major strategy in alleviating some of the homosexual's problems is to alter reactions to homosexuals. We now discuss what can be done toward this end with particular reference to the United States.

Institutions

Research on racial minorities has shown that one of the more effective ways to make societal reactions less negative is to change the institutions that sustain discrimination. When this is done, a change in individuals' attitudes often follows.[3] Therefore, those aspects of social organization that support the moral meanings of homosexuality as sinful, immoral, dangerous, perverted, revolting, or sick should be a primary target for change. The following arenas are seen by most commentators—homosexual and heterosexual alike—as most in need of change.

Law and law enforcement/As we discussed in detail in Chapters 2–4, the law and its enforcement discriminate against adult consenting homosexuals, despite the absence of evidence that such behavior is harmful to the persons involved or to society in general. Not only does this reinforce negative evaluations of homosexuality among the general public, but it causes great hardship for many individual homosexuals.

In the United States, for example, if one has ever been arrested for a homosexual offense, whether convicted or not, he may find his employment opportunities limited. Many employers, both public and private, ask whether a job applicant has ever been arrested. If the answer is "yes," the employer can obtain the specific offense from court records. In those cases where arrests do not lead to conviction, arrest records should be expunged. Otherwise, the employment chances of many persons are unjustly limited, and this is especially true for homosexuals.[4]

In addition, antihomosexual laws and law enforcement practices extract a price from the heterosexual majority. Proponents of homosexual law reform point out, for example, that civil liberties in general are threatened by such intrusions into the realm of private morality.[5] This realm, the Wolfenden Committee states bluntly, is "not the law's business." [6] Sodomy laws are considered by many to be unconstitutional in that they exceed the legitimate police powers of the state and attempt to sustain religious dictates.[7]

Perhaps more important than the sodomy laws are laws against soliciting, lewd conduct, and so forth, under which American homosexuals are most often actually prosecuted.

To obtain evidence, the police resort to entrapment and such devices as decoys, peepholes, and one-way mirrors in public rest rooms. Such practices degrade the ideals of the law and law enforcement, to say the least, and often make for police corruption. In addition, they are a waste of the time and resources of law enforcement agencies. We also see no reason why behavior such as homosexual solicitation should be a matter for the criminal law.

In conclusion, we recommend that antihomosexual laws be repealed and that the employment of other laws to harass homosexuals be stopped. Fears regarding the possible negative consequences of doing this are not supported by logic or data. Moreover, the burden of proof regarding the harmful effects of homosexuality should lie on the shoulders of those who insist on such laws and legal practices.[8]

The federal government/Government policies and practices in the United States attempt to exclude homosexuals from federal employment. The basis for such a position was a Senate report in 1950 (during the Communist scare) which claimed that homosexuals are unsuitable for government employment.[9] The report assumes that homosexuals are emotionally unstable, attempt to seduce heterosexuals, have a "corrosive" influence on other employees, attempt to hire other homosexuals for government jobs, and are susceptible to blackmail. The recommendations of that report became part of Civil Service policy, resulting in the removal or exclusion of suspected homosexuals from employment by the federal government.[10]

Exclusion of homosexuals from federal employment on such dubious grounds is clearly discriminatory. Furthermore, although there may be truth in some of the allegations—for example, susceptibility to blackmail—it is often overlooked that the same logic applies to others, such as married heterosexuals having extramarital affairs, and the government policy of firing persons found to be homosexual itself contributes to the potential for blackmail.[11]

Nonfederal government and private business/Although other employers may not have formal regulations to exclude homosexuals, informal procedures often discriminate against them. In many states, homosexuals are not allowed to be teachers, and arrests for homosexual acts (regardless of conviction) often disqualify a person from legally practicing certain professions, such as medicine, dentistry, and law. (Also, professional licenses are usually denied or withdrawn without a hearing.)

With private employers, the situation is no better. Even in a relatively liberal place like New York City:

> It is currently the practice of many companies . . . to refuse jobs to homosexuals, supposedly to "protect company morale" when, in reality, the applicant is rejected for being homosexual per se in spite of his qualifications and mode of behavior.
>
> Employers use several devices to discover whether an applicant is homosexual: special arrangements with employment agencies in which the agencies use a code to indicate whether, to their knowledge, the job seeker is homosexual; a request on the application form for the release of draft records, which disclose any references to homosexual behavior; a request for information regarding the draft classification of applicants who have not served in the military, and the marital status of all persons seeking employment; and employers sometimes contact private agencies whose sole purpose is to gather information on applicants in order to determine anything which might not be in what the firm considers its best interests.[12]

In this atmosphere, most homosexuals, and especially those in the more prestigious occupations, feel forced to hide or deny their homosexuality. Except perhaps for disclosure of one's homosexuality to his family, the threat to employment is probably (for the American homosexual) the most serious consequence of being publicly labeled homosexual.

The military/In line with federal employment policies, known homosexuals are excluded from the United States military.[13] Until recently, questions about homosexual behavior were asked at induction.[14] If a homosexual admitted his sexual orientation, he was disqualified from serving, and his homosexuality became a matter of official record (which could then become known to others). If he did not, the homosexual risked discovery while in the military. In the vast majority of cases, homosexuals who are discovered in the military are given a less than honorable discharge. Such a discharge makes the homosexual ineligible for veterans benefits. It also means that his future employment can be threatened, since discharge papers are often asked for by prospective employers. Injustice in this situation is clear in the manner in which homosexuals are processed by the military and in the fact that prior military record plays little part in the separation of homosexuals from the military.[15]

Religion/As we stated at the beginning of the book, religious dogma has played a large part in initiating and sustaining negative definitions of homosexuality in the Western world. And although today religion has less influence on people's daily lives, many of our customs and moralities are implicitly based upon religious codes. We believe that religion must be a primary target for change because the persons who are most negative toward homosexuals are often religious and because religious institutions are still influential enough to become catalysts for positive change.

One target for change should, therefore, be the clergy. If the perspective of the clergy can be changed, we may then persuade them to help dissipate the conception of "homosexual as sinner" among the laity.

Some churches have taken steps in this direction. This is best exemplified in the Netherlands. In the United States, the Unitarian General Assembly in 1970 rejected the "sickness theory" of homosexuality and endorsed homosexuals' civil rights. The Unitarians also called for a special effort on the part of their members to assist homosexuals and accept homosexuals in their ministry. National assemblies of the United Presbyterians and the Lutheran Church in America have also endorsed homosexual law reform. While it is difficult to determine the influence of such endorsements, at the very least they deny religious legitimation to intolerance and can be of some consolation to religious homosexuals.

Attitudes

The preceding institutional areas seem to us to be major targets for change because of their support of a moral meaning of homosexuality that leads to grave injustices for a large minority. Our data suggest, however, that in the long run, the attitudes of rejection, fear, and contempt, and the latent hostility in everyday encounters must be changed as well. Informal attitudes may be difficult to change due to various factors about which we can only speculate, namely, the psychological function that prejudice has for some persons, the sociological role of minority groups for majority groups, the phobia about sex found especially in America, and so forth. Nonetheless, attempts should be made to combat antihomosexual attitudes directly. The following suggestions are offered to that end.

Sex education/Sex education courses usually restrict themselves to heterosexual behavior and reproduction. It would seem that accurate information on homosexuality, introduced in a *nonmoralistic* framework, and as a not uncommon form of sexual expression, would affect heterosexuals' attitudes in a positive way.[16] While research in other areas of prejudice suggests that its impact is limited, education may help to dispel falsehoods about a phenomenon that is too often presented as sick, alien, and bizarre.[17] In addition to lessening rejection by heterosexuals, such education would also alleviate many of the unnecessary identity problems of homosexually oriented people who will also be among the students in such classes.

Also, sex education should not be limited to young people. Such courses should be compulsory for people who have much to do with homosexuals, including police, physicians, and especially psychiatrists. These groups have, in the past, played a major role in perpetuating negative views of homosexuality.

The mass media/The Task Force on Homosexuality noted the need to study the effects on the public of the portrayal of homosexuality in literature, drama, films, and so on. At present, the media seem to sustain prevailing stereotypes of the homosexual. The stereotype of the male homosexual as effeminate, flighty, and amusing often appears on television. Motion pictures have only begun to treat homosexuality in a more objective manner. Before the late 1960's, motion pictures used homosexuality, to quote one reviewer, "as a sensational third act revelation, after which the character discovered to be homosexual must obligingly commit suicide." [18] Whereas television has emphasized the effeminate aspect of the homosexual stereotype, movies have focused on homosexuals as sick and guilt-ridden.

How a more balanced picture of homosexuals might be gained through the media is difficult to determine. The greater openness that characterizes movies today may make for more representative films. For example, a character's homosexuality might be presented as secondary to his other attributes. A Western movie might explore the role of homosexuality in a society devoid of females. With regard to television, the presence of homosexuals on talk shows might counterbalance the stereotypes provided by comedy shows. The activities of ethnic minority groups against the dissemination of stereotypes in the media have provided a model that homosexual militants have copied; how successful they will be remains to be seen.

Research on the effectiveness of changing attitudes through the mass media is not encouraging.[19] Such research has shown that people avoid influence by perspectives contrary to their own by simply not exposing themselves to such perspectives or by misinterpreting them. By supporting more humane attitudes toward homosexuals, however, the changes we have suggested could make people more hesitant to act upon their negative attitudes.[20]

Other public support/Research has found that the more credible, attractive, and powerful the person who is urging a change in attitudes, the greater the likelihood of change.[21] Thus, if persons who are credible, attractive, and powerful present more favorable attitudes toward homosexuals, then other people's attitudes may be modified.

In terms of credibility, professionals such as physicians, psychiatrists, and social scientists could be effective. As greater sex education in medical schools provides physicians with up-to-date knowledge on homosexuality, their attitudes may become less negative. Psychiatrists seem to be moving increasingly away from the "sickness" model of homosexuality. Social scientists, too, are moving away from seeing homosexuality as intrinsically a "social problem" to viewing the societal reaction toward homosexuals as the major problem. As members of these professions in increasing numbers view homosexuality as a nonpathological variant of sexual expression, efforts must be made to get them to communicate these views to the general public.[22]

Sources who are attractive to the general public might

include professional entertainers and athletes. Consider, for example, the effect on stereotypes of homosexuals if a number of professional football players admitted to being homosexual. Consider also the effect of entertainers' plugging homosexual civil rights on television, as many do for ethnic minorities.

Finally, the power of the source is an important element in changing attitudes. Politicians in Great Britain have championed the rights of homosexuals, despite widespread lack of public support. In America today, an important gesture would be for those in power to acknowledge and support the recommendations of the Task Force on Homosexuality.

Homosexuals as a Minority Group

In addition to changing institutional discrimination against and negative attitudes toward homosexuals, a third strategy should be to obtain *positive* support for homosexuals from the larger society. For the time being, this would be facilitated, we feel, by a reconceptualization of homosexuals as a minority group and by accepting their life style as just one of many in a diversified society.[23] At the same time, it is our hope that ultimately homosexuals will not have to be differentiated as a group.

Until tolerance is translated into acceptance, the harmful effects of rejection will remain (as seen in Amsterdam and Copenhagen). Associated problems should be mitigated by providing special aid for homosexuals. Not only should opportunities for the integration of homosexuals into the wider society be available, but support should also be given to specifically homosexual institutions. The Netherlands can provide a model for such affirmative action in the governmental support given to homosexuals, for example, including homosexuals in the concerns of the Minorities Board.

Most important, however, we believe, will be the actions that homosexuals can take on their own behalf. First, homosexuals must develop the foundations for collective action. Although the homophile movement represents a trend in this direction, homosexuals in general have been characterized by their lack of group identity and unity. One finds among them nothing resembling the notion of "soul brother" or the reputed ethnocentrism of the Jewish people. Homosexuals must develop some sense of group identification and cohesion. To achieve this, we believe, they must be willing to be more open about being homosexual.

Compared with other minority groups such as blacks, homosexuals can pass easily, and in fact most do so.[24] While we appreciate the unpleasant effects disclosure of one's homosexuality might have, we feel that in the *long run* the beneficial effects of greater openness would be substantial in bringing about societal change. But, as one "gay liberationist" notes, ". . . the fear of coming out is not paranoia; the stakes are high. . . . Each . . . must make the steps toward openness at . . . [his] own speed and on . . . [his] own impulses."[25]

Greater openness on the part of an increasing number of homosexuals, however, would have cumulative effects. Homosexually oriented young people would be more likely to have positive homosexual role models with which to identify. And as heterosexuals realize that people they know are homosexual, they are likely to recognize that their stereotypes are distortions and to rethink their views on homosexuality.

More importantly, only when homosexuals are more willing to be known as such will they be able to use the techniques of social action which have proved effective for other minority groups. These would include political activism, the expansion of self-help organizations, and the investment of resources in homosexual institutions.

In short, homosexuals must, as a group, seek to end their tradition of silence and force the larger society to confront the issue of homosexuality and its treatment of homosexuals. By publicly acknowledging their homosexuality, and by using the methods of other minority groups, homosexuals may be able to change those features of society that have caused them problems in the past. In this, they will be assisted by the present flow of social change, especially the younger generation's greater acceptance of minority groups and different life-styles. Ultimately, however, it seems that the homosexuals' destiny lies in the efforts they make on their own behalf.

APPENDIX: QUESTIONNAIRE*

INSTRUCTIONS

Indicate the Extent to Which You Agree That the Statements Below Characterize You and Your Feelings.

AFTER READING EACH STATEMENT:

CIRCLE	*IF YOU . . .*
SA	STRONGLY AGREE
A	AGREE
?	ARE *NOT SURE*
D	DISAGREE
SD	STRONGLY DISAGREE

---

1. I feel that I have a number of good qualities	SA	A	?	D	SD
2. Being a homosexual is something that is completely beyond one's control	SA	A	?	D	SD
3. Homosexuals are *usually* superior in many ways to nonhomosexuals	SA	A	?	D	SD
4. I take a positive attitude toward myself .	SA	A	?	D	SD

* This questionnaire is the one which was distributed to the New York City samples. Questions which are specific to locale were deleted or modified for the other samples.

5. No one is going to care much what happens to you, when you get right down to it .... SA A ? D SD
6. What consenting adults do in private is nobody's business as long as they do not hurt other people .... SA A ? D SD
7. If you don't watch out for yourself, people will take advantage of you .... SA A ? D SD
8. Human nature is really cooperative ..... SA A ? D SD
9. I look effeminate .... SA A ? D SD
10. Most people can be trusted .... SA A ? D SD
11. Homosexuality may be best described as an illness .... SA A ? D SD
12. On the whole, I am satisfied with myself SA A ? D SD
13. I am not as happy as others seem to be . SA A ? D SD
14. I prefer to pass by friends or people I know but have not seen for a long time unless they speak to me first .... SA A ? D SD
15. I feel that I'm a person of worth, at least on an equal plane with others .... SA A ? D SD
16. I find that it is easier for me to talk to male homosexuals than to male heterosexuals .... SA A ? D SD
17. I find that it is easier for me to talk to male heterosexuals than to female heterosexuals .... SA A ? D SD
18. I tend to behave effeminately when in the heterosexual world .... SA A ? D SD
19. All in all, I am inclined to feel that I am a failure .... SA A ? D SD
20. I do not like to associate socially with a person who has a reputation (among heterosexuals) of being homosexual .... SA A ? D SD
21. I do not care who knows about my homosexuality .... SA A ? D SD
22. I have a harder time than other people in gaining friends .... SA A ? D SD
23. When I was a teenager I was unpopular with girls .... SA A ? D SD
24. I wish I were not homosexual .... SA A ? D SD
25. I would not want to give up my homosexuality even if I could .... SA A ? D SD
26. I certainly feel useless at times .... SA A ? D SD

27. I have a harder time than other people in making conversation .... SA A ? D SD
28. I often find myself "putting on an act" to impress people .... SA A ? D SD
29. People have made fun of me because I am a homosexual .... SA A ? D SD
30. Homosexuals and heterosexuals are basically different in more ways than simply sexual preference .... SA A ? D SD
31. I am able to do things as well as most other people .... SA A ? D SD
32. Most people are inclined to look out for themselves .... SA A ? D SD
33. I feel that I don't have enough friends . SA A ? D SD
34. Usually it is the most unethical, immoral, or hypocritical members of heterosexual society that are most likely to condemn homosexuals .... SA A ? D SD
35. I have noticed that my ideas about myself seem to change very quickly .... SA A ? D SD
36. I feel "closer" to a heterosexual of my own social class than to a homosexual who is of a much lower social class .... SA A ? D SD
37. I feel that nothing, or almost nothing, can change the opinion I currently hold of myself .... SA A ? D SD
38. It would not bother me if I had children who were homosexual .... SA A ? D SD
39. I am easily embarrassed .... SA A ? D SD
40. Some days I have a very good opinion of myself; other days I have a very poor opinion of myself .... SA A ? D SD
41. There have been times when I felt as though I were going to have a nervous breakdown .... SA A ? D SD
42. In general, I feel in low spirits most of the time .... SA A ? D SD
43. I get a lot of fun out of life .... SA A ? D SD
44. There is nothing immoral about being a homosexual .... SA A ? D SD
45. A person is born homosexual or heterosexual .... SA A ? D SD
46. I often feel downcast and dejected ..... SA A ? D SD

47. I am probably responsible for the fact that I am a homosexual .... SA A ? D SD
48. On the whole, I think I am quite a happy person .... SA A ? D SD
49. Homosexuality tends to have a negative effect on the society at large .... SA A ? D SD
50. Homosexuality may be best described as a mental illness .... SA A ? D SD
51. I tend to be a rather shy person .... SA A ? D SD
52. I would not mind being seen in public with a person who has the reputation (among heterosexuals) of being homosexual .... SA A ? D SD
53. I wish I could have more respect for myself .... SA A ? D SD
54. I often feel very self-conscious .... SA A ? D SD
55. I tend to behave effeminately when I'm with other homosexuals .... SA A ? D SD
56. I feel I do not have much to be proud of SA A ? D SD
57. At times I think I am no good at all .... SA A ? D SD
58. I often feel ill at ease when I'm in the presence of others .... SA A ? D SD

59. OF THE FOLLOWING PEOPLE, CHECK *HOW MANY* SUSPECT OR KNOW THAT YOU ARE HOMOSEXUAL:

	1 All	2 Most	3 More than Half	4 About Half	5 Less than Half	6 Only a Few	7 None
Heterosexuals whom you know	—	—	—	—	—	—	—
Male heterosexual friends ..	—	—	—	—	—	—	—
Female heterosexual friends	—	—	—	—	—	—	—
Aunts and uncles	—	—	—	—	—	—	—
Neighbors	—	—	—	—	—	—	—
Work associates	—	—	—	—	—	—	—
People whom *you* suspect or know are homosexual ..	—	—	—	—	—	—	—

60. DO ANY OF THE FOLLOWING PEOPLE KNOW OR SUSPECT THAT YOU ARE HOMOSEXUAL? (IF YOUR MOTHER OR FATHER IS DECEASED, CHECK WHETHER THEY DID KNOW OR SUSPECT AND PUT A "D" NEXT TO YOUR CHECK.) IF A CATEGORY DOES NOT PERTAIN TO YOU, CHECK "NOT APPLICABLE."

	1 Definitely Know(s)	2 Definitely or Probably Suspect(s)	3 Do(es) Not Seem to Know or Suspect	0 Not Applicable Have No Such Relationship
Your mother ...	—	—	—	—
Your father	—	—	—	—
Brother(s)	—	—	—	—
Sister(s)	—	—	—	—
Best heterosexual friend of same sex	—	—	—	—
Wife	—	—	—	—
Best heterosexual friend of opposite sex	—	—	—	—
Your employer ..	—	—	—	—

61. HOW DO YOU THINK EACH OF THE FOLLOWING PERSONS *WOULD* REACT (OR *HAS* REACTED) TO FINDING OUT THAT YOU ARE HOMOSEXUAL? (IF A CATEGORY DOES NOT PERTAIN TO YOU, CHECK "NOT APPLICABLE.")

	1 Accepting (Or It Would Not Matter)	2 Understanding (But Not Accepting)	3 Tolerant (But Not Understanding)	4 Intolerant (But Not Rejecting)	5 Rejecting	0 Not Applicable Have No Such Relationship
Your mother	—	—	—	—	—	—
Your father	—	—	—	—	—	—

	1 Accepting (Or It Would Not Matter)	2 Understanding (But Not Accepting)	3 Tolerant (But Not Understanding)	4 Intolerant (But Not Rejecting)	5 Rejecting	0 Not Applicable Have No Such Relationship
Brother(s)	—	—	—	—	—	—
Sisters(s)	—	—	—	—	—	—
Most of your aunts and uncles	—	—	—	—	—	—
Best heterosexual friend of same sex ...	—	—	—	—	—	—
Most other heterosexual friends of same sex ...	—	—	—	—	—	—
Wife ...	—	—	—	—	—	—
Best heterosexual friend of opposite sex ...	—	—	—	—	—	—
Most other heterosexual friends of opposite sex ...	—	—	—	—	—	—
Most of your work associates	—	—	—	—	—	—
Your employer	—	—	—	—	—	—

	1 Accepting (Or It Would Not Matter)	2 Understanding (But Not Accepting)	3 Tolerant (But Not Understanding)	4 Intolerant (But Not Rejecting)	5 Rejecting	0 Not Applicable Have No Such Relationship
Most of your neighbors ..	—	—	—	—	—	—
Most heterosexuals in general	—	—	—	—	—	—

62. CHECK HOW IMPORTANT YOU PERSONALLY THINK EACH OF THE FOLLOWING IS:

	1 Very Important	2 Somewhat Important	3 Not Very Important	4 Not at All Important
Formal religion	—	—	—	—
Traditional morality	—	—	—	—
Conformity in general	—	—	—	—

63. ALL OF US VALUE THE OPINIONS OF SOME PERSONS MORE THAN THE OPINIONS OF OTHERS. HOW IMPORTANT IS IT TO YOU THAT EACH OF THE FOLLOWING PERSONS HAS (OR HAD, IF DECEASED) A "GOOD" OPINION OF YOU? CHECK THE SPACE AS CLOSE TO, OR AS FAR FROM, "VERY IMPORTANT" AS CHARACTERIZES YOUR FEELING:

	Very Important 1	2	3	4	5	6	7 Very Unimportant	0 No Such Relation
Your mother ...	—	—	—	—	—	—	—	—
Your father	—	—	—	—	—	—	—	—

	Very Important 1	2	3	4	5	6	7 Very Unimportant	0 No Such Relation
Brother(s)	—	—	—	—	—	—	—	—
Sisters(s)	—	—	—	—	—	—	—	—
Most of your aunts and uncles	—	—	—	—	—	—	—	—
Best heterosexual friend of same sex	—	—	—	—	—	—	—	—
Other heterosexual friends of same sex	—	—	—	—	—	—	—	—
Wife	—	—	—	—	—	—	—	—
Best heterosexual friend of opposite sex	—	—	—	—	—	—	—	—
Other heterosexual friends of opposite sex ..	—	—	—	—	—	—	—	—
Most of your work associates	—	—	—	—	—	—	—	—
Your employer .	—	—	—	—	—	—	—	—
Most of your neighbors	—	—	—	—	—	—	—	—
Heterosexuals in general	—	—	—	—	—	—	—	—
Best homosexual friends	—	—	—	—	—	—	—	—
Homosexuals in general	—	—	—	—	—	—	—	—

64. TO WHAT DEGREE DO YOU THINK HOMOSEXUALITY VIOLATES THE FOLLOWING:

	1 Very Much	2 Somewhat	3 Not Too Much	4 Not at All
Formal religion	—	—	—	—
Traditional morality	—	—	—	—

	1 Very Much	2 Somewhat	3 Not Too Much	4 Not at All
Conformity in general	—	—	—	—

CHOOSE THE ALTERNATIVE THAT BEST CHARACTERIZES YOUR SITUATION. CIRCLE THE NUMBER OPPOSITE THE ANSWER YOU CHOOSE:

65. Of all your friends, how many are (to your knowledge) heterosexual?
    - All 1
    - Most 2
    - More than half 3
    - About half 4
    - Less than half 5
    - Only a few 6
    - None 7
66. How socially active were you in heterosexual circles when you first began to really view yourself as a homosexual?
    - Very active 1
    - Somewhat active 2
    - Not too active 3
    - Not active at all 4
67. How many close relationships did you have with heterosexuals (other than family members) when you first began to really view yourself as a homosexual?
    - Many 1
    - Some 2
    - Very few 3
    - None 4
68. How popular were you in heterosexual circles when you first began to really view yourself as homosexual?
    - Quite popular 1
    - Reasonably popular 2
    - Not very popular 3
    - Not at all popular 4
69. At the present time, how many close relationships do you have with heterosexuals (other than family members)?
    - Many 1

Some 2
Very few 3
None 4

70. At the present time, how socially active are you in heterosexual circles?
Very active 1
Somewhat active 2
Not too active 3
Not active at all 4

71. At the present time, how popular are you in heterosexual circles?
Quite popular 1
Reasonably popular 2
Not very popular 3
Not popular at all 4

72. From how many heterosexuals do you try to conceal your homosexuality?
All 1
Most 2
More than half 3
About half 4
Less than half 5
Only a few 6
None 7

73. Have there been problems on any job you've had because people suspected or knew that you were homosexual?
No 1
Yes, but only to a very small degree 2
Yes, to some degree 3
Yes, very much so 4

74. Would there be problems at work if people found out?
No 1
Yes, but only to a very small degree 2
Yes, to some degree 3
Yes, very much so 4
Most people I work with already know 5

75. Have you ever lost a job because your homosexuality became known?
Yes, more than once 1
Yes, once 2
No 3

76. Have you ever been labeled a homosexual on some official record (outside of homosexual or homophile organizational records)?

Yes, more than once 1
Yes, once 2
No 3

IF *YES:*

Does this bother you?
Yes, a great deal 1
Yes, somewhat 2
Yes, but not very much 3
No, not at all 4

IF *NO:*

Would this bother you?
Yes, a great deal 1
Yes, somewhat 2
Yes, but not very much 3
No, not at all 4

77. Has suspicion or knowledge of your homosexuality adversely affected your social relationships?

Yes, a great deal 1
Yes, somewhat 2
Yes, but only to a very small degree 3
No 4
No one knows or suspects that I am homosexual 5

78. Do you think people are likely to break off social relationships with someone if they suspect he is homosexual?

Yes, most people would 1
Yes, many would 2
Yes, a few would 3
No 4

79. Do you think people are likely to make life difficult for persons they suspect are homosexual?

Yes, most people would 1
Yes, many would 2
Yes, a few would 3
No 4

80. Has life been made difficult for you because someone knew or suspected that you were homosexual?

Yes, very much so 1
Yes, to some degree 2
Yes, but only to a very small degree 3
No 4

81. How do you think most people feel about homosexuals?
    They feel disgusted or repelled by homosexuals 1
    They dislike homosexuals 2
    They have a "live and let live" attitude toward homosexuals 3
    They have some liking for homosexuals 4

82. What proportion of your leisure-time socializing is with homosexuals?
    Most 1
    More than half 2
    About half 3
    Less than half 4
    Only a small amount 5
    None 6

83. How many of your friends are homosexual?
    All 1
    Most 2
    More than half 3
    About half 4
    Less than half 5
    Only a small amount 6
    None 7

84. For how long have you had mostly homosexuals as friends?
    I have never had mostly homosexuals as friends 1
    Only at some time in the past 2
    For the past 6 months or less 3
    For between 6 months and a year 4
    For between 1 and 2 years 5
    For longer than 2 years 6

85. Which category best describes your social situation among homosexuals?
    Not really known among homosexuals 1
    Not really a part of the group 2
    Well accepted 3
    Popular socially 4
    Very popular socially 5

86. How often do you ordinarily frequent homosexual bars or clubs?
    More than once a week 1
    About once a week 2
    About once every other week 3
    About once a month 4

About once every few months 5
Less often 6
Almost never 7
Never 8

87. Have you ever danced "slow" dances with another male?
Yes, often 1
Yes, a few times 2
Yes, once 3
No, never 4

88. Has "necking" (kissing) been a part of your sexual (homosexual) practices?
Yes, often 1
Yes, a few times 2
Yes, once 3
No, never 4

89. Have you ever appeared dressed in women's clothing in front of others?
Yes, many times 1
Yes, a few times 2
Yes, once 3
No, never 4

90. At the present time, are another homosexual and yourself limiting your sexual relationships primarily to each other?
No 1
Yes, we have been for less than a month 2
Yes, we have been for one to six months 3
Yes, we have been for six months to a year 4
Yes, we have been for more than a year 5

91. At some time in the past, did another homosexual and yourself limit your sexual relationships primarily to each other? (This should refer to a different relationship than the one considered in the previous question.)
No 1
Yes, for less than a month 2
Yes, for between one and six months 3
Yes, for between six months and a year 4
Yes, for more than a year 5

92. What do you think most homosexuals that know you think of you?
Think very well of me 1
Think fairly well of me 2
Do not really accept or reject me 3

Think fairly poorly of me 4
Think very poorly of me 5
Do not associate enough with homosexuals to answer this question 6

93. What do you think most heterosexuals that know you think of you?
Think very well of me 1
Think fairly well of me 2
Do not really accept or reject me 3
Think fairly poorly of me 4
Think very poorly of me 5
Do not associate enough with heterosexuals to answer this question 6

94. Even though it may be difficult, please specify the exact number of people whom you consider to be your close friends (e.g., 0, 1, 2, 3, 4, . . .): .... —
Of these close friends, write the number that are homosexual: .... —

95. Have you ever had sexual intercourse with a female?
Yes 1
No 2
If *YES:*
At what age did you first have sexual intercourse with a female? .... —
Did you enjoy sexual intercourse your first time?
Yes 1
No 2
Since then, do (did) you enjoy sexual intercourse with males?
Yes 1
No 2
Have had no subsequent experiences 3
If *NO:*
Do you think that you would enjoy having sexual intercourse with a female?
Yes 1
No 2

96. EVEN THOUGH IT MAY BE DIFFICULT, IN YOUR ANSWERS TO THESE QUESTIONS *PROVIDE NUMBERS:*

In the last 6 months, how many times have you had sexual relations with females? .... —

In the last 6 months, how many times have you had sexual relations with males? .... —
In the last month, how many times have you had sexual relations with males? .... —
At what age did you first have a homosexual experience? —

97. Are you presently:
Single and never married 1
Single, but have been married 2
Married, but not living with your wife 3
Married and living with your wife 4

98. If you are not married or are not presently living with your wife, how many dates with girls have you had in the last 12 months? .... —

99. Have you ever been arrested on any charge related to your homosexuality?
Yes 1
No 2
If *YES:*
What was the charge and what were the circumstances of your arrest (be specific as to where you were and with whom —e.g., an adult or a minor)?

100. Has anyone ever suggested that you seek psychiatric treatment regarding your homosexuality?
Yes, 3 or more persons 1
Yes, 2 persons 2
Yes, 1 person 3
No one has ever suggested this 4

101. *Regarding your homosexuality:*
Have you ever visited a psychiatrist?
Yes 1
No 2
Have you received psychiatric treatment?
Yes 1
No 2
Are you presently receiving psychiatric treatment?
Yes 1
No 2
IF *NO:*
Would you like to obtain psychiatric treatment regarding your homosexuality?
Yes 1
No 2

Have you ever had (or are you presently receiving) psychiatric treatment for reasons other than your homosexuality?

Yes 1
No 2

102. Do you ever find that on one day you have one opinion of yourself and on another day you have a different opinion?

Yes, this happens often 1
Yes, this happens sometimes 2
Yes, but this rarely happens 3
No, this never happens 4

103. Does the opinion you have of yourself tend to change a good deal?

Changes a great deal 1
Changes somewhat 2
Changes very little 3
Does not change at all 4

---

104. HOW OFTEN DO THE FOLLOWING THINGS HAPPEN TO YOU?

	Nearly All the Time	Pretty Often	Not Very Much	Never
a] Do you ever have any trouble getting to sleep or staying asleep?	—	—	—	—
b] Have you ever been bothered by nervousness, feeling fidgety and tense?	—	—	—	—
c] Are you ever troubled by headaches or pains in the head?	—	—	—	—
d] Do you have loss of appetite?	—	—	—	—
e] How often are you bothered by having an upset stomach?	—	—	—	—
f] Do you find it difficult to get up in the morning?	—	—	—	—

	Many Times	Some Times	Hardly Ever	Never
g] Have you ever been bothered by shortness of breath when you were not exercising or working hard?	—	—	—	—
h] Have you ever been bothered by your heart beating hard?	—	—	—	—
i] Do you ever drink more than you should?	—	—	—	—
j] Have you ever had spells of dizziness?	—	—	—	—
k] Are you ever bothered by nightmares?	—	—	—	—
l] Do you tend to lose weight when you have something important bothering you?	—	—	—	—
m] Do your hands ever tremble enough to bother you?	—	—	—	—
n] Are you troubled by your hands sweating so that you feel damp and clammy?	—	—	—	—
o] Have there ever been times when you couldn't take care of things because you just couldn't get going? ...	—	—	—	—

105. Does knowing that you are homosexual "weigh on your mind" (make you feel guilty, depressed, anxious, or ashamed)?
    - A great deal 1
    - Somewhat 2
    - Not very much 3
    - Not at all 4

106. At the present time do you ever experience shame, guilt, or anxiety after having sexual (homosexual) relations?

Nearly always 1
Pretty often 2
Not very much 3
Never 4

107. Did you feel guilt or shame after your first homosexual experience?
Yes, a great deal 1
Yes, some 2
Yes, but very little 3
No 4

108. Do you feel lonely?
Never 1
Seldom 2
Often 3
Very often 4

109. Taking all things together, how would you say things are these days—would you say you are:
Very happy 1
Pretty happy 2
Not too happy 3
Very unhappy 4

110. For how long have you thought of yourself as being homosexual?
Never 1
Only at some time in the past 2
For less than a year 3
For less than 3 years 4
For between 3 and 5 years 5
For between 6 and 9 years 6
For 10 years or more 7

111. Do you presently worry about the possible exposure of your homosexuality?
A great deal 1
Somewhat 2
Very little 3
Not at all 4

112. Which of the following homosexual practices have you engaged in at least *three* times?
Mutual masturbation 1
Full body stimulation to orgasm 2
Performing fellatio 3

Receiving fellatio 4
Performing anal intercourse 5
Receiving anal intercourse 6

113. Do you think of yourself as:
Exclusively homosexual 6
Predominantly homosexual, only insignificantly heterosexual 5
Predominantly homosexual, but significantly heterosexual 4
Equally homosexual and heterosexual 3
Predominantly heterosexual, but significantly homosexual 2
Predominantly heterosexual, only insignificantly homosexual 1
Exclusively heterosexual 0

114. How often do you presently go to the Mattachine office, Mattachine meetings, or West Side meetings? Do you go to any combination of these:
More than once a week 1
About once a week 2
2–3 times a month 3
Once a month 4
Once every few months 5
Once every six months 6
Less often... 7
Never 8

115. With whom do you live?
Both parents 1
Father 2
Mother 3
Alone 4
Male (homosexual) roommate(s) 5
Male (heterosexual) roommate(s) 6
Wife 7
Other (Specify: ________________) 8

IF YOU LIVE WITH ROOMMATE(S), IS (ARE) ROOMMATE(S) ALSO YOUR LOVER(S)? .... —

IF YOU DO *NOT* LIVE WITH PARENT(S):

Do your parents or close relatives live in the same city as you?
Yes 1
No 2

116. If you live in New York City, in what section of the city do you live?

The Village	1
East Side (Between 14th and 42nd)	2
East Side (Above 42nd)	3
West Side (Between 23rd and 59th)	4
West Side (Above 59th)	5
Brooklyn Heights	6
Another part of Brooklyn	7
Bronx	8
Queens	9
Metropolitan suburbs (Long Island, Westchester, etc.)	0
Other (Specify: ________________)	X

117. How old are you?

Under 21	1
21–25	2
26–30	3
31–35	4
36–40	5
41–45	6
46–50	7
51–60	8
Over 60	9

118. Are you employed in:

White collar work	1
Blue collar work	2

119. What kind of work do you do for a living? What is your job called, what kind of business or industry do you work in, and *what do you do?* (For example: "Sales clerk, wait on customers in a department store"; "Weaver, operate a loom in a cotton textile mill"; "Owner and operator of a grocery store"; or "Doctor of internal medicine in private practice.")

120. What kind of firm or outfit are you associated with in your work?

Own business, small firm (50 employees or less)	1
Own business, large firm (over 50 employees)	2
Own farm	3
Own professional office	4
Work for a private firm, organization, or factory:	
Small firm (50 employees or less)	5
Large firm (over 50 employees)	6
Educational institution	7

Social agency 8
Other non-profit organization (Specify: ___________) 9
Government bureau or agency 0
Other (Specify: _________________) X

121. How satisfied are you with your present job?
Very satisfied 1
Satisfied 2
Neither satisfied nor dissatisfied 3
Not sure 4
Dissatisfied 5

122. Would you like to change occupations if you could?
Yes 1
No 2
IF *YES:*
What occupation would you prefer? _______________
Why would you like to leave your present occupation?

123. How long have you been employed in your present job? —

124. How many job *changes* have you made in the last 5 years? —

125. How would you place your social class?
Upper 1
Upper middle 2
Lower middle 3
Working 4
Lower 5

126. How would you place your father's social class?
Upper 1
Upper middle 2
Lower middle 3
Working 4
Lower 5

127. Is (was) your father employed in primarily white collar or blue collar work?
White collar work 1
Blue collar work 2

128. What kind of work does (did) your father do for a living? What is (was) his job called, what kind of business or industry does (did) he work in, and what does (did) he do?

129. What kind of firm or outfit is (was) your father associated with in his work?
Own business, small firm (50 employees or less) 1

Own business, large firm (over 50 employees) 2
Own farm 3
Own professional office 4
Work for a private firm, organization, or factory:
  Small firm (50 employees or less) 5
  Large firm (over 50 employees) 6
Educational institution 7
Social agency 8
Other non-profit organization (Specify: ________) 9
Government bureau or agency 0
Other (Specify: ______________) X

130. How far have you gone in your education?
8th grade or less 1
Some high school 2
High school diploma 3
Some college 4
College degree 5
Graduate degree 6

131. What is your race?
Negro 1
White 2
Other 3

132. What is your religious background?
Catholic 1
Protestant 2
Jewish 3
Other 4

IF *PROTESTANT:*
State denomination:

____

IF *JEWISH:*
State whether your background was Orthodox, Conservative, or Reform:

____

IF *OTHER:*
Specify: ______________

133. How often do you usually attend church or synagogue?
Once a week or more 1
Two or three times a month 2
Once a month 3
Several times a year 4

Once a year 5
Less often 6
Never 7

134. How "religious" (in the traditional sense of the term) were your parents?
Very religious 1
Somewhat religious 2
Not very religious 3
Not at all religious 4

135. How "religious" (in the traditional sense of the term) were you as a teenager?
Very religious 1
Somewhat religious 2
Not very religious 3
Not at all religious 4

136. How "religious" (in the traditional sense of the term) are you now?
Very religious 1
Somewhat religious 2
Not very religious 3
Not at all religious 4

137. In which of the following categories does your annual income fit?
Less than $3,000 1
$3,000–$4,999 2
$5,000–$7,999 3
$8,000–$9,999 4
$10,000–$14,999 5
$15,000–$24,999 6
$25,000–$49,999 7
$50,000 or over 8

138. Were your teenage years spent primarily in a:
Large city 1
Medium-sized city 2
Small city 3
Small town 4
Suburbs 5
Country area 6

139. What is the approximate population of the town or city in which you spent most of your teenage years?
Less than 1,000 1

1,000–2,499 2
2,500–9,999 3
10,000–24,999 4
25,000–99,999 5
100,000–249,999 6
250,000 or over 7

140. Do you presently live in a:
Large city 1
Medium-sized city 2
Small city 3
Small town 4
Suburbs 5
Country area 6

141. What is the approximate population of the town or city in which you presently live?
Less than 1,000 1
1,000–2,499 2
2,500–9,999 3
10,000–24,999 4
25,000–99,999 5
100,000–249,999 6
250,000 or over 7

142. How long have you lived at your present address? ...... —

143. How long did you live at your previous address? .... —

144. Are you a member of the Mattachine Society?
Yes 1
No 2
IF *YES:*
Do you think you have gained something from your membership?
Yes 1
No 2
If so, what would you say you have gained?

145. Are there any ways that you would be directly affected by a change in the present laws pertaining to homosexuality?
Yes 1
No 2
If so, specify in what ways.

NOTES

Chapter 1 / The Study of Homosexuality

1. See Martin S. Weinberg and Alan P. Bell, *Homosexuality: An Annotated Bibliography* (New York: Harper and Row, 1972). This contains abstracts of more than 1,200 scholarly publications on homosexuality.

2. Irving Bieber et al., *Homosexuality: A Psychoanalytic Study* (New York: Basic Books, 1962), p. 220.

3. Ibid. p. 18.

4. Sandor Rado, "A Critical Examination of the Concept of Bisexuality," *Psychosomatic Medicine* 2 (October 1940). This idea is also held by Bieber and his associates.

5. Many items in the Institute for Sex Research bibliography (Ref. 1) report techniques for "curing" homosexuality. The range of techniques is impressive; a sampling includes aversion therapy, group psychotherapy, hypnotherapy, and drug therapy.

6. Weinberg and Bell, *Homosexuality*.

7. For an extension of this point, see Wainwright Churchill, *Homosexual Behavior Among Males: A Cross-Cultural and Cross-Species Investigation* (New York: Hawthorn Books, 1967), pp. 38ff.

8. Psychoanalytic theorists have been interested in testing Freudian hypotheses in other cultures. Most work in what is called "culture and personality" represents such efforts, although there has been little attention paid to homosexuality.

9. For an account of the early barriers to sex research, see Sophie D. Aberle and George W. Corner, *Twenty-Five Years of Sex Re-*

search: History of the National Research Council Committee for Research in Problems of Sex 1922–1947 (Philadelphia: W. B. Saunders Company, 1953), pp. 1–8. For a discussion of sociology and sex research in general, see Edward Sagarin, "Sex Research and Sociology: Retrospective and Prospective," in James M. Henslin (ed.), *Studies in the Sociology of Sex* (New York: Meredith Corporation, 1971), pp. 377–408.

10. Alfred C. Kinsey, Wardell B. Pomeroy, and Clyde E. Martin, *Sexual Behavior in the Human Male* (Philadelphia: W. B. Saunders Company, 1948); Alfred C. Kinsey, Wardell B. Pomeroy, Clyde E. Martin, and Paul H. Gebhard, *Sexual Behavior in the Human Female* (Philadelphia: W. B. Saunders Company, 1953). Note, however, that there were quantitative studies of sexual behavior that preceded Kinsey, though they were few in number. See Edward M. Brecher, *The Sex Researchers* (Boston: Little Brown, 1969). Also, for a comprehensive treatment of the development of sex research, see Winston Ehrmann, "Marital and Non-Marital Sexual Behavior," in Harold Christensen (ed.), *Handbook of Marriage and the Family* (New York: Rand McNally, 1964).

11. For example, while this book was in press the American Psychiatric Association removed homosexuality from the list of mental illnesses in its diagnostic manual. See *New York Times*, December 16, 1973.

12. Evelyn Hooker, "The Adjustment of the Male Overt Homosexual," *Journal of Projective Techniques* 21 (March 1957), p. 30.

13. Martin Hoffman, *The Gay World: Male Homosexuality and the Social Creation of Evil* (New York: Bantam Books, 1968), p. 176. Hoffman, a psychiatrist, presents a definite sociological perspective in his work.

14. William Simon and John H. Gagnon, "Homosexuality: The Formulation of a Sociological Perspective," *Journal of Health and Social Behavior* 8 (September 1967), p. 179. This article is by far the most articulate presentation of the sociological perspective.

15. Ibid. p. 181.

16. Cf. Mary McIntosh, "The Homosexual Role," *Social Problems* 16 (Fall 1968), pp. 182–92.

17. The major statements of this approach are found in Earl Rubington and Martin S. Weinberg, *Deviance: The Interactionist Perspective*, 2nd ed. (New York: Macmillan, 1973); Edwin Lemert, *Social Pathology* (New York: McGraw-Hill, 1951); Howard S. Becker, *Outsiders: Studies in the Sociology of Deviance* (New York: The Free Press, 1963); John I. Kitsuse, "Societal Reaction to Deviant Behavior: Problems of Theory and Method," *Social Problems* 9 (Winter 1962), pp. 247–56; Kai Erikson, "Notes on the

Sociology of Deviance," *Social Problems* 9 (Spring 1962), pp. 307–14; Thomas Scheff, *Being Mentally Ill* (Chicago: Aldine, 1966); Edwin M. Schur, "Reactions to Deviance: A Critical Assessment," *American Journal of Sociology* 75 (November 1969), pp. 309–22.

18. Other studies that could be subsumed under the societal reaction approach are Albert J. Reiss, "The Social Integration of Queers and Peers," *Social Problems* 9 (Fall 1961), pp. 102–20; Maurice Leznoff and William Westley, "The Homosexual Community," *Social Problems* 3 (April 1956), pp. 257–63; Nancy Achilles, "The Homosexual Bar as an Institution," in John H. Gagnon and William Simon (eds.), *Sexual Deviance* (New York: Harper and Row, 1967); Laud Humphreys, *Tearoom Trade: Impersonal Sex in Public Places* (Chicago: Aldine, 1970); David Sonenschein, "The Ethnography of Male Homosexual Relations," *Journal of Sex Research* 4 (May 1968), pp. 69–83; *U.C.L.A. Law Review*, "The Consenting Adult Homosexual and the Law: An Empirical Study of Enforcement and Administration in Los Angeles County" (March 1966), pp. 644–832, hereinafter referred to as *U.C.L.A. Law Review* throughout the book; Barry M. Dank, "Coming Out in the Gay World," *Psychiatry* 34 (May 1971), pp. 180–97; Colin J. Williams and Martin S. Weinberg, *Homosexuals and the Military: A Study of Less than Honorable Discharge* (New York: Harper and Row, 1971); Laud Humphreys, *Out of the Closets: The Sociology of Homosexual Liberation* (Englewood Cliffs, N.J.: Prentice-Hall, 1972). An analysis of homosexuality (rather than original research) utilizing the societal reaction perspective is provided by Edwin M. Schur, *Crimes Without Victims* (Englewood Cliffs, N.J.: Prentice-Hall, 1965).

19. In commenting on the implications of the societal reaction perspective for criminology, a criminologist writes: "Research in the vein of the new criminology . . . requires studies on a scale that many of us will find difficult to implement. To throw some light on the consequences of alternate legal and law enforcement arrangements requires some variations in those arrangements." Herbert L. Costner, *Newsletter: Society for the Study of Social Problems* 2 (Winter 1971), p. 7.

20. Rubington and Weinberg, *Deviance*, passim.

21. For a general account of the ways in which various types of social deviants handle the problem of being known about, see Erving Goffman, *Stigma: Notes on the Management of Spoiled Identity* (Englewood Cliffs, N.J.: Prentice-Hall, 1965).

22. This term is used by Matza in reference to juvenile delinquents. See David Matza, *Delinquency and Drift* (New York: Wiley, 1964).

23. One limiting case here is provided by the heterosexually married

homosexual. For many such persons, the motivation for marriage may be the rewards obtained from a heterosexual union, e.g., children. Marriage may, however, also reflect giving in to social pressures and can be seized upon as a further way of passing. See H. Laurence Ross, "Modes of Adjustment of Married Homosexuals," *Social Problems* 18 (Winter 1971), pp. 385–93.

24. George Serban, "The Phenomenological Concept of Homosexuality," *Existential Psychiatry* 7, No. 28 (1970).

25. For descriptions of homosexual relationships, see Evelyn Hooker, "Male Homosexuals and Their Worlds," in Judd Marmor (ed.), *Sexual Inversion: The Multiple Roots of Homosexuality* (New York: Basic Books, 1965); Achilles, "Homosexual Bar as an Institution"; Leznoff and Westley, "Homosexual Community." Sonenschein, "Ethnography of Male Homosexual Relations," makes use of the distinction between sexual and social gratifications in distinguishing various types of homosexual relationships.

26. Humphreys found over half his sample of persons using public rest rooms for sex were heterosexually married. Humphreys, *Tearoom Trade.*

27. Leznoff and Westley, "Homosexual Community."

28. Donald Webster Cory, *The Homosexual in America* (New York: Greenberg, 1951), p. 12.

29. Simon and Gagnon, "Homosexuality: The Formulation of a Sociological Perspective," pp. 182–83.

30. Hoffman, *The Gay World,* pp. 164ff.

31. Hooker, "Male Homosexuals and Their Worlds," pp. 103–5.

Chapter 2 / The United States

1. Robert R. Bell, *Premarital Sex in a Changing Society* (Englewood Cliffs, N.J.: Prentice-Hall, 1966), p. 13.

2. Wainwright Churchill, *Homosexual Behavior Among Males: A Cross-Cultural and Cross-Species Investigation* (New York: Hawthorn Books, 1967).

3. Alfred C. Kinsey et al., *Sexual Behavior in the Human Female* (Philadelphia: W. B. Saunders Company, 1953), p. 477.

4. Cf. Kinsey, *Sexual Behavior in the Human Female,* pp. 481ff; Churchill, *Homosexual Behavior Among Males,* Chap. IV. Also, Derek S. Bailey, *Homosexuality and the Western Christian Tradition* (London: Longmans, 1955). For an alternate explanation centering around the conflict between homosexuality and the institutionalization of male-female relationships, see Kingsley Davis, "Sexual

Behavior," in Robert K. Merton and Robert A. Nisbet (eds.), *Contemporary Social Problems* (New York: Harcourt, Brace and World, 1966), esp. pp. 339–42.

5. Also, the United States was not influenced, as were many European countries, by the Napoleonic codes, which were very liberal toward homosexuality.

6. For an account of Puritan attitudes and behavior concerning sex, see Robert M. Frumkin, "Early English and American Sex Customs," in Albert Ellis and Albert Abarbanel (eds.), *Encyclopaedia of Sexual Behavior*, 2nd ed. (New York: Hawthorn Books, 1967), pp. 350–65.

7. Donald Webster Cory, *Homosexuality: A Cross Cultural Approach* (New York: Julian Press, 1965), p. 428. Actual sexual behaviors rather than attitudes, however, are another matter, as the Kinsey research shows. For a sociological explanation of why cultural attitudes and laws lag behind behavior, see also John H. Gagnon, "Sexuality and Sexual Learning in the Child," in John H. Gagnon and William Simon (eds.), *Sexual Deviance* (New York: Harper and Row, 1967), pp. 19ff.

8. Colin J. Williams and Martin S. Weinberg, *Homosexuals and the Military: A Study of Less than Honorable Discharge* (New York: Harper and Row, 1971).

9. Boutilier v. Immigration and Naturalization Service, 87 S. Ct. 1563 (1967). For a discussion of this case in the light of what it shows about American attitudes toward homosexuals, see Thomas S. Szasz, *The Manufacture of Madness* (New York: Delta Books, 1970), pp. 242–59.

10. J. L. Simmons, "Public Stereotypes of Deviants," *Social Problems* 13 (Fall 1965), pp. 223–32.

11. The results of this survey are reproduced in *Drum* (a homophile magazine) 25 (August 1967). Ranked before homosexuality were: sale of salacious literature (45%) and teenage sex relations (38%).

12. *Washington Post*, September 27, 1965, as reported in *The Challenge and Progress of Homosexual Law Reform* (San Francisco: 1968), p. 68.

13. Reported in *Time*, October 31, 1969. The main feature of this edition is entitled "The Homosexual in America" and is instructive on recent depictions of the homosexual in the media.

14. Simmons, "Public Stereotypes of Deviants," *passim*.

15. Elizabeth A. Rooney and Don C. Gibbons, "Social Reactions to 'Crimes Without Victims,'" *Social Problems* 13 (Spring 1966), pp. 400–10.

16. Ibid. p. 405.

17. Though the more educated were more tolerant on this issue, no matter how the population was grouped (age, education, region, etc.) there was no majority approval in any of the subgroups. The report notes the inconsistency in that a majority regard homosexuality as an *illness* yet demand that it should be *punished* by law.

18. *Drum*, p. 11.

19. Eugene Levitt and Albert D. Klassen, "Public Attitudes Toward Sexual Behaviors: The Latest Investigation of the Institute for Sex Research" (unpublished manuscript).

20. *The Challenge and Progress of Homosexual Law Reform*, p. 16. This pamphlet put out by homophile organizations in the San Francisco area is an excellent compendium of knowledge on the homosexual and the law.

21. Thirteen states employ the term "sodomy"; nineteen, "crimes against nature"; one, "buggery"; six, a combination of "sodomy" and "the crime against nature"; two, a combination of "sodomy" and "buggery"; the remainder have other similar terms and combinations. See *U.C.L.A. Law Review* (1966), p. 659. Despite attempts to rewrite and clarify such statutes, however, ". . . there is no quick method of ascertaining exactly what acts are included or excluded under many of the present day sodomy laws," ibid. p. 662. (These data do not include the most recent legal changes.)

22. Hugh M. Hefner, "The Legal Enforcement of Morality," *University of Colorado Law Review* 40 (Winter 1968), pp. 199–221. For other discussions of homosexuality and the law, see Churchill, *Homosexual Behavior Among Males*, Chap. X; Morris Ploscowe, *Sex and the Law* (New York: Ace Books, 1962), Chap. VII; Gilbert M. Cantor, "The Need for Homosexual Law Reform," in Ralph Weltge (ed.), *The Same Sex* (Philadelphia: Pilgrim Press, 1969), pp. 83–94; Martin Hoffman, *The Gay World: Male Homosexuality and the Social Creation of Evil* (New York: Bantam Books, 1968), Chap. 5; Gilbert Geiss, *Not the Law's Business: An Examination of Homosexuality, Abortion, Prostitution, Narcotics and Gambling in the United States* (Washington, D.C., Government Printing Office, 1972).

23. *U.C.L.A. Law Review*, p. 663. (This does not include the most recent legal changes.)

24. For a discussion of such laws, see Alan H. Swanson, "Sexual Psychopath Statutes: Summary and Analysis," *Journal of Criminal Law, Criminology, and Police Science* 51 (July–August 1960), pp. 215–35; Karl Bowman and Bernice Engle, "Sexual Psychopath Laws," in Ralph Slovenko (ed.), *Sexual Behavior and the Law* (Springfield, Ill.: Charles C Thomas, 1965), pp. 757–78; Thomas

R. Byrne, Jr., and Francis M. Mulligan, "Psychopathic Personality and Sexual Deviation: Medical Terms or Legal Catch-Alls. Analysis of the Status of the Homosexual Alien," *Temple Law Quarterly* 40 (Spring–Summer 1967), pp. 328–47. Also, Churchill, *Homosexual Behavior Among Males,* pp. 221–24; *The Challenge and Progress of Homosexual Law Reform,* p. 8 and footnotes 8–13, pp. 42–43.

25. Churchill, *Homosexual Behavior Among Males,* p. 221.

26. The following is taken from the *U.C.L.A. Law Review* study, Part III, which is the best account of such techniques. For a shorter account, see Edwin M. Schur, *Crimes Without Victims* (Englewood Cliffs, N.J.: Prentice-Hall, 1965), pp. 77ff, and Hoffman, *The Gay World,* pp. 81–92.

27. *U.C.L.A. Law Review,* footnote 132, p. 707. The most frequent locale was public rest rooms—139 of 475 misdemeanor arrests (29%) occurred in such places. Ibid. footnote 138, p. 707.

28. *U.C.L.A. Law Review,* footnote 58, p. 695; the study revealed that only seven out of 463 misdemeanor arrests (1.6%) and 12 out of 493 felony arrests (2.4%) made by decoys were dismissed in court.

29. For evidence of such abuse, see *U.C.L.A. Law Review,* pp. 705–6, and *The Challenge and Progress of Homosexual Law Reform,* pp. 21–22.

30. Of 493 felony defendants studied, 459 (93%) were arrested through direct observation by the police, *U.C.L.A. Law Review,* footnote 133, p. 707; 274 (56%) of the arrests occurred in public rest rooms, ibid. footnote 134, p. 707. For a detailed study of homosexual practices in rest rooms, see Laud Humphreys, *Tearoom Trade: Impersonal Sex in Public Places* (Chicago: Aldine, 1970).

31. See *U.C.L.A. Law Review,* pp. 718–25, for further examples and *The Challenge and Progress of Homosexual Law Reform,* pp. 24–29.

32. For a discussion of the establishment and early history of American homophile societies, see Foster Gunnison, Jr., "The Homophile Movement in America," in Ralph W. Weltge (ed.), *The Same Sex* (Philadelphia: Pilgrim Press, 1969), pp. 113–45; and Edward Sagarin, *Odd Man In: Societies of Deviants in America* (Chicago: Quadrangle Books, 1969), pp. 78–110.

33. Before these changes, some Mattachine members had formed a separate organization, One, Inc., of Los Angeles, to concentrate on publishing materials relevant to homosexuality. Its fight against postal censorship of its material opened the mails to materials for other homophile organizations. See Gunnison, "Homophile Movement in America," p. 116.

34. See, for example, any issue of the G.L.F.'s newspaper *Come Out*. Other slogans include, "Better blatant than latent," "2, 4, 6, 8, Gay is just as good as straight."

35. *Gay Power*, Vol. 1, No. 12 (1970), p. 16.

36. Another comparison would be between black militants and the N.A.A.C.P. One radical pamphlet in fact refers to M.S.N.Y. as "the N.A.A.C.P. of the Gay movement." *Gay Liberation*, a Red Butterfly Publication, first published in New York, February 13, 1970, p. 3.

37. The strain is evident in the following comment by a member of G.L.F., New York: "I distinctly remember Dick Leitsch of Mattachine New York emphatically saying he wanted only one (1) gay organization in 'fun city' and it was his: tough titty dicky your organization is waning, it doesn't have the militant spirit once boasted of in the 50's. One doesn't wear a suit and tie anymore or sit at home hiding to demand equality." Ralph Hall, "Gay Liberation Front," *Gay Power*, Vol. 1, No. 8 (1969), p. 9.

38. For a response to the Gay Liberation movement and its aims from a Mattachine member, see Madolin Cervantes, "Is Militancy the Answer," *Gay Power*, Vol. 1, No. 14 (1970), p. 8. This, however, is not necessarily an M.S.N.Y. position. Like the other groups mentioned, M.S.N.Y. also has a variety of "spokesmen."

39. For sociological descriptions of the structure and functions of homosexual bars, see Evelyn Hooker, "The Homosexual Community," pp. 167–84, and Nancy Achilles, "The Development of the Homosexual Bar as an Institution," pp. 228–44, both in John H. Gagnon and William Simon (eds.), *Sexual Deviance* (New York: Harper and Row, 1967).

Chapter 3 / New York City

1. For a review and critique of the new laws insofar as they concern sex, see Morris Ploscowe, "Sex Offenses in the New Penal Law," *Brooklyn Law Review* 32 (1966), pp. 274–86.

2. Three degrees of sodomy are recognized under the code:

Sodomy in the first degree—A person is guilty of sodomy in the first degree when he engages in deviate sexual intercourse with another person:

(1) By forcible compulsion; or
(2) When the other person is incapable of consent by reason of being physically helpless; or
(3) When the other person is less than 11 years old.

Sodomy in the first degree is a Class B felony punishable by a maximum of 25 years imprisonment (Section 130.50).

Sodomy in the second degree—A person is guilty of sodomy in the second degree when being 18 years old or more, he engages in deviate sexual intercourse with another person less than 14 years old.

Sodomy in the second degree is a Class D felony punishable by a maximum of seven years imprisonment (Section 130.45).

Sodomy in the third degree—A person is guilty of sodomy in the third degree when:

(1) He engages in deviate sexual intercourse with a person who is incapable of consent by reason of some factor other than being less than 17 years old; or

(2) Being 21 years old or more, he engages in deviate sexual intercourse with a person less than 17 years old.

Sodomy in the third degree is a Class E felony punishable by a maximum of four years imprisonment (Section 130.40).

3. For a description of the demographic characteristics of M.S.N.Y., see Chapter 9 of this book. For an earlier study with demographic information on M.S.N.Y., see Edward Sagarin, "Structure and Ideology in an Organization of Deviants," unpublished Ph.D. thesis, New York University, 1966.

4. The case originated on complaint from two men who had passed the Civil Service exam for case workers in the Welfare Department but were turned down on the grounds they were homosexual. M.S.N.Y. acted with the N.Y.C.L.U., who brought suit to force the commission to give the men the jobs. Since that time, being homosexual has not been a bar to obtaining most city jobs. See *New York Times,* May 9, 1969.

5. Not all homosexuals, however, saw the Stonewall event in such a light. The more conservative Mattachine Society saw the Stonewall as a place that was hardly worth defending. It noted that the building was unsafe, it was a fire trap, its sanitation was bad, and it did not have a license. Furthermore, its manager, they said, had been implicated in a national blackmail ring that preyed on homosexuals. They concluded that ". . . police are doing us a favor by closing the Stonewall type places" (*Mattachine Newsletter,* April 1970, p. 4). This view can be contrasted with that of the Red Butterfly Cell of the Gay Liberation Front: "It was not the Mafia bar as such which was being defended. Rather, it was the idea of defending just one place, even in a gay ghetto, where people could meet without harassment and intimidation." *Gay Liberation,* New York: Red Butterfly, 1970. See also Steven V. Roberts, "Homosexuals in Revolt," *New York Times,* August 24, 1970.

6. For example, New York State Court of Appeals ruled Decem-

ber 29, 1967, that close dancing between members of the same sex is not illegal.

7. *Bay Area Reporter* 9 (August 1, 1971). For a more detailed account, including evidence of organized crime in these establishments, see Arthur Bell, "The After Hours 28: Greetings from the Feds," *Village Voice* 16 (December 23, 1971).

8. *New York Times,* November 30, 1967.

9. In estimating the number of gay bars in New York we used the "Gay Scene Guide" published by M.S.N.Y. in 1968, which listed thirty-three bars in Manhattan. To check the validity of this list we compared it with other lists, including the "Lavender Baedecker" (1966), "Bob Damron's Address Book" (1968), a list published by *Gay Power* (1970), and *Gay* (November 1970). Sixty per cent (twenty) of the bars listed by Mattachine were included on other lists. (It would be misleading to talk of a 40 per cent attrition rate. Obviously this cannot be done, since we do not know how extensive a search was made by the compilers of any of these lists.) Adding the remainder on the Mattachine list and the others on the rest of our lists to these "validated" bars, we came to our estimate of seventy gay bars. Two possible sources of error in this estimate are: Some bars changed their ownership and name over the period and therefore could have been counted twice (we did not double count bars whose names we knew had changed, but we do not know how many name changes we did not spot); our count is of gay bars, but what constitutes a "bar" rather than a nightclub or restaurant is not always clear. Thus, our count includes only those establishments that are not much more (as far as we could ascertain) than bars. If we had included nightclub/restaurant listings the number would be approximately ninety. Also, only public bars were counted. Thus, we did not include ten private clubs that were operating after 1968, which admit only members and their guests.

10. Brooklyn Heights has been referred to as a "homosexual suburbia," popular with "young marrieds." William J. Helmer, "New York's 'Middle Class' Homosexuals," *Harper's Magazine* 96 (March 1963), p. 91.

Chapter 4 / San Francisco

1. *U.C.L.A. Law Review,* "The Consenting Adult Homosexual and the Law: An Empirical Study of Enforcement and Administration in Los Angeles County" (March 1966), footnote 26, p. 651.

2. The following account of California law is based on ibid. pp. 674–85.

3. Ibid. p. 681.

4. In the case of Los Angeles, 95 per cent of all felonious homosexual convictions are converted to misdemeanors (by sentence or judicial declaration). Ibid. p. 765. However, the same sentences were also found to be given for felonies and misdemeanors, usually a fine, suspended jail sentence, and probation. Ibid. p. 736.

5. The history of these events can be followed in *Vector* from July 1970 onward.

6. The *U.C.L.A. Law Review* study also describes the law enforcement practices of the Department of Alcoholic Beverage Control. See *U.C.L.A. Law Review,* pp. 726–34.

7. The circulation of *Vector* was reported in the December 1970 issue to be over seven thousand. Note also that S.I.R.'s membership also includes fifty females.

8. For a report on this move, see *Vector* 6 (October 1970), p. 24. For its defeat, see *Vector* 7 (November 1971), pp. 10–11.

9. At the time of the study, the Tavern Guild had close ties with S.I.R. Its office was at the S.I.R. community center, its secretarial tasks were done on a contractual basis by S.I.R.'s full-time secretary, and sometimes it lent S.I.R. money.

10. For a sociological account of the San Francisco bar scene and its problems, see Nancy Achilles, "The Development of the Homosexual Bar as an Institution," in John H. Gagnon and William Simon (eds.), *Sexual Deviance* (New York: Harper and Row, 1967), pp. 228–44.

11. Achilles notes that only three of the thirty-seven San Francisco bars she studied were owned by persons not resident in the city. Ibid. p. 233.

12. Achilles also agrees with this and cites the openness of the gay life in San Francisco as a factor in making bars less subject to underworld control and hence police bribery. Ibid. In the early 1960's, however, the "gayola" scandals, which involved revelations of extensive payoffs by gay bar owners to both state liquor authorities and police, received considerable publicity and eventually led to changes in A.B.C. enforcement practices as described on page 70. See *San Francisco Chronicle,* May 3, 11, 12, 27, 1960; March 14, 1961; May 11, 1962, p. 3; and *Appellant's Opening Brief,* Stoumen v. Munro, 33 *Cal. Rptr.* 305 (1964), pp. 68–94.

13. In estimating the number of homosexual bars in San Francisco, we began with four lists published at the beginning of our period of interest: "Bob Damron's Address Book" for Spring 1965, late 1965, and mid-1966, and the "Lavender Baedecker" for 1966. (These lists include other cities as well as San Francisco.) There were forty-three bars mentioned for San Francisco in Damron's Spring 1965 list, of which thirty-one were listed in the 1966 "Lavender Baedecker."

Comparing Damron's Spring 1965 list with his late 1965 list, there was a loss of two bars and a gain of three. Comparing his late 1965 list with his mid-1966 list, there was a loss of ten bars and a gain of sixteen, giving a net gain of six bars across his lists. We estimate, therefore, that around 1965–66 there were at least fifty homosexual bars operating in San Francisco.

For the later part of our period of interest we used the 1971 "Homosexual National Classified Directory" and lists published in *Vector*. *Vector* began publishing lists of only "strictly homosexual spots" in June of 1970, and we selected the July 1970, February 1971, and August 1971 listings from which to work. We found eighteen bars on these *Vector* listings to be among the 1965–66 listings (and seven of these were on the 1963 "Lavender Baedecker" list), which shows a number of homosexual bars to have persisted (at least under the same name) over what is, for this type of establishment, quite some time. The 1970–71 listings give an estimated seventy-three homosexual bars in operation during this period. Although we do not know the extent to which the earlier and later lists are comparable, the increase in the number of bars accords with other knowledge we have about the bar scene.

Again, of course, this estimate is affected by the same considerations as those for New York. The possibility of double-counting was still a problem. By comparing addresses we found bars in operation, sometimes for a considerable period, at the same address but with different names. Again, how far we avoided double-counting in our estimations we do not know. As in New York, we attempted to include only homosexual *bars,* but in San Francisco bars more often serve meals as well. Five private clubs were not included in our counts, nor bars for women.

14. For a discussion of homosexuals and the Tenderloin, see *Vector* 4 (May–June 1968), pp. 16–18.

Chapter 5 / The Netherlands

1. An independent assessment of the Dutch situation which came to the same conclusion as ours and in fact used the same phraseology of tolerance and acceptance is that of Altman. See Dennis Altman, *Homosexual: Oppression and Liberation* (New York: Outerbridge and Dienstfrey, 1971).

2. *Report of the Committee on Homosexual Offenses and Prostitution* (London: HMSO, 1957), p. 150. After the paperback edition of

this book was in press, we received word that the Dutch law has been revised to what it was before 1911—viz., the age of consent for both heterosexuals and homosexuals is sixteen.

3. *Mattachine Review* 9 (November 1963), p. 12.

Chapter 6 / Denmark

1. Erik Manniche and Kaare Svalastoga, "The Family in Scandinavia," unpublished manuscript, p. 2. See also Kaare Svalastoga, "The Family in Scandinavia," *Marriage and Family Living* 16 (November 1954), pp. 374–80.

2. Manniche and Svalastoga, "Family in Scandinavia," p. 62.

3. See Kingsley Davis, "Sexual Behavior," in Robert K. Merton and Robert A. Nisbet (eds.), *Contemporary Social Problems* (New York: Harcourt, Brace and World, 1966), pp. 322–72.

4. For comparisons with the United States, see Harold T. Christensen, "Cultural Relativism and Premarital Sex Norms," *American Sociological Review* 25 (February 1960), pp. 31–39; and "Scandinavian and American Sex Norms: Some Comparisons with Sociological Implications," *Journal of Social Issues* 22 (April 1966), pp. 60–75.

5. Manniche and Svalastoga, "Family in Scandinavia." For example, over the period 1650–1880 the number of Danish women pregnant or with born children at time of marriage remained unchanged. During the post–World War II period the number decreased because of the increasing use of contraceptives.

6. These data can be found in Gordon Shindler (ed.), *A Report on Denmark's Legalized Pornography* (Torrance, Calif.: Banner Books, 1969), pp. 277–82.

7. For a discussion of this problem, see Jens Jersild, *The Normal Homosexual Male* (Copenhagen: NYT Nordisk Forlag Arnold Busck, 1967).

Chapter 7 / The Three Societies: Concluding Remarks

1. This does not mean they are entirely free from discrimination, however. Differences between homosexuals and heterosexuals concerning the "age of consent" and the military have been referred

to earlier. In addition, both C.O.C. and Forbundet are trying to reduce discrimination with regard to stable homosexual couples in the areas of tax relief, joint property, legacies, and housing.

2. Bryan Magee, *One in Twenty: A Study of Homosexuality in Men and Women* (London: Secker and Warburg, 1966), p. 99.

3. Carl Driver, *Los Angeles Advocate* (March 1970).

4. An interesting comparison with Denmark is England and Wales, where legal prohibitions have been recently lifted. Here, organized homophile activities are quite undeveloped, and the problems faced by homosexuals are similar to those of Denmark and the Netherlands. Cf. Anthony Grey and D. J. West, "Homosexuals: New Law but No New Deal," *New Society* 27 (March 27, 1969), pp. 476–79.

5. Evelyn Hooker, "Male Homosexuals and Their Worlds," in Judd Marmor (ed.), *Sexual Inversion: The Multiple Roots of Homosexuality* (New York: Basic Books, 1965), p. 98.

6. Martin Hoffman, *The Gay World: Male Homosexuality and the Social Creation of Evil* (New York: Basic Books, 1968), pp. 176–79.

Chapter 8 / Methods and Distributions

1. The translators for the initial translation were a professional translator (for Danish) and a Dutch student fluent in English. Translators for the subsequent steps were people recommended to us by the language departments at Indiana University.

2. As noted previously, every bar on our list was visited to confirm that it did indeed cater primarily to homosexuals. In some cases it was found that—due to a change in ownership, for example—the bar could no longer be defined as homosexual, and such bars were deleted from the lists.

For Manhattan and again for San Francisco, the random samples of bars were drawn from their lists by using a table of random numbers; the rare cases found not to be homosexual bars were deleted and replaced with bars randomly selected from the remaining bars on the list.

3. It is difficult to know the actual number of questionnaires mailed in Denmark. Forbundet handled the mailing to its membership and would not allow the researchers any access to the mailing list. For this reason the researchers have no way of checking Forbundet's estimate of the number mailed. Also, for Denmark as well as for the other countries, we made a very conservative estimate of the number of undeliverable mailed questionnaires in computing the corrected response rate. Furthermore, over 50 per cent of the base of

the computed Danish response rate is comprised by Forbundet's reported number of questionnaires mailed, and it is for these mailed questionnaires that the Danish response rate diverges most from the rates for the other countries.

4. The alpha coefficient is a measure of internal consistency of a composite measure (taking into account the number of items). Its computation is a generalized form of Kuder-Richardson formulas 20 and 21. (See L. J. Cronback, "Coefficient Alpha and the Internal Structure of Tests," *Psychometrika* 16 [1951], pp. 297–334.)

At times there was no strong theoretical rationale for computing alpha. In these instances (for example, the putative response of specific others to the respondent's homosexuality), each item has its own individual focus, and there is no reason to expect a high intercorrelation between the different items in the measure (although a high alpha is often obtained). In such instances items were combined into the composite measure for additive purposes (that is, multiple items with low intercorrelations can comprise a theoretically meaningful dimension). In these cases the alpha is presented primarily for readers who might be interested in the intercorrelation. Where such composites did not produce findings, the items comprising them were individually run. When no alpha is presented for a group of items, they were always used individually and not as a composite.

Even with the above in mind, other sets of items were *not* brought together into a composite measure for reasons presented by D. T. Campbell and D. W. Fiske ("Convergent and Discriminant Validation by the Multitrait-Multimethod Matrix," *Psychological Bulletin* 56 [1959], pp. 81–105), namely, that items *normally* should not be combined unless their intercorrelation is substantially higher than would be the correlation between these items and other variables.

5. William Simon and John H. Gagnon, "Homosexuality: The Formulation of a Sociological Perspective," *Journal of Health and Social Behavior* 8 (September 1967), p. 180.

6. Colin J. Williams and Martin S. Weinberg, *Homosexuals and the Military: A Study of Less Than Honorable Discharge* (New York: Harper and Row, 1971).

7. At the time of questionnaire completion, 27 per cent of our respondents indicate that their employers know or suspect they are homosexual.

8. Forty per cent of those not married or living with their wives had dated females in the last year.

9. One interesting feature of this distribution of sexual orientation and the data on sexual behavior is that they contradict the impression that some homosexuals give—that most homosexuals are really bisexual. This seems to be a technique of dissociating themselves

from a "sick" image by describing themselves as simply having extended their sexual horizons.

10. These items and many others in this section are from Morris Rosenberg, *Society and the Adolescent Self-Image* (Princeton, N.J.: Princeton University Press, 1965).

11. Hubert M. Blalock, Jr., *Social Statistics,* 2nd ed. (New York: McGraw-Hill, 1972), pp. 309–10.

Chapter 9 / Source-Respondent Variation

1. In a few cases, a respondent received more than one questionnaire. The respondent was asked to check the various sources from which he received a questionnaire if he received more than one. (Each individual questionnaire was coded for sample source before it was distributed.) If the respondent's questionnaire had more than one source checked, and "club" was one of the sources, he was put into the club sample. This was because persons receiving club questionnaires were more likely to have received bar and mail questionnaires than vice versa. Using a similar logic, if the bar and mail sources were checked, the respondent was placed in the mail sample because persons receiving mail questionnaires were more likely to have received bar questionnaires than vice versa. Very few respondents indicated, however, that they had received more than one questionnaire.

2. The greater residential stability of the mail source sample may, however, be due in part to the method by which these respondents were contacted. This method involved mailing questionnaires to persons on the mailing lists of homophile organizations. Presumably, this method would have missed those who are not stable in terms of residence, for example, those who had moved and left no forwarding address.

The number of residentially unstable people we missed for this reason would depend on how often these organizations cleared names of such people from their lists. We know that at the time the files for M.S.N.Y. had not been so cleaned. For the other organizations we have no information on this, although it seems unlikely that such names would be retained on the mailing list of these organizations for long (especially an organization as well staffed and run as C.O.C.), since this would mean unnecessary postal expense. Thus, while we must qualify the finding that mail source respondents are more stable in residence, given the large percentage differences, we do not disregard it as merely a methodological artifact.

3. Additional findings found only in the United States are reported in Martin S. Weinberg, "Homosexual Samples: Differences and Similarities," *Journal of Sex Research* 6 (November 1970), pp. 312–25.

Chapter 10 / Locale

1. "Outlying areas" are composed of towns and cities ranging in population size from under 25,000 to over 250,000. As noted in Chapter 8, 35 and 41 per cent of our respondents in the United States and the Netherlands, respectively, live in locales of less than 250,000. In Denmark, however, the proportion is lower, 24 per cent. For those living in communities of less than 25,000 population the percentages are, in the United States 18 per cent, in the Netherlands 14 per cent, and in Denmark 9 per cent.

2. Caution is suggested regarding our rejection of the traditional urbanism hypothesis. Since all our "outside" respondents are at least members of a homophile organization, the lack of city size differences justifies our collapsing of locales, but it may not do justice to a true test of the hypothesis.

3. The similarity of the Danish respondents in outlying areas to those in Copenhagen may be due in part to our methodological procedures. Since we were not allowed access to the Danish mailing list and since there was no information available on the number of persons in various locations, we have no knowledge of the geographical distribution of its addresses. Thus, in Denmark respondents in outlying areas may be geographically concentrated closer to the major city than in our other samples. We would expect this concentration if Forbundet were less known outside Copenhagen than are, for example, C.O.C. outside Amsterdam or M.S.N.Y. outside New York City.

If this is the case, our Danish homosexuals in outlying areas would be closer to Copenhagen than American and Dutch homosexuals in outlying areas would be to their major city. Hence, the Danes inside and outside Copenhagen would not be as differentiated. Our knowledge of the geographical distribution of C.O.C.'s mailing list (and the fact that nearly 50 per cent of a national sample of the Dutch population over twenty-one had heard of the organization) indicates that this is not a methodological problem for the Netherlands.

4. The terms "European" and "American" are used as convenient shorthand. Amsterdam and Copenhagen are not meant to be gen-

eralized to Europe, nor New York and San Francisco to the United States.

5. Frank E. Hartung, *Crime, Law and Society* (Detroit: Wayne State University Press, 1966), p. 40.

Chapter 11 / Homosexual–General Population Comparisons

1. Cf. Melvin L. Kohn, *Class and Conformity: A Study in Values* (Homewood, Illinois: Dorsey Press, 1969), p. 9.

2. The seventeen items are as follows: 1. I certainly feel useless at times. 2. I take a positive attitude toward myself. 3. I wish I could have more respect for myself. 4. I feel that I'm a person of worth, at least on an equal plane with others. 5. I am able to do things as well as most other people. 6. At times I think I am no good at all. 7. Do you ever have any trouble getting to sleep or staying asleep? 8. Have you ever been bothered by nervousness, feeling fidgety or tense? 9. Are you ever troubled by headaches or pains in the head? 10. How often are you bothered by having an upset stomach? 11. Are you troubled by your hands sweating, so that you feel damp and clammy? 12. I am not as happy as others seem to be. 13. On the whole, I think I am quite a happy person. 14. No one is going to care much what happens to you, when you get right down to it. 15. Human nature is really cooperative. 16. If you don't watch out for yourself, people will take advantage of you. 17. Most people can be trusted.

3. Derek L. Phillips and Kevin J. Clancy, "Response Biases in Field Studies of Mental Illness," *American Sociological Review* 35 (June 1970), p. 508. The studies using interviews done in the field which Phillips and Clancy cite are Thomas S. Langner, "A Twenty-two Items Screening Score of Psychiatric Symptoms Indicating Impairment," *Journal of Health and Human Behavior* 3 (Winter 1962), pp. 269–76; Bruce P. Dohrenwend, "Social Status and Psychiatric Disorder: An Issue of Substance and an Issue of Method," *American Sociological Review* 31 (February 1966), pp. 14–34; and Derek L. Phillips, "The 'True Prevalence' of Mental Illness in a New England State," *Community Mental Health Journal* 2 (Spring 1966), pp. 35–40.

4. One person in the Amsterdam sample and no one in the Copenhagen sample reports himself to be a homosexual on our sexual orientation item. The Kohn sample is taken to be representative of the general population with regard to sexual orientation.

5. For reviews of some of these studies, see Evelyn Hooker, "Homo-

sexuality," *International Encyclopedia of the Social Sciences* (New York: Macmillan, 1968), Vol. 14, pp. 222–32; Martin S. Weinberg and Alan P. Bell, *Homosexuality: An Annotated Bibliography* (New York: Harper and Row, 1972). Examples of such recent findings include Marvin Siegelman, "Adjustment of Male Homosexuals and Heterosexuals," *Archives of Sexual Behavior* 2 (June 1972), pp. 9–25; Norman L. Thompson, Boyd R. McCandless, and Bonnie R. Strickland, "Personal Adjustment of Male and Female Homosexuals and Heterosexuals," *Journal of Abnormal Psychology* 78 (October 1971), pp. 237–40; Robert Athanasiou, Philip Shaver, and Carol Tavris, "Sex," *Psychology Today* 4 (July 1970), p. 51; Jerrold S. Greenberg, "A Study of the Self-Esteem and Alienation of Male Homosexuals," *The Journal of Psychology* 83 (January 1973), pp. 137–43.

6. Cf. Martin Hoffman, *The Gay World: Male Homosexuality and the Social Creation of Evil* (New York: Basic Books, 1968), Chapter 9.

7. Cf., for example, William J. Goode, "A Theory of Role Strain," *American Sociological Review* 25 (August 1960), p. 486.

8. Regarding the actual nature of societal reactions to homosexuals, which are often very mild, see John I. Kitsuse, "Societal Reaction to Deviant Behavior," *Social Problems* 9 (Winter 1962), pp. 247–56.

9. Such typological delineations are beyond the scope of this work but will be investigated in a future Institute for Sex Research volume. Alan P. Bell and Martin S. Weinberg, *The Development and Management of Homosexuality* (tentative title).

10. Greenberg, "Self-Esteem and Alienation of Male Homosexuals," too, finds greater alienation for male homosexuals (which parallels our respondents' low faith in others) but no differences from heterosexuals in self-esteem.

Chapter 12 / Self-Other Processes

1. Slogan in the homophile publication *QQ (Queen's Quarterly)* 2 (Summer 1970), p. 46.

2. Self-acceptance does not explain the correlations between acceptance by heterosexuals (or homosexuals—next section) and other psychological variables.

3. The experience of frequent homosexual sex, however, is not unambiguous for many homosexuals. While frequent homosexual sex may be quite ego-enhancing, at the same time it may create considerable guilt and anxiety for the homosexual who has not become routinized to it. Our discussions with homosexuals indicate

that this dilemma is experienced by many male homosexuals who have just "come out," but that as time passes and the homosexual becomes routinized to homosexual sex, the associated guilt and anxiety subside.

4. These findings are in accord with those of B. A. Dickey, "Attitudes Toward Sex Roles and Feelings of Adequacy in Homosexual Males," *Journal of Consulting Psychology* 25 (April 1961), pp. 116–22; Marvin Siegelman, "Adjustment of Male Homosexuals and Heterosexuals," *Archives of Sexual Behavior* 2 (June 1972), pp. 9–25.

5. William Simon and John H. Gagnon, "Homosexuality: The Formulation of a Sociological Perspective," *Journal of Health and Social Behavior* 8 (September 1967), p. 182.

6. Most of our respondents are more or less exclusively homosexual (that is, 5 or 6 on the Kinsey Scale). It is really these homosexuals to whom the above discussion applies. For the bisexual, such a process of confrontation and acknowledgment could possibly create an even greater identity conflict. Looking at our bisexual respondents and our more exclusively homosexual respondents separately, however, there are no statistically significant differences. At the same time, we must again acknowledge our sampling problem which involves our obtaining all our respondents from homosexual bars, clubs, and organizations.

7. The former relationships hold when commitment is held constant.

8. A more complete consideration of this subject can be found in Sue Kiefer Hammersmith and Martin S. Weinberg, "Homosexual Identity: Commitment, Adjustment, and Significant Others," *Sociometry* 36 (March 1973), pp. 56–79.

9. The former relationships hold when normalization is held constant.

10. Cf. Albert K. Cohen, "The Sociology of the Deviant Act," *American Sociological Review* 30 (February 1965), pp. 5–14; Edwin M. Lemert, *Human Deviance, Social Problems, and Social Control* (Englewood Cliffs, N.J.: Prentice-Hall, 1967), p. 48.

Chapter 13 / Passing and Being Known About

1. Merle Miller, "What It Means to Be a Homosexual," *The New York Times Magazine*, January 17, 1971, p. 48.

2. Peter Wildeblood, *Against the Law* (New York: Julian Messner, 1959), p. 32.

3. Note, too, that many homosexuals who worry about exposure and anticipate discrimination sometimes find the excitement of passing a positive experience. See, for example, Humphreys's discussion of "ambisexuals." Laud Humphreys, "Impersonal Sex in Public Places," *Trans-action* 7 (January 1970), p. 20. Such a phenomenon is, of course, not limited to these types of homosexuals.

4. John I. Kitsuse, "Societal Reaction to Deviant Behavior: Problems of Theory and Method," *Social Problems* 9 (Winter 1962), pp. 247–56.

5. Colin J. Williams and Martin S. Weinberg, *Homosexuals and the Military: A Study of Less Than Honorable Discharge* (New York: Harper and Row, 1971), Chapter 9.

6. Seventy-eight per cent of those arrested in the United States also report having been labeled homosexual on some official record (other than homophile organization records). Of this 78 per cent, we do not know what proportion of the official labeling is in connection with arrest and what proportion is by other organizations such as the military or mental hospitals.

Chapter 14 / Social Involvement with Other Homosexuals

1. Howard S. Becker, *Outsiders: Studies in the Sociology of Deviance* (New York: Free Press, 1963), pp. 38–39.

2. We thus hoped to include both involvement in the more public institutions of the homosexual world (a great deal of leisure-time activities, for example, center around the homosexual bar) as well as more private settings, what Hooker calls the "loosely knit extended series of overlapping networks of friends." Evelyn Hooker, "The Homosexual Community," in John H. Gagnon and William Simon (eds.), *Sexual Deviance* (New York: Harper and Row, 1967), p. 180. For a typology and discussion of homosexual relationships, see David Sonenschein, "The Ethnography of Male Homosexual Relations," *Journal of Sex Research* 4 (May 1968), pp. 69–83.

3. For an indication of the variegated response of some heterosexuals toward homosexuals, see John I. Kitsuse, "Societal Reaction to Deviant Behavior: Problems of Theory and Method," *Social Problems* 9 (Winter 1962), pp. 247–56.

4. In addition to the above, of course, as a result of becoming more known about (whether voluntarily or not), a homosexual may feel freer to associate more with other homosexuals.

5. This relationship is not accounted for by the correlation between social involvement and exclusive relationships.

6. Sonenschein, "Ethnography of Male Homosexual Relationships," p. 73.

7. See Alfred C. Kinsey, Wardell B. Pomeroy, and Clyde E. Martin, *Sexual Behavior in the Human Male* (Philadelphia: W. B. Saunders Company, 1948), pp. 632ff, and David Sonenschein, "Are Homosexuals Really Oversexed?" *Sexology* 38 (October 1971), pp. 24–26, which show that frequency of sexual relations is lower for homosexuals than for heterosexuals of the same age.

Chapter 15 / Bisexuality

1. We are using the word "bisexuality" to refer to a person's being sexually attracted to both sexes. This is not to be confused with the biological use of the word, having both male and female sexual anatomy.

2. Angelo D'Arcangelo, *The Homosexual Handbook* (New York: Ophelia Press, Inc., 1969), pp. 199–200.

3. Alfred C. Kinsey, Wardell B. Pomeroy, and Clyde E. Martin, *Sexual Behavior in the Human Male* (Philadelphia: W. B. Saunders Company, 1948), p. 639.

4. This scale is well known and does not require a detailed description. For an extended discussion, see Wainwright Churchill, *Homosexual Behavior Among Males: A Cross-Cultural and Cross-Species Investigation* (New York: Hawthorn Books, 1967), Chapter 2.

5. For a critique of the position which sees homosexuality as a condition, see Mary McIntosh, "The Homosexual Role," *Social Problems* 16 (Fall 1968), pp. 182–92.

6. Ibid. pp. 184–85.

7. Donald Webster Cory and John P. LeRoy, *The Homosexual and His Society* (New York: The Citadel Press, 1963), p. 61.

8. Ibid.

9. Categories 2–4 and 5–6 on the Kinsey Scale were combined for three reasons: First, no differences were found *within* the categories 2–4 and 5–6; second, unless categories are collapsed, the number of respondents in some categories is too small for us to obtain meaningful comparisons; third, the combined categories (2–4 and 5–6) seem to adequately distinguish between the more exclusively homosexual respondents and the bisexuals.

10. See, for example, the case of Tom in Martin Hoffman, *The Gay*

World: Male Homosexuality and the Social Creation of Evil (New York: Basic Books, 1968), pp. 13–22.

Chapter 16 / Age

1. Jess Stearn, *The Sixth Man* (New York: Macfadden Publishers, 1961), pp. 201–2.

2. In the United States, 17 per cent more of those over 45—as compared with those 26–35 or 36–45—score low in social involvement with other homosexuals.

3. Other age-related findings also do not appear to reflect the aging process but rather generation differences or the fact that older homosexuals, merely by virtue of having lived longer, have had more time to undergo certain experiences. Thus, with regard to the latter, older homosexuals are more likely to report having thought of themselves as homosexual longer, to have been arrested, or to have been married. The last two findings, however, could reflect generation differences instead, for example, changes in law enforcement practices and the development of a more liberal social ethos whereby pressures on single males to get married are greatly reduced.

Other differences among age groups which appear to reflect generation differences are as follows. First, the younger respondent is more likely to report being known as homosexual by his mother and father (except in Denmark). With the more authoritarian family of past generations, and the correspondingly greater fear of parents, one might expect older homosexuals to have strived more to conceal their sexual proclivities. Second, our data seem to indirectly reflect a greater openness about being homosexual on the part of younger males with religious backgrounds in Catholicism or in the lower-status Protestant denominations. We suggest this because respondents with these religious backgrounds comprise a larger proportion of our samples among the younger cohorts than among the older ones. (Of course, the finding for lower-status Protestant denominations cannot be replicated in Europe.) Thus, this finding suggests that in younger cohorts homosexuals with Catholic or with lower-status Protestant denominational backgrounds are becoming less covert and, consequently, more likely to be included in our sample. We would also expect this finding if a higher proportion of males with Catholic or lower-status Protestant denominational religious background are now becoming homosexual.

This seems unlikely, however. Third, older homosexuals score lower on our acculturation measure, perhaps indicating that their sexual habits involve sexual encounters which are more anonymous and of shorter duration. This might also reflect changes in the homosexual subculture to which older homosexuals have not been socialized (for example, dancing in homosexual bars). Finally, generation differences are also evident with respect to beliefs regarding the determinants of human behavior. Such beliefs have generally changed over time from an emphasis on "nature" to an emphasis on "nurture." Thus, older homosexuals are more likely to believe they were born homosexual (although this might reflect more failures at attempts to "change," leading the homosexual to believe he must have been born "that way"). Also, the older homosexual is less likely to report that anyone ever suggested that he seek psychiatric help regarding his homosexuality.

4. Controlling for social involvement with other homosexuals or sexual frequency does not affect any of the findings in this chapter.

5. Gerald Gurin, Joseph Veroff, and Sheila Feld, *Americans View Their Mental Health: A Nationwide Interview Study* (New York: Basic Books, 1960), p. 214.

6. While the older persons in our study and those in the study by Gurin et al. generally seem to be lower in the psychological problems cited, Gurin et al., as well as others (Norman Bradburn and David Caplovitz, *Reports on Happiness* [Chicago: Aldine, 1965]), have found older respondents to be less "happy." In another study, Srole et al. (Leo Srole, Thomas Langner, Stanley Michael, Marvin Opler, and Thomas Rennie, *Mental Health in the Metropolis: The Midtown Manhattan Study* [New York: McGraw-Hill, 1962]) found more general psychological problems to increase with age. Bradburn, on the other hand, found no difference by age in psychosomatic symptoms.

These apparent contradictions regarding age and psychological problems may be due to the multidimensional nature of psychological well-being and the fact that different studies tap different dimensions. The Gurin et al. and Bradburn-Caplovitz studies are not in disagreement; both find an increase in "unhappiness" with age. (We find no difference by age; this may be due to the unusually stressful situation faced by younger homosexuals.) At the same time, the Gurin et al. study finds that other psychological problems decrease with age. In the Srole et al. study it is difficult to know the relative weights given to various psychological dimensions used in rating a respondent's "mental health." Also, in the Srole et al. study there are no age-related differences in "mild" or "moderate" symptom formation; the age differences were found largely among those persons who were labeled "impaired," with the greater difference between those in the 20–29 age group and those in the oldest group, ages 50–59. At this level of "impairment" such a finding need not be considered in conflict with the findings of Gurin and his associates, who may be tapping less severe psychological problems in a more adequate way (for example, in getting at the subjective feelings the respondent has regarding himself).

Another explanation could also be given. Srole and associates explain the positive relationship between age and psychological problems which they obtain for the general population through use of the concept "role discontinuity." This refers to the often dramatic transition and anomie resulting as one moves from one role to another in the life cycle, for example, adapting to parenthood, the loss of children from the household, and so on. Homosexuals, however, may face their major "discontinuity" crisis at an earlier age, for example, identity crises during early adulthood. The aging homosexual may also, of course, experience role discontinuity (as noted in our text). He, too, has stable relationships that can dissolve, and, as aging may reduce physical attraction, he may find that certain bars or beaches are no longer viable settings for finding sexual partners. By middle age, however, the homosexual may have grown accustomed to such experiences and, as a result, not find them so disturbing.

7. A number of questions certainly deserve further exploration: the multidimensionality of psychological problems, the nature of the supports employed by older homosexuals, the salience of sex for homosexuals over 45, and, in greater detail, the social and psychological character of their lives. These topics remain for future research.

Chapter 17 / Occupation

1. Maurice Leznoff and William A. Westley, "The Homosexual Community," *Social Problems* 3 (April 1956), pp. 259–60.

2. Respondents were classified in terms of occupational status according to their present occupation. Low occupational status includes skilled and semiskilled workers, machine operators, and unskilled labor. Medium occupational status includes administrative personnel, small-business owners, semiprofessionals, clerical and sales workers, and technicians. High occupational status includes executives, proprietors of large and medium-size businesses, man-

agers, and major and lesser professionals. A measure that asked the respondent to circle his social class (for example, upper-middle class) produces results similar to those reported in this chapter.

3. One potential problem with this social identification item is as follows. In order to tap whether the respondent identifies more strongly with other homosexuals (regardless of their social class) or with people in his social class (regardless of their sexual orientation), the item asks if the respondent feels closer to a heterosexual of his own social class than to a homosexual of a much lower social class. However, since there is less distance in social status "below" a lower-status occupation than there is "below" a higher-status occupation, the lower-status respondent may think of himself as closer in social status to "a homosexual of a much lower social class" than would a higher-status respondent. Thus, patterns of identification based on class versus sexual orientation may reflect this difference in status distance rather than differences in the strength of identification with other homosexuals. For example, a low-status respondent may feel closer to "a homosexual of a much lower social class" than would a high-status homosexual while at the same time feeling much more distant from a homosexual of a much *higher* social class than would a high-status respondent. In such a case, the low-status respondent's scoring higher in social identification with other homosexuals would be in part an artifact of his own low status.

4. Although a part of the passing scale, this sub-scale is presented here because of Leznoff and Westley's specific discussion of persons' willingness (or disinclination) to associate with known homosexuals.

5. The positive relationship between occupational status and covertness is, of course, not invariable. There are some higher-status occupations where disclosure would not pose a status threat, and some lower-status occupations where disclosure could cause great problems.

6. Leznoff and Westley, "Homosexual Community," p. 263.

7. Martin Stow, "Closet Queens," *Vector* 7 (January 1971), p. 4.

8. Morris Rosenberg, *Society and the Adolescent Self-Image* (Princeton, New Jersey: Princeton University Press, 1965), p. 39.

9. For example, ibid.; Norman Bradburn and David Caplovitz, *Reports on Happiness* (Chicago: Aldine, 1965); William Sewell and A. O. Haller, "Factors in the Relationship Between Social Status and the Personality Adjustment of the Child," *American Sociological Review* 24 (August 1959), pp. 511–20.

10. See George C. Homans, *The Human Group* (New York: Harcourt, Brace and Company, 1950).

11. For example, see William Parker, "Homosexuals and Employ-

ment," in *Essays on Homosexuality*, No. 4 (San Francisco: The Corinthian Foundation, 1970).

Chapter 18 / Living Arrangements

1. Homosexuals who live with heterosexual roommates are not discussed in this chapter because of the small number of respondents with that living arrangement (United States, 21; the Netherlands, 9; Denmark, 5).

2. Cf. Martin Hoffman, *The Gay World: Male Homosexuality and the Social Creation of Evil* (New York: Basic Books, 1968), Chapter 10. For some of the difficulties associated with such relationships, see Donald Webster Cory, *The Homosexual in America* (New York: Greenberg, 1951), Chapter 13.

3. Cory, *Homosexual in America,* p. 144.

4. See Chapter 14.

5. Among respondents with homosexual roommates, the majority report that their roommates are also their lovers. It should be noted, however, that this living arrangement does not preclude "extra-marital" activity or a roommate who is not their lover.

6. Among those in psychiatric treatment, the same residential pattern appears but with smaller percentage differences, bringing the data just under our requisite for substantive significance.

7. A discussion of why homosexuals do or do not marry is found in Cory, *Homosexual in America,* Chapter 19. For a general discussion of the married homosexual, see also H. Laurence Ross, "Modes of Adjustment of Married Homosexuals," *Social Problems* 18 (Winter 1971), pp. 385–93.

8. Because only five of the Danish respondents are married and living with their wives, none of the findings reported for homosexuals in this living arrangement could be replicated in Denmark.

Chapter 19 / Religious Background

1. Melvin DeFleur, William V. D'Antonio, and Lois DeFleur, *Sociology: Man in Society* (Glenview, Ill.: Scott, Foresman, 1971), p. 545.

2. The distribution on religious background varies somewhat between the United States and the Netherlands. The United States

sample is 28.6 per cent Catholic, 52.5 per cent Protestant, 9.0 per cent Jewish, and 10.0 per cent other. The Dutch sample is 44.2 per cent Catholic, 51.9 per cent Protestant, 1.5 per cent Jewish, and 2.4 per cent other.

In the United States, denominational background was also obtained. Of the 557 Protestants, 11.8 per cent are Baptist, 18.0 per cent Methodist, 9.5 per cent Lutheran, 19.4 per cent Episcopalian, 12.0 per cent Presbyterian, 5.1 per cent Congregational, 6.8 per cent Unitarian, and 17.5 per cent another denomination. Of the 98 Jewish respondents in our United States sample, 41 per cent are Reform, 36 per cent Conservative, and 23 per cent Orthodox. Such information was not obtained in Europe.

3. The differences between respondents of different religious backgrounds which seem to merely reflect differences in the general population are as follows. In class position, Catholics tend to be lower and Jews higher than average. The same is true for subjective class placement. With regard to residence, Jews are the most likely to be living in the same city as their parents (which is not explained by their concentration in New York City). In terms of declared religiosity, Jewish respondents define themselves as less religious than do Catholic and Protestant respondents. Jews are also the least likely, and Catholics the most likely, to attribute any importance to formal religion.

4. See, for example, Gerhard Lenski, *The Religious Factor: A Sociologist's Inquiry* (Garden City, N.Y.: Anchor Books, 1963); Bernice Milburn Moore and Wayne H. Holzman, *Tomorrow's Parents: A Study of Youth and Their Families* (Austin: University of Texas Press, 1965); Julius Cohen, Reginald A. H. Robson, and Alan P. Bates, *Paternal Authority: The Community and the Law* (New Brunswick, N.J.: Rutgers University Press, 1958); Martin S. Weinberg and Prudence Rains, "Religion, Familism, and the Commuting Student," paper delivered at the American Sociological Association meetings, Boston, Massachusetts, 1968.

5. Alfred C. Kinsey, Wardell B. Pomeroy, and Clyde E. Martin, *Sexual Behavior in the Human Male* (Philadelphia: W. B. Saunders Company, 1948), p. 486.

Chapter 20 / Religiosity

1. Alfred C. Kinsey, Wardell B. Pomeroy, and Clyde E. Martin, *Sexual Behavior in the Human Male* (Philadelphia: W. B. Saunders Company, 1948), p. 631. Kinsey defines religiosity in terms of religious participation; ibid. pp. 304–7.

2. Using another measure of religiosity, an item which asked, "How religious (in the traditional sense of the term) are you now?" provided no departures from the findings presented in this chapter, with relationships being similar in strength. It also should be noted that religiosity is a multidimensional phenomenon. Glock and Stark define five such dimensions. Using a scale based upon these dimensions, Ruppell found all five dimensions correlated negatively with heterosexual permissiveness; the ritualistic dimension (behavior, church attendance, and so on), however, was found to be of lesser importance than the others. Charles Y. Glock and Rodney Stark, *Religion and Society in Tension* (Chicago: Rand McNally, 1965); Howard J. Ruppell, "Religiosity and Pre-Marital Sexual Permissiveness: A Response to the Reiss-Heltsley and Broderick Debate," *Journal of Marriage and the Family* 32 (November 1970), pp. 647–55.

3. Among our United States respondents, those who are more religious are less educated and more likely to live in a community of under 25,000 people. (While these trends were replicated in the Netherlands and Denmark, the differences in Europe were statistically or substantively significant.)

4. In the United States, less religious homosexuals are less likely to continue to experience guilt, shame, or anxiety after having homosexual relations. This trend, however, is not replicated in Europe.

5. Rev. Dr. Billy Hudson, *Christian Homosexuality* (North Hollywood, Calif.: Now Library Press, 1970), pp. 46, 90.

6. The relationship is monotonic and strong—with a 34.5 per cent difference between the low and high violation categories—but it is not replicated in Europe.

7. The relationships between psychological problems, the values of traditional morality and conformity in general, and perceived conflict between homosexuality and these values follow the same pattern as those found for religion. In general, however, the pattern is weaker for morality than for religion and weakest for conformity.

8. Emile Durkheim, *Sociology and Philosophy* (Glencoe, Ill.: The Free Press, 1953), p. 40.

Chapter 21 / Race

1. Compared with white homosexuals in the United States sample, our black homosexuals have less income and education and lower occupational status. (However, our black respondents are better educated than are blacks in general and even better educated than the United States population as a whole.) In addition, most of the

black homosexuals in our sample live in New York City, and of these, most live in the Bronx. Whether they live in a predominantly black area we do not know.

2. Robert Staples, "The Sexuality of Black Women," *Sexual Behavior* 2 (June 1972), pp. 4–15.

3. Ibid. p. 11. Also, black prostitutes are less likely than white prostitutes to experience complete parental rejection. See Diana Gray, "Turning Out: A Study of Teenage Prostitution," *Urban Life and Culture* 1 (January 1973), p. 418. At the same time, blacks appear more likely to view masturbation, oral-genital relations, and group sex as "abnormal." Staples, "Sexuality of Black Women," p. 11.

4. Staples, "Sexuality of Black Women," pp. 6ff. For corroborating research appearing since Staples' codification, see John F. Kanter and Melvin Zelnick, "Sexual Experience of Young Unmarried Women in the United States," *Family Planning Perspectives* 4 (October 1972), pp. 9–18.

5. Bass-Hass reports that black lesbians have more often had heterosexual experiences than have white lesbians. See Rita Bass-Hass, "The Lesbian Dyad," *Journal of Sex Research* 4 (May 1968), pp. 108–26. We find a similar pattern among our male homosexuals; however, the difference between our black and white respondents is not statistically significant ($p < .10$).

6. We originally thought that this difference might be explained by the black respondents' perception of tolerance, but this does not seem to be the case. Holding constant our respondents' perceived reactions to homosexuality, the original gamma of .29 is only reduced to a partial gamma of .20. Holding constant anticipated discrimination, it is reduced to a partial gamma of .17.

7. Yancey, Rigsby, and McCarthy have recently reported that, controlling for socioeconomic status, sex, and marital status, the relationship between race and self-acceptance varies between cities. They find that in Nashville, Tennessee, blacks have more self-acceptance than whites, while in Philadelphia whites have more self-acceptance. See William L. Yancey, Leo Rigsby, and John D. McCarthy, "Social Position and Self-Evaluation: The Relative Importance of Race," *American Journal of Sociology* 78 (September 1972), pp. 338–59.

In addition, Morris Rosenberg did not find the black adolescents to be particularly low in self-acceptance in comparison with white adolescents. See Morris Rosenberg, *Society and the Adolescent Self-Image* (Princeton, N.J.: Princeton University Press, 1965), pp. 56–57.

For a critique of other research on race and self-acceptance, see

John D. McCarthy and William L. Yancey, "Uncle Tom and Mr. Charlie: Metaphysical Pathos in the Study of Racism and Personal Disorganization," *American Journal of Sociology* 76 (January 1971), pp. 648–72.

Chapter 22 / Theoretical Implications

1. Gibbs has pointed out that current notions of societal reaction constitute a theoretical perspective rather than a theory in that they do not provide any body of empirically testable propositions. See Jack Gibbs, "Conceptions of Deviant Behavior: The Old and the New," *Pacific Sociological Review* 9 (Spring 1966), pp. 9–14.

2. Cf. also Colin J. Williams and Martin S. Weinberg, *Homosexuals and the Military: A Study of Less than Honorable Discharge* (New York: Harper and Row, 1971), for similar considerations.

3. See, for example, John I. Kitsuse, "Societal Reaction to Deviant Behavior: Problems of Theory and Method," *Social Problems* 9 (Winter 1962), pp. 247–56.

4. See Jack D. Douglas, *American Social Order: Social Rules in a Pluralistic Society* (New York: The Free Press, 1971).

5. Ibid. p. 139.

6. Cf. also Williams and Weinberg, *Homosexuals and the Military*, p. 184.

7. Irving Louis Horowitz and Martin Liebowitz, "Social Deviance and Political Marginality: Toward a Redefinition of the Relation between Sociology and Politics," *Social Problems* 15 (Winter 1968), pp. 280–96.

8. For a sociological study of homosexual militancy, see Laud Humphreys, *Out of the Closets: The Sociology of Homosexual Liberation* (Englewood Cliffs, N.J.: Prentice-Hall, 1972).

9. Although a far more sophisticated analysis is presented, the most extensive consideration of passing, by Erving Goffman, also suffers from an overly rational, cognitive emphasis. Goffman's actor appears always to be on stage, always managing a performance, always poised on the brink of disaster. Erving Goffman, *Stigma: Notes on the Management of Spoiled Identity* (Englewood Cliffs, N.J.: Prentice-Hall, 1963). For a critique similar to ours, see Sheldon Messenger, H. Sampson, and R. D. Towne, "Life as Theater: Some Notes on the Dramaturgical Approach to Social Reality," *Sociometry* 25 (March 1962), pp. 98–110.

10. Note the compartmentalization between unconventional sexual behavior and an otherwise conventional life reported by some of

Humphreys's respondents, who have homosexual sex in public rest rooms, and Bartell's respondents who engage in group sex. Laud Humphreys, *Tearoom Trade: Impersonal Sex in Public Places* (Chicago: Aldine, 1970); Gilbert Bartell, *Group Sex* (New York: Peter H. Wyden, 1971).

11. Cf. Goffman, *Stigma,* pp. 41ff. Being known about may produce more harmful effects for other types of "deviants," however—for example, the unwed mother whose interests (perhaps dating "respectable" men, getting married) may be hampered by being known about, or the abstinent drug addict who, if known about, might be ostracized by people not into drugs.

12. Not all background characteristics, of course, have important effects on how the individual manages his homosexuality. For example, it will be remembered that religious affiliation exerts few, if any, independent effects.

13. Mary McIntosh, "The Homosexual Role," *Social Problems* 16 (Fall 1968), pp. 182–92.

14. This is not a new idea. Hartung has written about the cultural reality (despite no evidence or scientific reality) of such clinical "entities" as kleptomaniacs, compulsive criminals, psychopaths, and so forth. See Frank E. Hartung, *Crime, Law and Society* (Detroit: Wayne State University Press, 1966). And, of course, the whole societal reaction literature is replete with examples of how all kinds of labels come to have lives of their own.

15. Barry M. Dank, "Coming Out in the Gay World," *Psychiatry* 34 (May 1971), p. 189.

16. For an extended discussion of this point, see Dennis Altman, *Homosexual: Oppression and Liberation* (New York: Outerbridge and Dienstfrey, 1971), Chap. 7.

Chapter 23 / Practical Considerations

1. For a discussion of the various processes by which organizations of "deviants" can help to alleviate the problems of their members, see Martin S. Weinberg, "The Problems of Midgets and Dwarfs and Organizational Remedies: A Study of the Little People of America," *Journal of Health and Social Behavior* 9 (March 1968), pp. 65–71.

2. Dick Leitsch, *Mattachine Times,* January, 1971, p. 61.

3. Earl Raab and Seymour Martin Lipset, "The Prejudiced Society," in Earl Raab (ed.), *American Race Relations Today* (New York: Anchor Books, 1962), p. 41. For other commentaries on the

relationship between attitudes and behavior, see Frank R. Westie and Melvin DeFleur, "Verbal Attitudes and Overt Acts: An Experiment on the Salience of Attitudes," *American Sociological Review* 23 (December 1958), pp. 667–73; Irving Deutscher, "Words and Deeds: Social Science and Social Policy," *Social Problems* 13 (Winter 1966), pp. 235–54; Howard J. Ehrlich, "Attitudes, Behavior, and Intervening Variables," *American Sociologist* 4 (February 1969), pp. 29–34.

4. M.S.N.Y.'s legislative program for 1971 proposes that it be a misdemeanor for an employer to ask a job applicant if he has ever been arrested. They also propose the same for anyone divulging information about persons acquitted of any crime. They recommend sealing records to this end. Another proposal makes bonding companies which refuse to bond a homosexual guilty of a misdemeanor. *Mattachine Times,* November/December, 1970, p. 15.

5. See, for example, *Report of the Committee on Homosexual Offenses and Prostitution* (The Wolfenden Report) (London: Her Majesty's Stationery Office, 1957); Edwin M. Schur, *Crimes Without Victims* (Englewood Cliffs, N.J.: Prentice-Hall, 1965); Gilbert M. Cantor, "The Need for Homosexual Law Reform," in Ralph W. Weltge (ed.), *The Same Sex* (Philadelphia: The Pilgrim Press, 1969), pp. 83–94; Sanford H. Kadish, "The Crisis of Overcriminalization," *Annals of the American Academy of Political and Social Science* (November 1967), pp. 157–70.

6. *Committee on Homosexual Offenses and Prostitution,* p. 24.

7. Cantor, "Need for Homosexual Law Reform." Nonetheless, it seems difficult to get sodomy laws repealed. In October 1971 the California legislature defeated a bill (the "Brown Bill") that would have legalized all forms of sexual behavior between consenting adults in private.

8. Some of the arguments for retaining laws against homosexuality are considered by the Wolfenden Committee, *Committee on Homosexual Offenses and Prostitution,* pp. 21ff; and Schur, *Crimes Without Victims,* pp. 107ff.

9. U.S. Senate, Committee on Expenditures in the Executive Departments, Subcommittee on Investigations. Interim Report: "Employment of Homosexuals and Other Sex Perverts in Government," Senate Document No. 241, December 1950.

10. See, for example, a letter written by John W. Macy, Jr., former chairman of the Civil Service Commission, to the Mattachine Society of Washington, February 25, 1966, reprinted in Lewis I. Maddocks, "The Law and the Church vs. the Homosexual," in Ralph W. Weltge (ed.), *The Same Sex,* p. 101. These recommendations, however, have since been somewhat mitigated by the Federal Appellate Court,

Washington, D.C., which stated that a homosexual cannot be dismissed from a government agency without proof that his homosexuality interfered with the agency's efficiency (Norton v. Macy, 417 Fed. 2d 1161 [D.C. Circ. 1969]). However, government officials still try to perpetuate such exclusionary practices; see "Government-Created Employment Disabilities of the Homosexual," *Harvard Law Review* 82 (June 1969), pp. 1738–51, and Franklin Kameny, "Gays and the U.S. Civil Service," *Vector* (February 1973), pp. 8, 39–41.

11. For a convincing argument against federal employment policies, see William Parker, "Homosexuals and Employment," in *Essays on Homosexuality,* No. 4 (San Francisco: The Corinthian Foundation, 1970), pp. 13–19. Also note the similar recommendations of the National Institute of Mental Health Task Force on Homosexuality.

12. *Mattachine Times,* January 1971, p. 1.

13. For an account of military policy and treatment regarding homosexuals, see Colin J. Williams and Martin S. Weinberg, *Homosexuals and the Military: A Study of Less than Honorable Discharge* (New York: Harper and Row, 1971).

14. Until it was recently eliminated, every inductee for the last twenty years has had to answer the following question during his preinduction physical exam (under penalty of perjury): "Have you ever had, or have you now, homosexual tendencies?" Even after this question was abolished, the law still provided for automatic exemption for the homosexual who could prove his homosexuality.

15. Colin J. Williams and Martin S. Weinberg, "The Military: Its Processing of Accused Homosexuals," *American Behavioral Scientist* 14 (November/December 1970), pp. 203–17.

16. We recognize that some people might object on the ground that this would encourage experimentation with homosexuality. First, there is no evidence that homosexual behavior would increase. Second, even if people did experiment more with homosexual behavior, we have no evidence that in a tolerant and nonmoralistic atmosphere this would be harmful. Third, to exclude homosexuality from sex education courses on such grounds would be to perpetuate for the sake of one moral stand an ignorance which is itself immoral in its consequences for a substantial number of persons.

17. For example, Stember reviewed a number of studies of the relationship between education and ethnic and racial prejudice and concluded that "its chief effect is to reduce traditional provincialism —to counteract the notion that members of minorities are strange creatures with exotic ways, and to diminish fear of casual personal contact. But the limits of acceptance are sharply drawn; while legal

equality is supported, full social participation is not." Charles H. Stember, *Education and Attitude Change* (New York: Institute of Human Relations Press, 1961), p. 171.

18. Gene D. Phillips, "Homosexuality in the Movies," *Sexual Behavior* (May 1971), p. 21.

19. See, for example, Arthur R. Cohen, *Attitude Change and Social Influence* (New York: Basic Books, 1964).

20. Perhaps we have given less attention to the written media here than is warranted. We do agree, however, with the Wolfenden Committee's proposal that the press report homosexual offenses or homosexual conduct in such a way as to avoid the public labeling of those involved. *Committee on Homosexual Offenses and Prostitution,* p. 78.

21. See William J. McGuire, "The Nature of Attitudes and Attitude Change," in Gardner Lindzey and Elliot Aronson (eds.), *The Handbook of Social Psychology,* Second Edition (Reading, Mass.: Addison-Wesley, 1969), Vol. 3, especially pp. 177–200.

22. Unfortunately, "experts" and "professionals" in the area of sexual behavior are often self-appointed. This is problematic when their popularity is high but their knowledge is low. A case in point is the collage of misinformation and stereotyped thinking about homosexuality found in David Reuben's *Everything You Always Wanted to Know About Sex (But Were Afraid to Ask)* (New York: McKay Company, 1969).

23. See the essays by Frank Kameny and Helen Hacker in Edward Sagarin (ed.), *The Other Minorities* (Waltham, Mass.: Ginn & Co., 1971). Similar proposals are made by Anthony Grey and D. J. West in "Homosexuals: New Law But No New Deal," *New Society* (March 27, 1969).

24. The ease of passing is a major basis for the lack of group cohesiveness and identification on the part of homosexuals. One source of cohesiveness lies in a group's having to stand openly as a minority, surrounded by a hostile majority. These are experiences that homosexuals *as a group* need never face. The individual homosexual usually blends imperceptibly into the heterosexual mass. There is often no sense of sharing his differentness with other homosexuals, no cohesiveness or easy sense of identification, when the only occasions on which he chooses to present himself as a homosexual are those where he is exempt from the gaze of the heterosexual majority.

In addition, two other aspects of the ease of passing contribute to the lack of group cohesion and identification among homosexuals. First, since it is in his daily round of activities that the homosexual passes as a member of the majority, he is less likely than other minority group members to feel that he is considered an outsider by those with whom he comes into everyday contact. The black, for example, is more likely to interpret interpersonal occurrences as a function of his being black, which produces a stronger sense of minority group identification. Second, there is the fact that homosexuality is "achieved," whereas race or ethnicity is "ascribed." There is the realization of the ethnic or racial minority group member, sometime in his childhood, that he is irrevocably a member of that minority group. For the homosexual, however, it appears less likely that such a moment will arrive when he realizes that he will be socially identified as homosexual for the rest of his life. In terms of *personal* identity, the person may think of himself as homosexual, but the ability to pass allows him to avoid an irrevocable *public* identity as homosexual. Thus, a person can gradually emerge into homosexuality without any intense feeling of being in fact socially differentiated from the majority or of having strong ties to others who share that differentness.

25. Carl Whittman, *The Gay Manifesto* (New York: Red Butterfly, 1970), p. 5.

INDEX

Jack Nichols

MEN'S LIBERATION
A New Definition of Masculinity

This pioneering book shows how men's liberation can enrich the lives of both sexes. An organizer and leader since 1961 of groups promoting sex-role freedom, Jack Nichols wants to free men from destructive competition, from the fear of being called "effeminate," from the nervousness that inhibits male friendship, from the terror of sexual failure, and from all the psychological and sociological stereotypes that warp their attitudes and behavior. *Men's Liberation* tells, among much else, why many men are afraid to be gentle and loving, why they are taught to avoid certain thoughts and activities, why, since the advent of women's liberation, there has been a startling increase in male impotence, how traditional male toughness has affected society and politics, and why men should be passive as well as active. It all adds up to a new and revolutionary definition of masculinity.

Richard Green, M.D.

SEXUAL IDENTITY CONFLICT IN CHILDREN AND ADULTS

This is an intimate look at children and adults so unhappy with their anatomical sexuality that they seek magical or surgical change. Richard Green considers historical and cross-cultural examples of transsexualism and reviews experimental and clinical material from psychology and other fields. The topics he discusses include the treatment of transsexuals, husbands of male-to-female transsexuals and wives of female-to-male transsexuals, feminine boys and masculine girls, and problems for future research. Among the book's outstanding features are its interviews with adult transsexuals, but the chief emphasis is on children who already want to change at an early age. The experiences of these children are analyzed in a way that throws new light on the mysterious process by which sexual identity is formed. Richard Green is Professor of Psychiatry at the State University of New York, at Stony Brook.

Joseph Epstein

DIVORCED IN AMERICA
Marriage in an Age of Possibility

What is it like to go through the experience of divorce? To break the news to children, family, friends? To become a weekend parent? To cope with loneliness and a sense of failure? To face your first sexual encounter as a divorced person? In this firsthand report on getting a divorce in America today, Joseph Epstein answers these and many other questions as he recounts his own divorce from his wife of ten years and, in alternating sections, explores divorce as a nationwide phenomenon. His concern is not only with laws and statistics but also with the emotions and ideals that combine to make—and often to break—the American marriage. A teacher and editor, Epstein describes himself as "a divorced man whose bias is on behalf of the nuclear family, a man who, despite all its flaws, really cannot imagine any other arrangement being any better."